Strange Maine

Strange Maine

Edited by Charles G. Waugh,
Martin H. Greenberg & Frank D. McSherry Jr.

Illustrated by Peter Farrow

Lance Tapley, Publisher

"The Children of Noah" by Richard Matheson. Copyright © 1957 by H.S.D. Publishing, Inc.; renewed © 1985 by Richard Matheson. Reprinted by permission of Don Congdon Associates, Inc.
"The Phantom Farmhouse" by Seabury Quinn. Copyright © 1923 by *Wierd Tales*. Reprinted by permission of the agents for the author's Estate, the Scott Meredith Literary Agency, Inc., 845 Third Avenue, New York, NY 10022.
"Longtooth" by Edgar Pangborn. Copyright © 1970 by Mercury Press, Inc. From *The Magazine of Fantasy and Science Fiction*. Reprinted by permission of Richard Curtis Associates, Inc.
"One for the Road" by Stephen King appeared in *Maine Magazine*, March/April, 1977. Copyright © 1977 by Maine Magazine Company, Inc. From the book *Night Shift*; reprinted by permission of Doubleday & Company, Inc.
"Four Dreams of Gram Perkins" by Ruth Sawyer. Copyright © 1926 by American Mercury, Inc. Reprinted by permission of Ruth Sawyer's heirs.
"The Prevaricator" by Carlos Baker. Copyright © 1976 by Carlos Baker. Reprinted by permission of the author.
"One Old Man, with Seals" by Jane Yolen. Copyright © 1982 by Jane Yolen. Reprinted by permission of Curtis Brown, Ltd.
"Safe Harbor" by Donald Wismer. Copyright © 1986 by Donald Wismer. Reprinted by permission of the author.
"Mood Wendigo" by Thomas Easton. Copyright © 1980 by Davis Publications, Inc. Reprinted by permission of the author.
"Death Is a White Rabbit" by Fredric Brown. Copyright © 1942 by *Strange Detective Mysteries*. Reprinted by permission of Roberta Pryor, Inc.
"Yesterday House" by Fritz Leiber. Copyright © 1952 by Galaxy Publishing Corporation. Reprinted by permission of Richard Curtis Associates, Inc.
"Three-Day Magic" by Charlotte Armstrong. Copyright © 1952 by Charlotte Armstrong Levi. Copyright renewed © 1980 by Charlotte Armstrong. Reprinted by permission of Brandt & Brandt Literary Agency, Inc.

Library of Congress Cataloging-in-Publication Data
Strange Maine.

1. Fantastic fiction, American.   2. Maine--Fiction.
I. Waugh, Charles. II. Greenberg, Martin Harry. III. McSherry, Frank D.
PS648.F3S7   1986   813'.0876'0832741   86-14566
ISBN 0-912769-10-6

Designed by Diane de Grasse

Composed by Type & Design, Brunswick, Maine

Printed in the United States of America

Contents

Richard Matheson

THE CHILDREN OF NOAH

IT WAS JUST past three a.m. when Mr. Ketchum drove past the sign that read *Zachry: pop. 67*. He groaned. Another in an endless string of Maine seaside towns. He closed his eyes hard a second, then opened them again and pressed down on the accelerator. The Ford surged forward under him. Maybe, with luck, he'd reach a decent motel soon. It certainly wasn't likely there'd be one in Zachry: pop. 67.

Mr. Ketchum shifted his heavy frame on the seat and stretched his legs. It had been a sour vacation. Motoring through New England's historic beauty, communing with nature and nostalgia was what he'd planned. Instead, he'd found only boredom, exhaustion and over-expense.

Mr. Ketchum was not pleased.

The town seemed fast asleep as he drove along its Main Street. The only sound was that of the car's engine, the only sight that of his raised headbeams splaying out ahead, lighting up another sign. *Speed 15 Limit*.

"Sure, sure," he muttered disgustedly, pressing down on the gas pedal. Three o'clock in the morning and the town fathers expected him to creep through their lousy hamlet. Mr. Ketchum watched the dark buildings rush past his window. Good-by Zachry, he thought. Farewell, pop. 67.

Then the other car appeared in the rear-view mirror. About half a block behind, a sedan with a turning red spotlight on its roof. He knew what kind of car it was. His foot curled off the accelerator and he felt his heartbeat quicken. Was it possible they hadn't noticed how fast he was going?

The question was answered as the dark car pulled up to the Ford and a man in a big hat leaned out of the front window. "Pull over!" he barked.

Swallowing dryly, Mr. Ketchum eased his car over to the curb. He drew up the emergency brake, turned the ignition key and the car was still. The police car nosed in toward the curb and stopped. The right front door opened.

The glare of Mr. Ketchum's headlights outlined the dark figure approaching. He felt around quickly with his left foot and stamped down on the knob, dimming the lights. He swallowed again. Damned nuisance this. Three a.m. in the middle of nowhere and a hick policeman picks him up for speeding. Mr. Ketchum gritted his teeth and waited.

The man in the dark uniform and wide-brimmed hat leaned over into the window. "License."

Mr. Ketchum slid a shaking hand into his inside pocket and drew out his billfold. He felt around for his license. He handed it over, noticed how expressionless the face of the policeman was. He sat there quietly while the policeman held a flashlight beam on the license.

"From New Jersey."

"Yes, that . . . that's right," said Mr. Ketchum.

The policeman kept staring at the license. Mr. Ketchum stirred restlessly on the seat and pressed his lips together. "It hasn't expired," he finally said.

He saw the dark head of the policeman lift. Then, he gasped as the narrow circle of flashlight blinded him. He twisted his head away.

The light was gone. Mr. Ketchum blinked his watering eyes.

"Don't they read traffic signs in New Jersey?" the policeman asked.

"Why, I . . . You mean the sign that said p-population sixty-seven?"

"No, I don't mean that sign," said the policeman.

"Oh." Mr. Ketchum cleared his throat. "Well, that's the only sign I saw," he said.

"You're a bad driver then."

"Well, I'm—"

"The sign said the speed limit is fifteen miles an hour. You were doing fifty."

"Oh. I . . . I'm afraid I didn't see it."

"The speed limit is fifteen miles an hour whether you see it or not."

"Well . . . at—at *this* hour of the morning?"

"Did you see a timetable on the sign?" the policeman asked.

"No, of course not. I mean, I didn't see the sign at all."

"*Didn't* you?"

Mr. Ketchum felt hair prickling along the nape of his neck. "Now, now see here," he began faintly, then stopped and stared at the policeman. "May I have my license back?" he finally asked when the policeman didn't speak.

The policeman said nothing. He stood on the street, motionless.

"May I—?" Mr. Ketchum started.

"Follow our car," said the officer abruptly and strode away.

Mr. Ketchum stared at him, dumbfounded. *Hey wait!* he almost yelled. The officer hadn't even given him back his license. Mr. Ketchum felt a sudden coldness in his stomach.

"What *is* this?" he muttered as he watched the policeman getting back into his car. The police car pulled away from the curb, its roof light spinning again.

Mr. Ketchum followed.

"This is ridiculous," he said aloud. They had no right to do this. Was this the Middle Ages? His thick lips pressed into a jaded mouth line as he followed the police car along Main Street.

Two blocks up, the police car turned. Mr. Ketchum saw his headlights splash across a glass storefront. *Hand's Groceries* read the weather-worn letters.

There were no lamps on the street. It was like driving along an inky passage. Ahead were only the three red eyes of the police car's rear lights and spotlight; behind only impenetrable blackness. The end of a perfect day, thought Mr. Ketchum; picked up for speeding in Zachry, Maine. He shook his head and groaned. Why hadn't he just spent his vacation in Newark; slept late, gone to shows, eaten, watched television?

The police car turned right at the next corner, then, a block block up, turned left again and stopped. Mr. Ketchum pulled up behind it as its lights went out. There was no sense in this. This was only cheap melodrama. They could just as easily have fined him on Main Street. It was the rustic mind. Debasing someone from a big city gave them a sense of vengeful eminence.

Mr. Ketchum waited. Well, he wasn't going to haggle. He'd pay his fine without a word and depart. He jerked the hand brake. Suddenly he frowned, realizing that they could fine him anything they wanted. They could charge him $500 if they chose! The heavy man had heard stories about small-town police, about the absolute authority they wielded. He cleared his throat viscidly. Well, this is absurd, he thought. What foolish imagination.

The policeman opened the door.

"Get out," he said.

There was no light in the street or in any building. Mr. Ketchum swallowed. All he could really see was the black figure of the policeman.

"Is this the—station?" he asked.

"Turn out your lights and come on," said the policeman.

Mr. Ketchum pushed in the chrome knob and got out. The policeman slammed the door. It made a loud, echoing noise; as if they were inside an unlighted warehouse instead of on a street. Mr. Ketchum glanced upward. The illusion was complete. There were neither stars nor moon. Sky and earth ran together blackly.

The policeman's hard fingers clamped on his arm. Mr. Ketchum lost balance a moment, then caught himself and fell into a quick stride beside the tall figure of the policeman.

"Dark here," he heard himself saying in a voice not entirely familiar.

The policeman said nothing. The other policeman fell into step on the other side of him. Mr. Ketchum told himself: These damned hick-town nazis were doing their best to intimidate him. Well, they wouldn't succeed.

Mr. Ketchum sucked in a breath of the damp, sea-smelling air and let it shudder out. A crumby town of 67 and they have two policemen patrolling the streets at three in the morning. Ridiculous.

He almost tripped over the step when they reached it. The policeman on his left side caught him under the elbow.

"Thank you," Mr. Ketchum muttered automatically. The policeman didn't reply. Mr. Ketchum licked his lips. Cordial oaf, he thought and managed a fleeting smile to himself. There, that was better. No point in letting this get to him.

He blinked as the door was pulled open and, despite himself, felt a sign of relief filtering through him. It was a police station all right. There was the podiumed desk, there a bulletin board, there a black, pot-bellied stove unlit, there a scarred bench against the wall, there a door, there the floor covered with a cracked and grimy linoleum that had once been green.

"Sit down and wait," said the policeman.

Mr. Ketchum looked at his lean, angled face, his swarthy skin. There was no division in his eyes between iris and pupil. It was all one darkness. He wore a dark uniform that fitted him loosely.

Mr. Ketchum didn't get to see the other policeman because both of them went into the next room. He stood watching the closed door a moment. Should he leave, drive away? No, they'd have his address on the license. Then again, they might actually want him to attempt to leave. You never knew what sort of warped minds these small-town police had. They might even—shoot him down if he tried to leave.

Mr. Ketchum sat heavily on the bench. No, he was letting imagination run amuck. This was merely a small town on the Maine seacoast and they were merely going to fine him for—

Well, why didn't they fine him then? What was all this play-acting? The heavy man pressed his lips together. Very well, let them play it the way they chose. This was better than driving anyway. He closed his eyes. I'll just rest them, he thought.

After a few moments he opened them again. It was damned quiet. He looked around the dimly lit room. The walls were dirty and bare except for a clock and one picture that hung behind the desk. It was a painting—more likely a reproduction—of a bearded man. The hat he wore was a seaman's hat. Probably one of Zachry's ancient mariners. No; probably not even that. Probably a Sears Roebuck print: *Bearded Seaman.*

Mr. Ketchum grunted to himself. Why a police station should have such a print was beyond him. Except, of course, that Zachry was on the Atlantic. Probably its main source of income was from fishing. Anyway, what did it matter? Mr. Ketchum lowered his gaze.

In the next room he could hear the muffled voices of the two policemen. He tried to hear what they were saying but he couldn't. He glared at the closed door. Come *on*, will you? he thought. He looked at the clock again. Three twenty-two. He checked it with his wrist watch. About right. The door opened and the two policemen came out.

One of them left. The remaining one—the one who had taken Mr. Ketchum's license—went over to the raised desk and switched on the gooseneck lamp over it, drew a big ledger out of the top drawer and started writing in it. *At last,* thought Mr. Ketchum.

A minute passed.

"I—" Mr. Ketchum cleared his throat. "I beg your—"

His voice broke off as the cold gaze of the policeman raised from the ledger and fixed on him.

"Are you . . . That is, am I to be—fined now?"

The policeman looked back at the ledger. "Wait," he said.

"But it's past three in the mor—" Mr. Ketchum caught himself. He tried to look coldly belligerent. "Very well," he said curtly. "Would you kindly tell me how long it will be?"

The policeman kept writing in the ledger. Mr. Ketchum sat there stiffly, looking at him. *Insufferable,* he thought. This was the last damned time he'd ever go within a hundred miles of this damned New England.

The policeman looked up. "Married?" he asked.

Mr. Ketchum stared at him.

"Are you married?"

"No, I—it's on the license," Mr. Ketchum blurted. He felt a tremor of pleasure at his retort and, at the same time, an impaling of strange dread at talking back to the man.

"Family in Jersey?" asked the policeman.

"Yes. I mean no. Just a sister in Wiscons—"

Mr. Ketchum didn't finish. He watched the policeman write it down. He wished he could rid himself of this queasy distress.

"Employed?" asked the policeman.

Mr. Ketchum swallowed. "Well," he said, "I—I have no one particular em—"

"Unemployed," said the policeman.

"Not at all; not at *all,*" said Mr. Ketchum stiffly. "I'm a—a free-lance salesman. I purchase stocks and lots from . . ." His voice faded as the policeman looked at him. Mr. Ketchum swallowed three times before the lump stayed down. He realized that he was sitting on the very edge of the bench as if poised to spring to the defense of his life. He forced himself to settle back. He drew in a deep breath. Relax, he told himself. Deliberately, he closed his eyes. There. He'd catch a few winks. May as well make the best of this, he thought.

The room was still except for the tinny, resonant ticking of the clock. Mr. Ketchum felt his heart pulsing with slow, dragging beats. He shifted his heavy frame uncomfortably on the hard bench. *Ridiculous,* he thought.

Mr. Ketchum opened his eyes and frowned. That damned picture. You could almost imagine that bearded seaman was looking at you.

"Uh!"

Mr. Ketchum's mouth snapped shut, his eyes jerked open, irises flaring. He started forward on the bench, then shrank back.

A swarthy-faced man was bent over him, hand on Mr. Ketchum's shoulder.

"Yes?" Mr. Ketchum asked, heart jolting.

The man smiled.

"Chief Shipley," he said. "Would you come into my office?"

"Oh," said Mr. Ketchum. "Yes. Yes."

He straightened up, grimacing at the stiffness in his back muscles. The man stepped back and Mr. Ketchum pushed up with a grunt, his eyes moving automatically to the wall clock. It was a few minutes past four.

"Look," he said, not yet awake enough to feel intimidated. "Why can't I pay my fine and leave?"

Shipley's smile was without warmth.

"We run things a little different here in Zachry," he said.

They entered a small, musty-smelling office.

"Sit down," said the chief, walking around the desk while Mr. Ketchum settled into a straight-backed chair that creaked.

"I don't understand why I can't pay my fine and leave."

"In due course," said Shipley.

"But—" Mr. Ketchum didn't finish. Shipley's smile gave the impression of being no more than a diplomatically veiled warning. Gritting his teeth, the heavy man cleared his throat and waited while the chief looked down at the sheet of paper on his desk. He noticed how poorly Shipley's suit fitted. Yokels, the heavy man thought, don't even know how to dress.

"I see you're not married," Shipley said.

Mr. Ketchum said nothing. Give them a taste of their own no-talk medicine he decided.

"Have you friends in Maine?" Shipley asked.

"Why?"

"Just routine questions, Mr. Ketchum," said the chief. "Your only family is a sister in Wisconsin?"

Mr. Ketchum looked at him without speaking. What had all this to do with a traffic violation?

"Sir?" asked Shipley.

"I already told you; that is, I told the officer. I don't see—"

"Here on business?"

Mr. Ketchum's mouth opened soundlessly.

"Why are you asking me all these questions?" he asked. *Stop shaking!* he ordered himself furiously.

"Routine. Are you here on business?"

"I'm on my vacation. And I don't see this at all! I've been patient up to now, but, *blast it*, I demand to be fined and released!"

"I'm afraid that's impossible," said the chief.

Mr. Ketchum's mouth fell open. It was like waking up from a nightmare and discovering that the dream was still going on. "I—I don't understand," he said.

"You'll have to appear before the judge."

"But that's ridiculous."

"Is it?"

"Yes, it is. I'm a citizen of the United States. I demand my rights."

Chief Shipley's smile faded.

"You limited those rights when you broke our law," he said. "Now you have to pay for it as we declare."

Mr. Ketchum stared blankly at the man. He realized that he was completely in their hands. They could fine him anything they pleased or put him in jail indefinitely. All these questions he'd been asked; he didn't know why they'd asked them but he knew that his answers revealed him as almost rootless, with no one who cared if he lived or—

The room seemed to totter. Sweat broke out on his body.

"You can't *do* this," he said; but it was not an argument.

"You'll have to spend the night in jail," said the chief. "In the morning you'll see the judge."

"But this is ridiculous!" Mr. Ketchum burst out. *"Ridiculous!"*

He caught himself. "I'm entitled to one phone call," he said quickly. "I can make a telephone call. It's my legal right."

"It would be," said Shipley, "if there was any telephone service in Zachry."

When they took him to his cell, Mr. Ketchum saw a painting in the hall. It was of the same bearded seaman. Mr. Ketchum didn't notice if the eyes followed him or not.

Mr. Ketchum stirred. A look of confusion lined his sleep-numbed face. There was a clanking sound behind him; he reared up on his elbow.

A policeman came into the cell and set down a covered tray.

"Breakfast," he said. He was older than the other policemen, even older than Shipley. His hair was iron-gray, his cleanly shaved face seamed around the mouth and eyes. His uniform fitted him badly.

As the policeman started relocking the door, Mr. Ketchum asked, "When do I see the judge?"

The policeman looked at him a moment. "Don't know," he said and turned away.

"Wait!" Mr. Ketchum called out.

The receding footsteps of the policeman sounded hollowly on the cement floor. Mr. Ketchum kept staring at the spot where the policeman had been. Veils of sleep peeled from his mind.

He sat up, rubbed deadened fingers over his eyes and held up his wrist. Seven minutes past nine. The heavy man grimaced. By God, they were going to hear about this! His nostrils twitched. He sniffed, started to reach for the tray; then pulled back his hand.

"No," he muttered. He wouldn't eat their damned food. He sat there stiffly, doubled at the waist, glaring at his sock-covered feet.

His stomach grumbled uncooperatively.

"Well," he muttered after a minute. Swallowing, he reached over and lifted off the tray cover.

He couldn't check the *oh* of surprise that passed his lips.

The three eggs were fried in butter, bright yellow eyes focused straight on the ceiling, ringed about with long crisp lengths of meaty, corrugated bacon. Next to them was a platter of four book-thick slices of toast spread with creamy butter swirls, a paper cup of jelly leaning on them. There was a tall glass of frothy orange juice, a dish of strawberries bleeding in alabaster cream. Finally, a tall pot from which wavered the pungent and unmistakable fragrance of freshly brewed coffee.

Mr. Ketchum picked up the glass of orange juice. He took a few drops in his mouth and rolled them experimentally over his tongue. The citric acid tingled deliciously on his warm tongue. He swallowed. If it was poisoned it was by a master's hand. Saliva tided in his mouth. He suddenly remembered that, just before he was picked up, he had been meaning to stop at a café for food.

While he ate, warily but decidedly, Mr. Ketchum tried to figure out the motivation behind this magnificent breakfast.

It was the rural mind again. They regretted their blunder. It seemed a flimsy notion, but there it was. The food was superb. One thing you had to say for these New Englanders; they could cook like a son-of-a-gun. Breakfast for Mr. Ketchum was usually a sweet roll, heated, and coffee. Since he was a boy in his father's house he hadn't eaten a breakfast like this.

He was just putting down his third cup of well-creamed coffee when footsteps sounded in the hall. Mr. Ketchum smiled. Good timing, he thought. He stood.

Chief Shipley stopped outside the cell. "Had your breakfast?"

Mr. Ketchum nodded. If the chief expected thanks he was in for a sad surprise. Mr. Ketchum picked up his coat.

The chief didn't move.

"Well . . .?" said Mr. Ketchum after a few minutes. He tried to put it coldly and authoritatively. It came out somewhat less.

Chief Shipley looked at him expressionlessly. Mr. Ketchum felt his breath faltering.

"May I inquire—?" he began.

"Judge isn't in yet," said Shipley.

"But . . ." Mr. Ketchum didn't know what to say.

"Just came in to tell you," said Shipley. He turned and was gone.

Mr. Ketchum was furious. He looked down at the remains of his breakfast as if they contained the answer to this situation. He drummed a fist against his thigh. *Insufferable!* What were they trying to do—intimidate him? Well, by God—

—they were succeeding.

Mr. Ketchum walked over to the bars. He looked up and down the empty hallway. There was a cold knot inside him. The food seemed to have turned to dry lead in his stomach. He banged the heel of his right hand once against the cold bar. By God! *By God!*

It was two o'clock in the afternoon when Chief Shipley and the old policeman came to the cell door. Wordlessly the policeman opened it. Mr. Ketchum stepped into the hallway and waited again, putting on his coat while the door was relocked.

He walked in short, inflexible strides between the two men, not even glancing at the picture on the wall. "Where are we going?" he asked.

"Judge is sick," said Shipley. "We're taking you out to his house to pay your fine."

Mr. Ketchum sucked in his breath. He wouldn't argue with them; he just wouldn't. "All right," he said. "If that's the way you have to do it."

"Only way to do it," said the chief, looking ahead, his face an expressionless mask.

Mr. Ketchum pressed down the corners of a slim smile. This was better. It was almost over now. He'd pay his fine and clear out.

It was foggy outside. Sea mist rolled across the street like driven smoke. Mr. Ketchum pulled on his hat and shuddered. The damp air seemed to filter through his flesh and drew itself around his bones. Nasty day, he thought. He moved down the steps, eyes searching for his Ford.

The old policeman opened the back door of the police car and Shipley gestured toward the inside.

"What about *my* car?" Mr. Ketchum asked.

"We'll come back here after you see the judge," said Shipley.

"Oh, I . . ."

Mr. Ketchum hesitated. Then he bent over and squeezed into the car, dropping down on the back seat. He shivered as the cold of the leather pierced trouser wool. He edged over as the chief got in.

The policeman slammed the door shut. Again that hollow sound, like the slamming of a coffin lid in a crypt. Mr. Ketchum grimaced as the simile occurred to him.

The policeman got into the car and Mr. Ketchum heard the motor cough into liquid life. He sat there breathing slowly and deeply while the policeman out-choked warmth into the engine. He looked out the window at his left.

The fog was *just* like smoke. They might have been parked in a burning garage. Except for that bone-gripping dampness. Mr. Ketchum cleared his throat. He heard the chief shift on the seat beside him.

"Cold," Mr. Ketchum said, automatically.

The chief said nothing.

Mr. Ketchum pressed back as the car pulled away from the curb, U-turned and started slowly down the fog-veiled street. He listened to the crisp sibilance of tires on wet paving, the rhythmic swish of the wipers as they cleared off circle segments on the misted windshield.

After a moment he looked at his watch. Almost three. Half a day shot in this blasted Zachry.

He looked out through the window again as the town ghosted past. He thought he saw brick buildings along the curb but he wasn't sure. He looked down at his white hands, then glanced over at Shipley. The chief was sitting stiffly upright on the seat, staring straight ahead. Mr. Ketchum swallowed. The air seemed stagnant in his lungs.

On Main Street the fog seemed thinner. Probably the sea breezes, Mr. Ketchum thought. He looked up and down the street. All the stores and offices looked closed. He glanced at the other side of the street. Same thing.

"Where is everybody?" he asked.

"What?"

"I said where *is* everybody?"

"Home," the chief said.

"But it's Wednesday," said Mr. Ketchum. "Aren't your—stores open?"

"Bad day," said Shipley. "Not worth it."

Mr. Ketchum glanced at the sallow-faced chief, then withdrew his look hastily. He felt cold premonition spidering in his stomach again. What in God's name *is* this? he asked himself. It had been bad enough in the cell. Here, tracking through this sea of mist, it was altogether worse.

"That's right," he heard his nerve-sparked voice saying. "There are only sixty-seven people, aren't there?"

The chief said nothing.

"How . . . h-how old is Zachry?"

In the silence he heard the chief's finger joints crackle dryly.

"Hundred fifty years," said Shipley.

"That old," said Mr. Ketchum. He swallowed with effort. His throat hurt a little. Come *on*, he told himself. *Relax.*

"How come it's named Zachry?" The words spilled out, uncontrolled.

"Noah Zachry founded it," said the chief.

"Oh. Oh. I see. I guess that picture in the station . . . ?"

"That's right," said Shipley.

Mr. Ketchum blinked. So that was Noah Zachry, founder of this town they were driving through—

—*block after block after block.* There was a cold, heavy sinking in Mr. Ketchum's stomach as the idea came to him.

In a town so big, why were there only 67 people?

He opened his mouth to ask it, then couldn't. The answer might be wrong.

"Why are there only —?" The words came out anyway before he could stop them. His body jolted at the shock of hearing them.

"What?"

"Nothing, nothing. That is—" Mr. Ketchum drew in a shaking breath. No help for it. He had to know.

"How come there are only sixty-seven?"

"They go away," said Shipley.

Mr. Ketchum blinked. The answer came as such an anticlimax. His brow furrowed. Well, what else? he asked himself defensively. Remote, antiquated, Zachry would have little attraction for its younger generations. Mass gravitation to more interesting places would be inevitable.

The heavy man settled back against the seat. Of course. Think how much *I* want to leave the dump, he thought, and I don't even live here.

His gaze slid forward through the windshield, caught by something. A banner hanging across the street. BARBECUE TONIGHT. Celebration, he thought. They probably went berserk every fortnight and had themselves a rip-roaring taffy pull or fishnet-mending orgy.

"Who was Zachry anyway?" he asked. The silence was getting to him again.

"Sea captain," said the chief.

"Oh?"

"Whaled in the South Seas," said Shipley.

Abruptly, Main Street ended. The police car veered left onto a dirt road. Out the window Mr. Ketchum watched shadowy bushes glide by. There was only the sound of the engine laboring in second and of gravelly dirt spitting out from under the tires. Where does the judge live, on a mountain top? He shifted his weight and grunted.

The fog began thinning now. Mr. Ketchum could see grass and trees, all with a grayish cast to them. The car turned and faced the ocean. Mr. Ketchum looked down at the opaque carpet of fog below. The car kept turning. It faced the crest of the hill again.

Mr. Ketchum coughed softly. "Is . . . uh, that the judge's house up there?" he asked.

"Yes," the chief answered.

"High," said Mr. Ketchum.

The car kept turning on the narrow, dirt road, now facing the ocean, now Zachry, now the bleak, hill-topping house. It was a grayish-white house, three stories high, at each end of it the crag of an attic tower. It looked as old as Zachry itself, thought Mr. Ketchum. The car turned. He was facing the fog-crusted ocean again.

Mr. Ketchum looked down at his hands. Was it a deception of the light or were they really shaking? He tried to swallow but there was no moisture in his throat and he coughed instead, rattlingly. This is so *stupid*, he thought; there's no reason in the world for this. He saw his hands clench together.

The car was moving up the final rise toward the house now. Mr. Ketchum felt his breaths shortening. *I don't want to go,* he heard someone saying in his mind. He felt a sudden urge to shove out the door and run. Muscles tensed emphatically.

He closed his eyes. For God's sake, *stop* it! he yelled at himself. There was nothing wrong about this but his distorted interpretation of it. These were modern times. Things had explanations and people had reasons. Zachry's people had a reason too; a narrow distrust of city dwellers. This was their socially acceptable revenge. That made sense. After all—

The car stopped. The chief pushed open the door on his side and got out. The policeman reached back and opened the other door for Mr. Ketchum. The heavy man found one of his legs and foot to be numb. He had to clutch at the top of the door for support. He stamped the foot on the ground.

"Went to sleep," he said.

Neither of the men answered. Mr. Ketchum glanced at the house; he squinted. Had he seen a dark green drape slip back into place? He winced and made a startled noise as his arm was touched and the chief gestured toward the house. The three men started toward it.

"I, uh . . . don't have much cash on me, I'm afraid," he said. "I hope a traveler's check will be all right."

"Yes," said the chief.

They went up the porch steps, stopped in front of the door. The policeman turned a big, brass key-head and Mr. Ketchum heard a bell ring tinnily inside. He stood looking through the door curtains. Inside, he could make out the skeletal form of a hat rack. He shifted weight and the boards creaked under him. The policeman rang the bell again.

"Maybe he's—too sick," Mr. Ketchum suggested faintly.

Neither of the men looked at him. Mr. Ketchum felt his muscles tensing. He glanced back over his shoulder. Could they catch him if he ran for it?

He looked back disgustedly. You pay your fine and you leave, he explained patiently to himself. That's all; you pay your fine and you leave.

Inside the house there was dark movement. Mr. Ketchum looked up, startled in spite of himself. A tall woman was approaching the door.

The door opened. The woman was thin, wearing an ankle-length black dress with a white oval pin at her throat. Her face was swarthy, seamed with threadlike lines. Mr. Ketchum slipped off his hat automatically.

"Come in," said the woman.

Mr. Ketchum stepped into the hall.

"You can leave your hat there," said the woman, pointing toward the hat rack that looked like a tree ravaged by flame. Mr. Ketchum dropped his hat over one of the dark pegs. As he did, his eye was caught by a large painting near the foot of the staircase. He started to speak but the woman said, "This way."

They started down the hall. Mr. Ketchum stared at the painting as they passed it.

"Who's that woman," he asked, "standing next to Zachry?"

"His wife," said the chief.

"But she—"

Mr. Ketchum's voice broke off suddenly as he heard a whimper rising in his throat. Shocked, he drowned it out with a sudden clearing of the throat. He felt ashamed of himself. Still . . . Zachry's wife?

The woman opened a door. "Wait in here," she said.

The heavy man walked in. He turned to say something to the chief. Just in time to see the door shut.

"Say, uh . . ." He walked to the door and put his hand on the knob. It didn't turn.

He frowned. He ignored the pile-driver beats of his heart. "Hey, what's going on?" Cheerily bluff, his voice echoed off the walls. Mr. Ketchum turned and looked around. The room was empty. It was a square, empty room.

He turned back to the door, lips moving as he sought the proper words.

"Okay," he said abruptly, "it's very—" He twisted the knob sharply. "Okay, it's a very funny joke." By God, he was mad. "I've taken all I'm—"

He whirled at the sound, teeth bared.

There was nothing. The room was empty. He looked around dizzily. What was that sound? A dull sound, like water rushing.

"Hey," he said automatically. He turned to the door. "Hey!" he yelled, "cut it out! Who do you think you are anyway?"

He turned on weakening legs. The sound was louder. Mr. Ketchum ran a hand over his brow. It was covered with sweat. It was warm in there.

"Okay, okay," he said, "it's a fine joke but—"

Before he could go on, his voice had corkscrewed into an awful, wracking sob. Mr. Ketchum staggered a little. He stared at the room. He whirled and fell back against the door. His outflung hand touched the wall and jerked way.

It was hot.

"*Huh?*" he asked incredulously.

That was impossible. This was a joke. This was their deranged idea of a little joke. It was a game they played. Scare the City Slicker was the name of the game.

"Okay!" he yelled. "*Okay!* It's funny, it's very funny! Now let me out of here or there's going to be trouble!"

He pounded at the door. Suddenly he kicked it. The room was getting

hotter. It was almost as hot as an—

Mr. Ketchum was petrified. His mouth sagged open.

The questions they'd asked him. The loose way the clothes fit everyone he'd met. The rich food they'd given him to eat. The empty streets. The savagelike swarthy coloring of the men, of the woman. The way they'd all looked at him. And the woman in the painting, Noah Zachry's wife—*a native woman with her teeth filed to a point.*

BARBECUE TONIGHT.

Mr. Ketchum screamed. He kicked and pounded on the door. He threw his heavy body against it. He shrieked at the people outside.

"Let me out! *Let me out!* LET . . . ME . . . OUT!"

The worst part about it was, he just couldn't believe it was really happening.

Seabury Quinn

THE PHANTOM FARMHOUSE

I HAD BEEN at the New Briarcliff Sanitarium nearly three weeks before I actually saw the house.

Every morning, as I lay abed after the nurse had taken my temperature, I wondered what was beyond the copse of fir and spruce at the turn of the road. The picture seemed incomplete without chimneys rising among the evergreens. I thought about it so much I finally convinced myself there really was a house in the wood. A house where people lived and worked and were happy.

All during the long, trying days when I was learning to navigate a wheelchair, I used to picture the house and the people who lived in it. There would be a father, I was sure; a stout, good-natured father, somewhat bald, who sat on the porch and smoked a cob pipe in the evening. And there was a mother, too; a waistless, plaid-skirted mother with hair smoothly parted over her forehead, who sat beside the father as he rocked and smoked, and who had a brown workbasket in her lap. She spread the stocking feet over her outstretched fingers and her vigilant needle spied out and closed every hole with a cunning no mechanical loom could rival.

Then there was a daughter. I was a little hazy in my conception of her; but I knew she was tall and slender as a hazel wand, and that her eyes were blue and wide and sympathetic.

Picturing the house and its people became a favorite pastime with me during the time I was acquiring the art of walking all over again. By the time I was able to trust my legs on the road I felt I knew my way to my vision-friends' home as well as I knew the byways of my own parish; though I had as yet not set foot outside the sanitarium.

Oddly enough, I chose the evening for my first long stroll. It was unusually warm for September in Maine, and some of the sturdier of the convalescents had been playing tennis during the afternoon. After dinner they sat on the veranda, comparing notes on their respective cases of influenza, or matching experiences in appendicitis operations.

After building the house bit by bit from my imagination, as a child

23

pieces together a picture puzzle, I should have been bitterly disappointed if the woods had proved empty; yet when I reached the turn of the road and found my dream house a reality, I was almost afraid. Bit for bit and part for part, it was as I had visualized it.

A long, rambling, comfortable-looking farmhouse it was, with a wide porch screened by vines, and a whitewashed picket fence about the little clearing before it. There was a tumbledown gate in the fence, one of the kind that is held shut with a weighted chain. Looking closely, I saw the weight was a disused ploughshare. Leading from gate to porch was a path of flat stones, laid unevenly in the short grass, and bordered with a double row of clam shells. A lamp burned in the front room, sending out cheerful golden rays to meet the silver moonlight.

A strange, eerie sensation came over me as I stood there. Somehow, I felt I had seen that house before; many, many times before; yet I had never been in that part of Maine till I came to Briarcliff, nor had anyone ever described the place to me. Indeed, except for my idle dreams, I had had no intimation that there was a house in those pines at all.

"Who lives in the house at the turn of the road?" I asked the fat man who roomed next to me.

He looked at me as blankly as if I had addressed him in Choctaw, then countered, "What road?"

"Why, the south road," I explained. "I mean the house in the pines—just beyond the curve, you know."

If such a thing had not been obviously absurd, I should have thought he looked frightened at my answer. Certainly his already prominent eyes started a bit further from his face.

"Nobody lives there," he assured me. "Nobody's lived there for years. There isn't any house there."

I became angry. What right had this fellow to make my civil question the occasion for an ill-timed jest? "As you please," I replied. "Perhaps there isn't any house there for *you*; but I saw one there last night."

"My God!" he ejaculated, and hurried away as if I'd just told him I was infected with smallpox.

Later in the day I overheard a snatch of conversation between him and one of his acquaintances in the lounge.

"I tell you it's so," he was saying with great earnestness. "I thought it was a lot of poppycock, myself; but that clergyman saw it last night. I'm going to pack my traps and get back to the city, and not waste any time about it, either."

"Rats!" his companion scoffed. "He must have been stringing you."

Turning to light a cigar, he caught sight of me. "Say, Mr. Weatherby," he called, "you didn't mean to tell my friend here that you really saw a house down by those pines last night, did you?"

"I certainly did," I answered, "and I tell you, too. There's nothing unusual about it, is there?"

"Is there?" he repeated. "Is there? Say, what'd it look like?"

I described it to him as well as I could, and his eyes grew as wide as those of a child hearing the story of Bluebeard.

"Well, I'll be a Chinaman's uncle!" he declared as I finished. "I sure will!"

"See here," I demanded. "What's all the mystery about that farmhouse? Why shouldn't I see it? It's there to be seen, isn't it?"

He gulped once or twice, as if there were something hot in his mouth, before he answered:

"Look here, Mr. Weatherby, I'm telling you this for your own good. You'd better stay in nights; and you'd better stay away from those pines in particular."

Nonplussed at this unsolicited advice, I was about to ask an explanation, when I detected the after-tang of whisky on his breath. I understood, then. I was being made the butt of a drunken joke by a pair of race course followers.

"I'm very much obliged, I'm sure," I replied with dignity, "but if you don't mind, I'll choose my own comings and goings."

"Oh, go as far as you like"—he waved his arms wide in token of my complete free-agency—"go as far as you like. I'm going to New York."

And he did. The pair of them left the sanitarium that afternoon.

A slight recurrence of my illness held me housebound for several days after my conversation with the two sportively inclined gentlemen, and the next time I ventured out at night the moon had waxed to the full, pouring a flood of light upon the earth that rivaled midday. The minutest objects were as readily distinguished as they would have been before sunset; in fact, I remember comparing the evening to a silver-plated noon.

As I trudged along the road to the pine copse I was busy formulating plans for intruding into the family circle at the farmhouse; devising all manner of pious frauds by which to scrape acquaintance.

"Shall I feign having lost my way, and inquire direction to the sanitarium; or shall I ask if some mythical acquaintance, a John Squires, for instance, lives there?" I asked myself as I neared the turn of the road.

Fortunately for my conscience, all these subterfuges were unnecessary, for as I neared the whitewashed fence, a girl left the porch and walked quickly to the gate, where she stood gazing pensively along the moonlit road. It was almost as if she were coming to meet me, I thought, as I slacked my pace and assumed an air of deliberate casualness.

Almost abreast of her, I lessened my pace still more, and looked directly at her. Then I knew why my conception of the girl who lived in that house had been misty and indistinct. For the same reason the venerable John had faltered in his description of the New Jerusalem until his vision in the Isle of Patmos.

From the smoothly parted hair above her wide, forget-me-not eyes, to the hem of her white cotton frock, she was as slender and lovely as a Rossetti saint; as wonderful to the eye as a mediaeval poet's vision of his lost love in paradise. Her forehead, evenly framed in the beaten bronze of her hair, was wide and high, and startlingly white, and her brows were delicately penciled as if laid on by an artist with a camel's-hair brush. The eyes themselves were sweet and clear as forest pools mirroring the September sky, and lifted a little at the corners, like an Oriental's, giving her face a quaint, exotic look in the midst of these Maine woods.

So slender was her figure that the swell of her bosom was barely perceptible under the light stuff of her dress, and, as she stood immobile in the nimbus of moon rays, the undulation of the line from her shoulders to ankles was what painters call a "curve of motion."

One hand rested lightly on the gate, a hand as finely cut as a bit of Italian sculpture, and scarcely less white than the limed wood supporting it. I noticed idly that the forefinger was somewhat longer than its fellows, and that the nails were almond shaped and very pink—almost red—as if they had been rouged and brightly polished.

No man can take stock of a woman thus, even in a cursory, fleeting glimpse, without her being aware of the inspection, and in the minute my eyes drank up her beauty, our glances crossed and held.

The look she gave back was as calm and unperturbed as though I had been nonexistent; one might have thought I was an invisible wraith of the night; yet the faint suspicion of a flush quickening in her throat and cheeks told me she was neither unaware nor unappreciative of my scrutiny.

Mechanically, I raised my cap, and, wholly without conscious volition, I heard my own voice asking:

"May I trouble you for a drink from your well? I'm from the sanitarium—only a few days out of bed, in fact—and I fear I've overdone myself in my walk."

A smile flitted across her rather wide lips, quick and sympathetic as a mother's response to her child's request, as she swung the gate open for me.

"Surely—" she answered, and her voice had all the sweetness of the south wind soughing through her native pines—"surely you may drink at our well, and rest yourself, too—if you wish."

She preceded me up the path, quickening her pace as she neared the house, and running nimbly up the steps to the porch. From where I stood beside the old-fashioned well, fitted with windlass and bucket, I could hear the sound of whispering voices in earnest conversation. Hers I recognized, lowered though it was, by the flutelike purling of its tones; the other two were deeper, and, it seemed to me, hoarse and throaty. Somehow, odd as it seemed, there was a queer, canine note in them, dimly reminding me of the muttering of not too friendly dogs—such fractious growls I had heard while doing missionary duty in Alaska, when the savage, half-wolf malemutes were not fed promptly at the relay stations.

Her voice rose a trifle higher, as if in argument, and I fancied I heard her whisper, "This one is mine, I tell you; mine. I'll brook no interference. Go to your own hunting."

An instant later there was a reluctant assenting growl from the shadow of the vines curtaining the porch, and a light laugh from the girl as she descended the steps, swinging a bright tin cup in her hand. For a second she looked at me, as she sent the bucket plunging into the stone-curbed well; then she announced, in explanation:

"We're great hunters here, you know. The season is just in, and Dad and I have the worst quarrels about whose game is whose."

She laughed in recollection of their argument, and I laughed with her. I had been quite a Nimrod as a boy, myself, and well I remembered the heated controversies as to whose charge of shot was responsible for some luckless bunny's demise.

The well was very deep, and my breath was coming fast by the time I had helped her wind the bucket-rope upon the windlass; but the water was cold as only spring-fed well water can be. As she poured it from the bucket it shone almost like foam in the moonlight, and seemed to whisper with a half-human voice, instead of gurgling as other water does when poured.

I had drunk water in nearly every quarter of the globe; but never such water as that. Cold as the breath from a glacier: limpid as visualized air, it was yet so light and tasteless in substance that only the chill in my throat and the sight of the liquid in the cup told me that I was doing more than going through the motions of drinking.

"And now, will you rest?" she invited, as I finished my third draught. "We've an extra chair on the porch for you."

Behind the screen of vines I found her father and mother seated in the rays of the big kitchen lamp. They were just as I had expected to find them; plain, homely, sincere country folk, courteous in their reception and anxious to make a sick stranger welcome. Both were stout, with the comfortable stoutness of middle age and good health; but both had surprisingly slender hands. I noticed, too, that the same characteristic of an over-long forefinger was apparent in their hands as in their daughter's, and that both their nails were trimmed to points and stained almost a brilliant red.

"My father, Mr. Squires," the girl introduced, "and my mother, Mrs. Squires."

I could not repress a start. These people bore the very name I had casually thought to use when inquiring for some imaginary person. My lucky stars had surely guided me away from that attempt to scrape an acquaintance. What a figure I should have cut if I had actually asked for Mr. Squires!

Though I was not aware of it, my curious glance must have stayed longer on their reddened nails than I had intended, for Mrs. Squires looked deprecatingly at her hands. "We've all been turning, putting up fox grapes"—she included her husband and daughter with a comprehensive gesture. "And the stain just won't wash out; has to wear off, you know."

I spent, perhaps, two hours with my new-found friends, talking of everything from the best methods of potato culture to the surest way of landing a nine-pound bass. All three joined in the conversation and took a lively interest in the topics under discussion. After the vapid talk of the guests at the sanitarium, I found the simple, interested discourse of these country people as stimulating as wine, and when I left them it was with a hearty promise to renew my call at an early date.

"Better wait until after dark," Mr. Squires warned. "We'd be glad to see you any time; but we're so busy these fall days, we haven't much time for company."

I took the broad hint in the same friendly spirit it was given.

It must have grown chillier than I realized while I sat there, for my new friends' hands were clay-cold when I took them in mine at parting.

Homeward bound, a whimsical thought struck me so suddenly I laughed aloud. There was something suggestive of the dog tribe about the Squires family, though I could not for the life of me say what it was. Even Mildred, the daughter, beautiful as she was, with her light eyes, her rather prominent nose and her somewhat wide mouth, reminded me in some vague way of a lovely silver collie I had owned as a boy.

I struck a tassel of dried leaves from a cluster of weeds with my walking stick as I smiled at the fanciful conceit. The legend of the werewolf— those horrible monsters, formed as men, but capable of assuming bestial shape at will, and killing and eating their fellows, was as old as mankind's fear of the dark, but no mythology I had ever read contained a reference to dog-people.

Strange fancies strike us in the moonlight, sometimes.

September ripened to October, and the moon, which had been as round and bright as an exchange-worn coin when I first visited the Squires house, waned as thin as a shaving from a silversmith's lathe.

I became a regular caller at the house in the pines. Indeed, I grew to look forward to my nightly visits with those homely folk as a welcome relief from the tediously gay companionship of the over-sophisticated people at the sanitarium.

My habit of slipping away shortly after dinner was the cause of considerable comment and no little speculation on the part of my fellow convalescents, some of whom set it down to the eccentricity which, to their minds, was the inevitable concomitant of a minister's vocation, while others were frankly curious. Snatches of conversation I overheard now and then led me to believe that the objective of my strolls was the subject of wagering, and the guarded questions put to me in an effort to solve the mystery became more and more annoying.

I had no intention of taking any of them to the farmhouse with me. The Squires were my friends. Their cheerful talk and unassuming manners were as delightful a contrast to the atmosphere of the sanitarium as a breath of mountain balsam after the fetid air of a hothouse; but to the city-centered crowd at Briarcliff they would have been only the objects of less than half scornful patronage, the source of pitying amusement.

It was Miss Leahy who pushed the impudent curiosity further than any of the rest, however. One evening, as I was setting out, she met me at the gate and announced her intention of going with me.

"You must have found something *dreadfully* attractive to take you off every evening this way, Mr. Weatherby," she hazarded as she pursed her rather pretty, rouged lips at me and caught step with my walk. "We girls really *can't* let some little country lass take you away from us, you know. We simply can't."

I made no reply. It was scarcely possible to tell a pretty girl, even such a vain little flirt as Sara Leahy, to go home and mind her business. Yet that was just what I wanted to do. But I would not take her with me; to that I made up my mind. I would stop at the turn of the road, just out of sight of the farmhouse, and cut across the fields. If she wanted to accompany me on a cross-country hike in high-heeled slippers, she was welcome to do so.

Besides, she would tell the others that my wanderings were nothing more mysterious than nocturnal explorations of the nearby woods; which bit of misinformation would satisfy the busybodies at Briarcliff and relieve me of the espionage to which I was subjected, as well.

I smiled grimly to myself as I pictured her climbing over fences and ditches in her flimsy party frock and beaded pumps, and lengthened my stride toward the woods at the road's turn.

We marched to the limits of the field bordering the Squires' grove in silence, I thinking of the mild revenge I should soon wreak upon the pretty little busybody at my side, Miss Leahy too intent on holding the pace I set to waste breath in conversation.

As we neared the woods she halted, an expression of worry, almost fear, coming over her face.

"I don't believe I'll go any farther," she announced.

"No?" I replied, a trifle sarcastically. "And is your curiosity so easily satisfied?"

"It's not that." She turned half round, as if to retrace her steps. "I'm afraid of those woods."

"Indeed?" I queried. "And what is there to be afraid of? Bears, Indians, or wildcats. I've been through them several times without seeing anything terrifying." Now she had come this far, I was anxious to take her through the fields and underbrush.

"No-o," Miss Leahy answered, a nervous quaver in her voice, "I'm not afraid of anything like that; but—oh, I don't know what you call it. Pierre told me all about it the other day. Some kind of dreadful thing—loop—loop—something or other. It's a French word, and I can't remember it."

I was puzzled. Pierre Geronte was the ancient French-Canadian gardener at the sanitarium, and, like all doddering old men, would talk for hours to anyone who would listen. Also, like all *habitants*, he was full of wild folklore his ancestors brought overseas with them generations ago.

"What did Pierre tell you?" I asked.

"Why, he said that years ago some terrible people lived in these woods. They had the only house for miles 'round; and travelers stopped there for the night, sometimes. But no stranger was ever seen to leave that place, once he went in. One night the farmers gathered about the house and burned it, with the family that lived there. When the embers had cooled down they made a search, and found nearly a dozen bodies buried in the cellar. That was why no one ever came away from that dreadful place.

"They took the murdered men to the cemetery and buried them; but they dumped the charred bodies of the murderers into graves in the barnyard, without even saying a prayer over them. And Pierre says—Oh, Look! *Look!*"

She broke off her recital of the old fellow's story, and pointed a trembling hand across the field to the edge of the woods. A second more and she shrank against me, clutching at my coat with fear-stiffened fingers and crying with excitement and terror.

I looked in the direction she indicated, myself a little startled by the abject fear that had taken such sudden hold on her.

Something white and ungainly was running diagonally across the field from us, skirting the margin of the woods and making for the meadow that adjoined the sanitarium pasture. A second glance told me it was a sheep; probably one of the flock kept to supply our table with fresh meat.

I was laughing at the strength of the superstition that could make a girl see a figure of horror in an innocent mutton that had strayed away from its fellows and was scared out of its silly wits, when something else attracted my attention.

Loping along in the trail of the fleeing sheep, somewhat to the rear and a little to each side, were two other animals. At first glance they appeared to be a pair of large collies; but as I looked more intently, I saw that these animals were like nothing I had ever seen before. They were much larger than any collie—nearly as high as St. Bernards—yet shaped in a general way like Alaskan sledge-dogs—huskies.

The farther one was considerably the larger of the two, and ran with a slight limp, as if one of its hind paws had been injured. As nearly as I could tell in the indifferent light, they were a rusty brown color, very thick-haired and unkempt in appearance. But the strangest thing about them was the fact that both were tailless, which gave them a terrifyingly grotesque look.

As they ran, a third form, similar to the other two in shape, but smaller, slender as a greyhound, with much lighter-hued fur, broke from the thicket of short brush edging the wood and took up the chase, emitting a series of short, sharp yelps.

"Sheep-killers," I murmured, half to myself. "Odd. I've never seen dogs like that before."

"They're not dogs," wailed Miss Leahy against my coat. "They're not dogs. Oh, Mr. Weatherby, let's go away. Please, please take me home."

She was rapidly becoming hysterical, and I had a difficult time with her on the trip back. She clung whimpering to me, and I had almost to carry her most of the way. By the time we reached the sanitarium, she was crying bitterly, shivering, as if with a chill, and went in without stopping to thank me for my assistance.

I turned and made for the Squires farm with all possible speed, hoping to get there before the family had gone to bed. But when I arrived the house was in darkness, and my knock at the door received no answer.

As I retraced my steps to the sanitarium I heard faintly, from the fields beyond the woods, the shrill, eerie cry of the sheep-killing dogs.

A torrent of rain held us marooned the next day. Miss Leahy was confined to her room, with a nurse in constant attendance and the house doctor making hourly calls. She was on the verge of a nervous collapse, he told me, crying with a persistence that bordered on hysteria, and responding to treatment very slowly.

An impromptu dance was organized in the great hall and half a dozen bridge tables set up in the library; but as I was skilled in neither of these rainy day diversions, I put on a waterproof and patrolled the veranda for exercise.

On my third or fourth trip around the house I ran into old Geronte shuffling across the porch, wagging his head and muttering portentously to himself.

"See here, Pierre," I accosted him, "what sort of nonsense have you been telling Miss Leahy about those pine woods down the south road?"

The old fellow regarded me unwinkingly with his beady eyes, wrinkling his age-yellowed forehead for all the world like an elderly baboon inspecting a new sort of edible. "*M'seiur* goes out alone much at nights, *n'est-ce-pas?*" he asked, at length.

"Yes, Monsieur goes out alone much at night," I echoed, "but what Monsieur particularly desires to know is what sort of tales have you been telling Mademoiselle Leahy. *Comprenez vous?*"

The network of wrinkles about his lips multiplied as he smiled enigmatically, regarding me askance from the corners of his eyes.

"*M'sieur* is *Anglais,*" he replied. "He would not understand—or believe."

"Never mind what I'd believe," I retorted. "What is this story about murder and robbery being committed in those woods? Who were the murderers, and where did they live? *Hein?*"

For a few seconds he looked fixedly at me, chewing the cud of senility between his toothless gums, then, glancing carefully about, as if he feared being overheard, he tiptoed up to me and whispered:

"*M'sieur* mus' stay indoors these nights. There are evil things abroad at the dark of the moon, *M'sieur.* Even las' night they keel t'ree of my bes' sheep. Remembair, *M'sieur,* the *loup-garou,* he is out when the moon hide her light."

And with that he turned and left me; nor could I get another word from him save his cryptic warning, "Remembair, *M'sieur;* the *loup-garou.* Remembair."

In spite of my annoyance, I could not get rid of the unpleasant sensation the old man's words left with me. The *loup-garou*—werewolf— he had said, and to prove his goblin-wolf's presence, he had cited the death of his three sheep.

As I paced the rain-washed porch I thought of the scene I had witnessed the night before, when the sheep-killers were at their work.

"Well," I reflected, "I've seen the *loup-garou* on his native heath at last. From causes as slight as this, no doubt, the horrible legend of the werewolf had sprung. Time was when all France quaked at the sound of the *loup-garou's* hunting call and the bravest knights in Christendom trembled in their castles and crossed themselves fearfully because some renegade shepherd dog quested his prey in the night. On such a foundation are the legends of a people built."

Whistling a snatch from *Pinafore* and looking skyward in search of a patch of blue in the clouds, I felt a tug at my raincoat sleeve, such as a neglected terrier might give. It was Geronte again.

"*M'sieur,*" he began in the same mysterious whisper, "the *loup-garou* is a verity, certainly. I, myself, have nevair seen him"—he paused to bless himself—"but my cousin, Baptiste, was once pursued by him. Yes.

"It was near the shrine of the good Sainte Anne that Baptiste lived. One night he was sent to fetch the curé for a dying woman. They rode fast through the trees, the curé and my cousin Baptiste, for it was at the dark of the moon, and the evil forest folk were abroad. And as they galloped, there came a *loup-garou* from the woods, with eyes as bright as hell-fire. It followed hard, this tailless hound from the devil's kennel; but they reached the house before it, and the curé put his book, with the Holy Cross on its cover, at the doorstep. The *loup-garou* wailed under the windows like a child in pain until the sun rose; then it slunk back to the forest.

"When my cousin Baptiste and the curé came out, they found its hand marks in the soft earth around the door. Very like your hand, or mine, they were, *M'sieur*, save that the first finger was longer than the others."

"And did they find the *loup-garou?*" I asked, something of the old man's earnestness communicated to me.

"Yes, *M'sieur;* but of course," he replied gravely. "T'ree weeks before a stranger, drowned in the river, had been buried without the office of the Church. W'en they opened his grave they found his fingernails as red as blood, and sharp. Then they knew. The good curé read the burial office over him, and the poor soul that had been snatched away in sin slept peacefully at last."

He looked quizzically at me, as if speculating whether to tell me more; then, apparently fearing I would laugh at his outburst of confidence, started away toward the kitchen.

"Well, what else, Pierre?" I asked, feeling he had more to say.

"*Non, non, non,*" he replied. "There is nothing more, *M'sieur.* I did but want M'sieur should know my own cousin, Baptiste Geronte, had seen the *loup-garou* with his very eyes."

"Heresay evidence," I commented, as I went in to dinner.

During the rainy week that followed I chafed at my confinement like a privileged convict suddenly deprived of his liberties, and looked as wistfully down the south road as any prisoned gypsy ever gazed upon the open trail.

The quiet home circle at the farmhouse, the unforced conversation of the old folks, Mildred's sweet companionship, all beckoned me with an almost irresistible force. For in this period of enforced separation I discovered what I had dimly suspected for some time. I loved Mildred Squires. And, loving her, I longed to tell her of it.

No lad intent on visiting his first sweetheart ever urged his feet more eagerly than I when, the curtains of rain at last drawn up, I hastened toward the house at the turn of the road.

As I hoped, yet hardly dared expect, Mildred was standing at the gate to meet me as I rounded the curve, and I yearned toward her like a hummingbird seeking its nest.

She must have read my heart in my eyes, for her greeting smile was as tender as a mother's as she bends above her babe.

"At last you have come, my friend," she said, putting out both hands in welcome. "I am very glad."

We walked silently up the path, her fingers still resting in mine, her face averted. At the steps she paused, a little embarrassment in her voice as she explained, "Father and mother are out; they have gone to a—meeting. But you will stay?"

"Surely," I acquiesced. And to myself I admitted my gratitude for this chance of Mildred's unalloyed company.

We talked but little that night. Mildred was strangely distrait, and, much as I longed to, I could not force a confession of my love from my lips. Once, in the midst of a long pause between our words, the cry of the sheep-killers came faintly to us, echoed across the fields and woods, and as the weird, shrill sound fell on our ears, she threw back her head, with something of the gesture of a hunting dog scenting its quarry.

Toward midnight she turned to me, a panic of fear having apparently laid hold of her.

"You must go!" she exclaimed, rising and laying her hand on my shoulder.

"But your father and mother have not returned," I objected. "Won't you let me stay until they get back?"

"Oh, no, no," she answered, her agitation increasing. "You must go at once—please." She increased her pressure on my shoulder, almost as if to shove me from the porch.

Taken aback by her sudden desire to be rid of me, I was picking up my hat, when she uttered a stifled little scream and ran quickly to the edge of the porch, interposing herself between me and the yard. At the same moment, I heard a muffled sound from the direction of the front gate, a sound like a growling and snarling of savage dogs.

I leaped forward, my first thought being that the sheep-killers I had seen the other night had strayed to the Squires place. Crazed with blood, I knew, they would be almost as dangerous to men as to sheep, and every nerve in my sickness-weakened body cried out to protect Mildred.

To my blank amazement, as I looked from the porch I beheld Mr. and Mrs. Squires walking sedately up the path, talking composedly together. There was no sign of the dogs or any other animals about.

As the elderly couple neared the porch I noticed that Mr. Squires walked with a pronounced limp, and that both their eyes shone very brightly in the moonlight, as though they were suffused with tears.

They greeted me pleasantly enough; but Mildred's anxiety seemed increased, rather than diminished, by their presence, and I took my leave after a brief exchange of civilities.

On my way back I looked intently in the woods bordering the road for some sign of the house of which Pierre had told Miss Leahy; but everywhere the pines grew as thickly as though neither axe nor fire had ever disturbed them.

"Geronte is in his second childhood," I reflected, "and like an elder child, he loves to terrify his juniors with fearsome witch-tales."

Yet an uncomfortable feeling was with me till I saw the gleam of the sanitarium's lights across the fields; and as I walked toward them it seemed to me that more than once I heard the baying of the sheep-killers in the woods behind me.

A buzz of conversation, like the sibilant arguments of a cloud of swarming bees, greeted me as I descended the stairs to breakfast next morning.

It appeared that Ned, one of the pair of great mastiffs attached to the sanitarium, had been found dead before his kennel, his throat and brisket torn open and several gaping wounds in his flanks. Boris, his fellow, had been discovered whimpering and trembling in the extreme corner of the doghouse, the embodiment of canine terror.

Speculation as to the animal responsible for the outrage was rife, and, as usual, it ran the gamut of possible and impossible surmises. Every sort of beast from a grizzly bear to a lion escaped from the circus was in turn indicted for the crime, only to have a complete alibi straightway established.

The only one having no suggestion to offer was old Geronte, who stood Sphinx-like in the outskirts of the crowd, smiling sardonically to himself and wagging his head sagely. As he caught sight of me he nodded, sapiently, as if to include me in the joint tenancy to some weighty secret.

Presently he worked his way through the chattering group and whispered, "*M'sieur*, he was here last night—and with him was the other tailless one. Come and see."

Plucking me by the sleeve, he led me to the rear of the kennels, and, stooping, pointed to something in the moist earth. "You see?" he asked, as if a printed volume lay for my reading in the mud.

"I see that someone has been on his hands and knees here," I answered, inspecting the hand prints he indicated.

"*Something,*" he corrected, as if reasoning with an obstinate child. "Does not *M'sieur* behol' that the first finger is the longest?"

"Which proves nothing," I defended. "There are many hands like that."

"Oh—yes?" he replied with that queer upward accent of his. "And where has *M'sieur* seen hands like that before?"

"Oh, many times," I assured him somewhat vaguely, for there was a catch at the back of my throat as I spoke. Try as I would, I could recall only three pairs of hands with that peculiarity.

His little black eyes rested steadily on me in an unwinking stare, and the corners of his mouth curved upward in a malicious grin. It seemed, almost, as if he found a grim pleasure in thus driving me into a corner.

"See here, Pierre," I began testily, equally annoyed at myself and him, "you know as well as I that the *loup-garou* is an old woman's tale. Someone was looking here for tracks, and left his own while doing it. If we look among the patients here we shall undoubtedly find a pair of hands to match these prints."

"God forbid!" he exclaimed, crossing himself. "That woud be an evil day for us, *M'sieur*. "Here, Bor-ees," he snapped his fingers to the surviving mastiff, "come and eat."

The huge beast came wallowing over to him with the ungainly gait of all heavily-muscled animals, stopping on his way to make a nasal investigation of my knees. Scarcely had his nose come into contact with my trousers when he leaped back, every hair in his mane and along his spine stiffly erect, every tooth in his great mouth bared in a savage snarl. But instead of the mastiff's fighting growl, he emitted only a low, frightened whine, as though he were facing some animal of greater power than himself, and knew his own weakness.

"Good heavens!" I cried, thoroughly terrified at the friendly brute's sudden hostility.

"Yes, *M'sieur*," Geronte cut in quickly, putting his hand on the dog's collar and leading him a few paces away. "It is well you should call upon the heavenly ones; for surely you have the odor of hell upon your clothes."

"What do you mean?" I demanded angrily . "How dare you—?"

He raised a thin hand deprecatingly. "*M'sieur* knows that he knows," he replied evenly; "and what I also know."

And leading Boris by the collar, he shuffled to the house.

Mildred was waiting for me at the gate that evening, and again her father and mother were absent at one of their meetings.

We walked silently up the path and seated ourselves on the porch steps where the waning moon cast oblique rays through the pine branches.

I think Mildred felt the tension I was drawn to, for she talked trivialities with an almost feverish earnestness, stringing her sentences together, and changing her subjects as a Navajo rug weaver twists and breaks her threads.

At last I found an opening in the abatis of her small talk.

"Mildred," I said, very simply, for great emotions tear the ornaments from our speech, "I love you, and I want you for my wife. Will you marry me, Mildred?" I laid my hand on hers. It was cold as lifeless flesh, and seemed to shrink beneath my touch.

"Surely, dear, you must have read the love in my eyes," I urged, as she averted her face in silence. "Almost from the night I first saw you. I've loved you! I—"

"O-o-h, don't!" Her interruption was a strangled moan, as if wrung from her by my words.

I leaned nearer her. "Don't you love me, Mildred?" I asked. As yet she had not denied it.

For a moment she trembled, as if a sudden chill had come on her, then, leaning to me, she clasped my shoulders in her arms, hiding her face against my jacket.

"John, John, you don't know what you say," she whispered disjointedly, as though a sob had torn the words before they left her lips. Her breath was on my cheek, moist and cold as air from a vault.

I could feel the litheness of her through the thin stuff of her gown, and her body was as devoid of warmth as a dead thing.

"You're cold," I told her, putting my arms shieldingly about her. "The night has chilled you."

A convulsive sob was her only answer.

"Mildred," I began again, putting my hand beneath her chin and lifting her face to mine, "tell me, dear, what is the matter?" I lowered my lips to hers.

With a cry that was half scream, half weeping, she thrust me suddenly from her, pressing her hands against my breast and lowering her head until her face was hidden between her outstretched arms. I, too, started back, for in the instant our lips were about to meet, hers had writhed back from her teeth, like a dog's when he is about to spring, and a low, harsh noise, almost a growl, had risen in her throat.

"For God's sake," she whispered hoarsely, agony in every note of her shaking voice, "never do that again! Oh, my dear, dear love, you don't know how near to a horror worse than death you were."

"A—horror—worse—than—death?" I echoed dully, pressing her cold little hands in mine. "What do you mean, Mildred?"

"Loose my hands," she commanded with a quaint reversion to the speech of our ancestors, "and hear me. I do love you. I love you better than life. Better than death. I love you so I have overcome something stronger than the walls of the grave for your sake, but John, my very love, this is our last night together. We can never meet again. You must go, now, and not come back until tomorrow morning."

"Tomorrow morning?" I repeated blankly. What wild talk was this?

Heedless of my interruption, she hurried on. "Tomorrow morning, just before the sun rises over those trees, you must be here, and have your prayer book with you."

I listened speechless, wondering which of us was mad.

"By that corncrib there"—she waved a directing hand—"you will find three mounds. Stand beside them and read the office for the burial of the dead. Come quickly, and pause for nothing on the way. Look back for nothing; heed no sound from behind you. And for your own safety, come no sooner than to allow yourself the barest time to read your office."

Bewildered, I attempted to reason with the mad woman; begged her to explain this folly; but she refused all answer to my fervid queries, nor would she suffer me to touch her.

Finally, I rose to go. "You will do what I ask?" she implored.

"Certainly not," I answered firmly.

"John, John, have pity!" she cried, flinging herself to the earth before me and clasping my knees. "You say you love me. I only ask this one favor of you; only this. Please, for my sake, for the peace of the dead and the safety of the living, promise you will do this thing for me."

Shaken by her abject supplication, I promised, though I felt myself a figure in some grotesque nightmare as I did it.

"Oh, my love, my precious love," she wept, rising and taking both my hands. "At last I shall have peace, and you shall bring it to me. No," she forbade me as I made to take her in my arms at parting. "The most I can give you, dear, is this." She held her icy hands against my lips. "It seems so little, dear; but oh! it is so much."

Like a drunkard in his cups I staggered along the south road, my thoughts gone wild with the strangeness of the play I had just acted.

Across the clearing came the howls of the sheep-killers, a sound I had grown used to of late. But tonight there was a deeper, fiercer *timbre* in their bay; a note that boded ill for man as well as beast. Louder and louder it swelled; it was rising from the field itself, now, drawing nearer and nearer the road.

I turned and looked. The great beasts I had seen pursuing the luckless sheep the other night were galloping toward me. A cold finger seemed traced down my spine; the scalp crept and tingled beneath my cap. There was no other object of their quest in sight. I was their elected prey.

My first thought was to turn and run; but a second's reasoning told me this was worse than useless. Weakened with long illness, with an uphill road to the nearest shelter, I should soon be run down.

No friendly tree offered asylum; my only hope was to stand and fight. Grasping my stick, I spread my feet, bracing myself against their charge.

And as I waited their onslaught, there came from the shadow of the pines the shriller, sharper cry of the third beast. Like the crest of a flying, wind-lashed wave, the slighter, silver-furred brute came speeding across the meadow, its ears laid back, its slender paws spurning the sod daintily. Almost, it seemed as if the pale shadow of a cloud were racing toward me.

The thing dashed slantwise across the field, its flight converging on the line of the other two's attack. Midway between me and them it paused; hairs bristling, limbs bent for a spring.

All the savageness of the larger beasts' hunting cry was echoed in the smaller creature's bay, and with it a defiance that needed no interpretation.

The attackers paused in their rush; halted, and looked speculatively at my ally. They took a few tentative steps in my direction; and a fierce whine, almost an articulate curse, went up from the silver-haired beast. Slowly the tawny pair circled and trotted back to the woods.

I hurried toward the sanitarium, grasping my stick firmly in readiness for another attack.

But no further cries came from the woods, and once, as I glanced back, I saw the light-haired beast trotting slowly in my wake, looking from right to left, as if to ward off danger.

Half an hour later I looked from my window toward the house in the pines. Far down the south road, its muzzle pointed to the moon, the bright-furred animal crouched and poured out a lament to the night. And its cry was like the wail of a child in pain.

Far into the night I paced my room, like a condemned convict when the vigil of the death watch is on him. Reason and memory struggled for the mastery; one urging me to give over my wild act, the other bidding me obey my promise to Mildred.

Toward morning I dropped into a chair, exhausted with my objectless marching. I must have fallen asleep, for when I started up the stars were dimming in the zenith, and bands of slate, shading to amethyst slanted across the horizon.

A moment I paused, laughing cynically at my fool's errand, then, seizing cap and book, I bolted down the stairs, and ran through the paling dawn to the house in the pines.

There was something ominous and terrifying in the two-toned pastel of the house that morning. Its windows stared at me with blank malevolence, like the half-closed eyes of one stricken dead in mortal sin. The little patches of hoarfrost on the lawn were like leprous spots on some unclean thing. From the trees behind the clearing an owl hooted mournfully, as if to say, "Beware, beware!" and the wind soughing through the black pine boughs echoed the refrain ceaselessly.

Three mounds, sunken and weed-grown, lay in the unkempt thicket behind the corncrib. I paused beside them, throwing off my cap and adjusting my stole hastily. Thumbing the pages to the committal service, I held the book close, that I might see the print through the morning shadows, and commenced: "I know that my redeemer liveth . . ."

Almost beside me, under the branches of the pines, there rose such a chorus of howls and yelps I nearly dropped my book. Like all the hounds in the kennels of hell, the sheep-killers clamored at me, rage and fear and mortal hatred in their cries. Through the bestial cadences, too, there seemed to run a human note; the sound of voices heard before beneath these very trees. Deep and throaty, and raging mad, two of the voices came to me, and, like the tremolo of a violin lightly played in an orchestra of brass, the shriller cry of a third beast sounded.

As the infernal hubbub rose at my back, I half turned to fly. Next instant I grasped my book more firmly and resumed my office, for like a beacon in the dark, Mildred's words flashed on my memory: *"Look back for nothing; heed no sound behind you."*

Strangely, too, the din approached no nearer; but as though held by an invisible bar, stayed at the boundary of the clearing.

"Man that is born of a woman hath but a short time to live and is full of misery . . . deliver us from all our offenses . . . O, Lord, deliver us not into the bitter pains of eternal death . . ." and to such an accompaniment, surely, as no priest ever before chanted the office, I pressed through the brief service to the final *Amen.*

Tiny grouts of moisture stood out on my forehead, my breath struggled in my throat as I gasped out the last word. My nerves were frayed to shreds and my strength nearly gone as I let fall my book, and turned upon the beasts among the trees.

They were gone. Abruptly as it had begun, their clamor stopped, and only the rotting pine needles, lightly gilded by the morning sun, met my gaze. A light touch fell in the palm of my open hand, as if a pair of cool, sweet lips had laid a kiss there.

A vaporlike swamp-fog enveloped me. The outbuildings, the old, stone-curbed well where I had drunk the night I first saw Mildred, the house itself—all seemed fading into mist and swirling away in the morning breeze.

"Eh, eh, eh; but *M'sieur* will do himself an injury, sleeping on the wet earth!" Old Geronte bent over me, his arm beneath my shoulders. Behind him, great Boris, the mastiff, stood wagging his tail, regarding me with doggish good humor.

"Pierre," I muttered thickly, "how came you here?"

"This morning, going to my tasks, I saw *M'sieur* run down the road like a thing pursued. I followed quickly, for the woods hold terrors in the dark, *M'sieur.*"

I looked toward the farmhouse. Only a pair of chimneys, rising stark and bare from a crumbling foundation were there. Fence, well, barn—all were gone, and in their place a thicket of sumac and briars, tangled and overgrown as though undisturbed for thirty years.

"The house, Pierre! Where is the house?" I croaked, sinking my fingers into his withered arm.

"'Ouse?" he echoed. "Oh, but of course. There is no 'ouse here. *M'sieur;* nor has there been for years. This is an evil place, *M'sieur;* it is best we quit it, and that quickly. There be evil things that run by night—"

"No more," I answered, staggering toward the road, leaning heavily on him. "I brought them peace, Pierre."

He looked dubiously at the English prayer book I held. A Protestant clergyman is a thing of doubtful usefulness to the orthodox French-Canadian. Something of the heartsick misery in my face must have touched his kind old heart, for at last he relented, shaking his head pityingly and patting my shoulder gently, as one would soothe a sorrowing child.

"Per'aps, *M'sieur*," he conceded. "Per'aps; who shall say no? Love and sorrow are the purchase price of peace. Yes. Did not *le bon Dieu* so buy the peace of the world?"

Edgar Pangborn

LONGTOOTH

MY WORD IS good. How can I prove it? Born in Darkfield, wasn't I? Stayed away thirty more years after college, but when I returned I was still Ben Dane, one of the Darkfield Danes, Judge Marcus Dane's eldest. And they knew my word was good. My wife died and I sickened of all cities; then my bachelor brother Sam died too, who'd lived all his life here in Darkfield, running his one-man law office over in Lohman—our nearest metropolis, pop. 6437. A fast coronary at fifty; I had loved him. Helen gone, then Sam—I wound up my unimportances and came home, inheriting Sam's housekeeper Adelaide Simmons, her grim stability and celestial cooking. Nostalgia for Maine is a serious matter, late in life: I had to yield. I expected a gradual drift into my childless old age playing correspondence chess, translating a few of the classics. I thought I could take for granted the continued respect of my neighbors. I say my word is good.

I will remember again that middle of March a few years ago, the snow skimming out of an afternoon sky as dirty as the bottom of an old aluminum pot. Harp Ryder's back road had been plowed since the last snowfall; I supposed Bolt-Bucket could make the mile and a half in to his farm and out again before we got caught. Harp had asked me to get him a book if I was making a trip to Boston, any goddamn book that told about Eskimos, and I had one for him, De Poncins' *Kabloona*. I saw the midget devils of white running crazy down a huge slope of wind, and recalled hearing at the Darkfield News Bureau, otherwise Cleve's General Store, somebody mentioning a forecast of the worst blizzard in forty years. Joe Cleve, who won't permit a radio in the store because it pesters his ulcers, inquired of his Grand Inquisitor who dwells ten yards behind your right shoulder: "Why's it always got to be the worst in so-and-so many years, that going to help anybody?" The Bureau was still analyzing this difficult inquiry when I left, with my cigarettes and as much as I could remember of Adelaide's grocery list after leaving it on the dining table. It wasn't yet three when I turned in on Harp's back road, and a gust slammed at Bolt-Bucket like death with a shovel.

I tried to win momentum for the rise to the high ground, swerved to avoid an idiot rabbit and hit instead a patch of snow-hidden melt-and-freeze, skidding to a full stop from which nothing would extract me but a tow.

I was fifty-seven that year, my wind bad from too much smoking and my heart (I now know) no stronger than Sam's. I quit cursing—gradually, to avoid sudden actions—and tucked *Kabloona* under my parka. I would walk the remaining mile to Ryder's, stay just to leave the book, say hello, and phone for a tow; then, since Harp never owned a car and never would, I could walk back and meet the truck.

If Leda Ryder knew how to drive, it didn't matter much after she married Harp. They farmed it, back in there, in almost the manner of Harp's ancestors of Jefferson's time. Harp did keep his two hundred laying hens by methods that were considered modern before the poor wretches got condemned to batteries, but his other enterprises came closer to antiquity. In his big kitchen garden he let one small patch of weeds fool themselves for an inch or two, so he'd have it to work at; they survived nowhere else. A few cows, a team, four acres for market crops, and a small dog Droopy, whose grandmother had made it somehow with a dachshund. Droopy's only menace in obese old age was a wheezing bark. The Ryders must have grown nearly all vital necessities except chewing tobacco and once in a while a new dress for Leda. Harp could snub the 20th Century, and I doubt if Leda was consulted about it in spite of his obsessive devotion for her. She was almost thirty years younger, and yes, he should not have married her. Other side up just as scratchy; she should not have married him, but she did.

Harp was a dinosaur perhaps, but I grew up with him, he a year the younger. We swam, fished, helled around together. And when I returned to Darkfield growing old, he was one of the few who acted glad to see me, so far as you can trust what you read in a face like a granite promontory. Maybe twice a week Harp Ryder smiled.

I pushed on up the ridge, and noticed a going-and-coming set of wide tire-tracks already blurred with snow. That would be the egg-truck I had passed a quarter-hour since on the main road. Whenever the west wind at my back lulled, I could swing around and enjoy one of my favorite prospects of birch and hemlock lowland. From Ryder's Ridge there's no sign of Darkfield two miles southwest except one church spire. On clear days you glimpse Bald Mountain and his two big brothers, more than twenty miles west of us.

The snow was thickening. It brought relief and pleasure to see the black shingles of Harp's barn and the roof of his Cape Codder. Foreshortened, so that it looked snug against the barn; actually house and barn were connected by a two-story shed fifteen feet wide and forty feet long—woodshed below, hen-loft above. The Ryders' sunrise-facing bedroom window was set only three feet above the eaves of that shed roof. They truly went to bed with the chickens. I shouted, for Harp was about to close the big shed door. He held it for me. I ran, and the storm ran after me. The west wind was bouncing off the barn; eddies howled at us. The temperature had tumbled ten degrees since I left Darkfield. The thermometer by the shed door read 15 degrees, and I knew I'd been a damn fool. As I helped Harp fight the shed door closed, I thought I heard Leda, crying.

A swift confused impression. The wind was exploring new ranges of passion, the big door squawked, and Harp was asking: "Ca' break down?" I do still think I heard Leda wail. If so, it ended as we got the door latched and Harp drew a newly fitted two-by-four bar across it. I couldn't understand that: the old latch was surely proof against any wind short of a hurricane.

"Bolt-Bucket never breaks down. Ought to get one, Harp—lots of company. All she did was go in the ditch."

"You might see her again come spring." His hens were scratching overhead, not yet scared by the storm. Harp's eyes were small gray glitters of trouble. "Ben, you figure a man's getting old at fifty-six?"

"No." My bones (getting old) ached for the warmth of his kitchen-dining-everything room, not for sad philosophy. "Use your phone, okay?"

"If the wires ain't down," he said, not moving, a man beaten on by other storms. "Them loafers didn't cut none of the overhang branches all summer. I told 'em of course, I told 'em how it would be . . . I meant, Ben, old enough to get dumb fancies?" My face may have told him I thought he was brooding about himself with a young wife. He frowned, annoyed that I hadn't taken his meaning. "I meant, *seeing* things. Things that can't be so, but—"

"We can all do some of that at any age, Harp."

That remark was a stupid brush-off, a stone for bread, because I was cold, impatient, wanted in. Harp had always a tense one-way sensitivity. His face chilled. "Well, come in, warm up. Leda ain't feeling too good. Getting a cold or something."

When she came downstairs and made me welcome, her eyes were reddened. I don't think the wind made that noise. Droopy waddled from her basket behind the stove to snuff my feet and give me my usual low passing mark.

Leda never had it easy there, young and passionate with scant mental resources. She was twenty-eight that year, looking tall because she carried her firm body handsomely. Some of the sullenness in her big mouth and lucid gray eyes was sexual challenge, some pure discontent. I liked Leda; her nature was not one for animosity or meanness. But she did have the smoldering power that draws men without word or gesture. After her abrupt marriage to Harp—Sam told me all this; I wasn't living in Darkfield then and hadn't met her—the garbage-gossip about her went hastily underground; enraging Harp Ryder was never healthy.

The phone wires weren't down, yet. While I waited for the garage to answer, Harp said, "Ben, I can't let you walk back in that. Stay over, huh?"

I didn't want to. It meant extra work and inconvenience for Leda, and I was ancient enough to crave my known safe burrow. But I felt Harp wanted me to stay for his own sake. I asked Jim Short at the garage to go ahead with Bolt-Bucket if I wasn't there to meet him. Jim roared: "Know what it's doing right now?"

"Little spit of snow, looks like."

"Jesus!" He covered the mouthpiece imperfectly. I heard his enthusiastic voice ring through cold-iron echoes: "Hey, old Ben's got that thing into the ditch again! Ain't that something . . . ? Listen, Ben, I can't make no promises. Got both tow trucks out already. You better stop over and praise the Lord you got that far."

"Okay," I said. "It wasn't much of a ditch."

Leda fed us coffee. She kept glancing toward the landing at the foot of the stairs where a night-darkness already prevailed. A closed-in stairway slanted down at a never-used front door; beyond that landing was the other ground floor room-parlor, spare, guest room—where I would sleep. I don't know what Leda expected to encounter in that shadow. Once when a chunk of firewood made an odd noise in the range, her lips clamped shut on a scream.

The coffee warmed me. By that time the weather left no loophole for argument. Not yet 3:30, but west and north were lost in furious black. Through the hissing white flood I could just see the front of the barn forty feet away. "Nobody's going no place into that," Harp said. His little house shuddered, enforcing the words, "Leda, you don't look too brisk. Get you some rest."

"I better see to the spare room for Ben."

Neither spoke with much tenderness, but it glowed openly in him when she turned her back. Then some other need bent his granite face out of its normal seams. His whole gaunt body leaning forward tried to help him talk. "You wouldn't figure me for a man'd go off his rocker?" he asked.

"Of course not. What's biting, Harp?"

"There's something in the woods; got no right to be there." To me that came as a letdown of relief; I would not have to listen to another's marriage problems. "I wish, b' Jesus Christ, it would hit somebody else once, so I could say what I know and not be laughed at all to hell. I *ain't* one for dumb fancies."

You walked on eggs, with Harp. He might decide any minute that *I* was laughing. "Tell me," I said. "If anything's out there now it must feel a mite chilly."

"Ayah." He went to the north window, looking out where we knew the road lay under white confusion. Harp's land sloped down the other side of the road to the edge of mighty evergreen forest. Katahdin stands more than fifty miles north and a little east of us. We live in a withering, shrinking world, but you could still set out from Harp's farm and, except for the occasional country road and the rivers—not many large ones— you could stay in deep forest all the way to the tundra, or Alaska. Harp said, "This kind of weather is when it comes."

He sank into his beat-up kitchen armchair and reached for *Kabloona.* He had barely glanced at the book while Leda was with us. "Funny name."

"Kabloona's an Eskimo word for white man."

"He done these pictures . . . ? Be they good, Ben?"

"I like 'em. Photographs in the back."

"Oh." He turned the pages hastily for those, but studied only the ones that showed the strong Eskimo faces, and his interest faded. Whatever he wanted was not here. "These people, be they—civilized?"

"In their own way, sure."

"Ayah, this guy looks like he could find his way in the woods."

"Likely the one thing he couldn't do, Harp. They never see a tree unless they come south, and they hate to do that. Anything below the Arctic is too warm."

"That a fact . . . ? Well, it's a nice book. How much was it?" I'd found it second-hand; he paid me to the exact penny. "I'll be glad to read it." He never would. It would end up on the shelf in the parlor with the Bible, an old almanac, a Longfellow, until some day this place went up for auction and nobody remembered Harp's way of living.

"What's this all about, Harp?"

"Oh . . . I was hearing things in the woods, back last summer. I'd think, fox, then I'd know it wasn't. Make your hair stand right on end. Lost a cow, last August, from the north pasture acrosst the rud. Section of board fence tore out. I mean, Ben, the two top boards was *pulled out from the nail holes.* No hammer marks."

"Bear?"

"Only track I found looked like bear except too small. You know a bear wouldn't *pull* it out, Ben."

"Cow slamming into it, panicked by something?"

He remained patient with me. "Ben, would I build a cow-pasture fence nailing the cross-pieces from the outside? Cow hit it with all her weight she might bust it, sure. And kill herself doing it, be blood and hair all over the split boards, and she'd be there, not a mile and a half away into the woods. Happened during a big thunderstorm. I figured it had to be somebody with a spite ag'inst me, maybe some son of a bitch wanting the prop'ty, trying to scare me off that's lived here all my life and my family before me. But that don't make sense. I found the cow a week later, what was left. Way into the woods. The head and the bones. Hide tore up and flang around. Any *person* dressing off a beef, he'll cut whatever he wants and take off with it. He don't sit down and chaw the meat off the *bones*, b' Jesus Christ. He don't tear the thighbone out of the joint . . . All right, maybe bear. But no bear did that job on that fence and then driv old Nell a mile and a half into the woods to kill her. Nice little Jersey, clever's a kitten. Leda used to make over her, like she don't usually do with the stock . . . I've looked plenty in the woods since then, never turned up anything. Once and again I did smell something. Fishy, like bear-smell but—*different.*"

"But Harp, with snow on the ground—"

"Now you'll really call me crazy. When the weather is clear, I ain't once found his prints. I hear him then, at night, but I go out by daylight where I think the sound was, there's no trail. Just the usual snow tracks. I know. He lives in the trees and don't come down except when it's storming. I got to believe that? Because then he does come, Ben, when the weather's like now, like right now. And old Ned and Jerry out in the stable go wild, and sometimes we hear his noise under the window. I shine my flashlight through the glass—never catch sight of him. I go out with the ten-gauge if there's any light to see by, and there's prints around the house—holes filling up with snow. By morning there'll be maybe some marks left, and they'll lead off to the north woods, but under the trees you won't find it. So he gets up in the branches and travels that way? . . . Just once I have seen him, Ben. Last October. I better tell you one other thing first. A day or so after I found what was left of old Nell, I lost six roaster chickens. I made over a couple box stalls, maybe you remember, so the birds could be out on range and roost in the barn at night. Good doors, and I always locked 'em. Two in the morning, Ned and Jerry go crazy. I got out through the barn into the stable, and they was spooked, Ned trying to kick his way out. I got 'em quiet, looked all over the stable—loft, harness room, everywhere. Not a thing. Dead quiet night, no moon. It had to be something the horses smelled. I come back into the barn, and found one of the chicken-pen doors open—*tore* out from the lock. Chicken thief would bring along something to pry with—wouldn't he be a Christly idjut if he didn't . . . ? Took six birds, six nice eight-pound roasters, and left the heads on the floor—bitten off."

"Harp—some lunatic. People *can* go insane that way. There are old stories—"

"Been trying to believe that. Would a man live the winter out there?

Twenty below zero?"

"Maybe a cave—animal skins."

"I've boarded up the whole back of the barn. Done the same with the hen-loft windows—two-by-fours with four-inch spikes driv slantwise. They be twelve feet off the ground, and he ain't come for 'em, not yet... So after that happened I sent for Sheriff Robart. Son of a bitch happens to live in Darkfield, you'd think he might've took an interest."

"Do any good?"

Harp laughed. He did that by holding my stare, making no sound, moving no muscle except a disturbance at the eye corners. A New England art; maybe it came over on the *Mayflower*. "Robart he come by, after a while. I showed him that door. I showed him them chicken heads. Told him how I'd been spending my nights out there on my ass, with the ten-gauge." Harp rose to unload tobacco juice into the rage fire; he has a theory it purifies the air. "Ben, I might've showed him them chicken heads a shade close to his nose. By the time he got here, see, they wasn't all that fresh. He made out he'd look around and let me know. Mid-September. Ain't seen him since."

"You spoke of—seeing it, Harp?"

"Could call it seeing... All right. It was during them Indian summer days—remember? Like June except them pretty colors, smell of wind-falls—God I like that, I like October. I'd gone down to the slope acrosst the rud where I mended my fence after losing old Nell. Just leaning there, guess I was tired. Late afternoon, sky pinking up. You know how the fence cuts acrosst the slope to my east wood lot. I've let the bushes grow free—lot of elder, other stuff the birds come for. I was looking down toward that little break between the north woods and my wood lot, where a bit of old growed-up pasture shows through. Pretty spot. Painter fella come by a few years ago and done a picture of it, said the place looked like a coro; dunno what the hell that is, he didn't say."

I pushed at his brown study. "You saw it there?"

"No. Off to my right in them elder bushes. Fifty feet from me, I guess. By God I didn't turn my head. I got it with the tail of my eye and turned the other way as if I meant to walk back to the rud. Made like busy with something in the grass, come wandering back to the fence some nearer. He stayed for me, a brownish patch in them bushes by the big yellow birch. Near the height of a man. No gun with me, not even a stick... Big shoulders, couldn't see his goddamn feet. He don't stand more'n five feet tall. His hands, if he's got real ones, hung out of my sight in a tangle of elder bushes. He's got brown fur, Ben, reddy-brown fur all over him. His face too, his head, his big thick neck. There's a shine to fur in sunlight, you can't be mistook. So—I did look at him direct. Tried to act like I still didn't see him, but he knowed. He melted back and got the birch between him and me. Not a sound." And then Harp was listening for Leda upstairs. He went on softly: "Ayah, I ran back for a gun, and searched the woods, for all the good it did me. You'll want to know about his face. I ain't told Leda all this part. See, she's scared, I don't want to make it no worse, I just said it was some animal that snuck off before I could see it good. A big face, Ben. Head real human except it sticks out too much around the jaw. Not much nose—open spots in the fur. Ben, the—the *teeth!* I seen his mouth drop open and he pulled up one side of his lip to show me them stabbing things. I've seen as big as that on a full-growed bear. That's what I'll hear, I ever try to tell this. They'll say I seen a bear. Now I shot my first bear when I was sixteen and Pa took me over toward Jackman. I've got me one maybe every other year since then. I know 'em, all their ways. But that's what I'll hear if I tell the story."

I am a frustrated naturalist, loaded with assorted facts. I know there aren't any monkeys or apes that could stand our winters except maybe the harmless Himalayan langur. No such beast as Harp described lived anywhere on the planet. It didn't help. Harp was honest; he was rational; he wanted reasonable explanation as much as I did. Harp wasn't the village atheist for nothing. I said, "I guess you will, Harp. People mostly won't take the—unusual."

"Maybe you'll hear him tonight, Ben."

Leda came downstairs, and heard part of that. "He's been telling you, Ben. What do you think?"

"I don't know what to think."

"Led', I thought, if I imitate that noise for him—"

"No!" She had brought some mending and was about to sit down with it, but froze as if threatened by attack. "I couldn't stand it, Harp. And—it might bring them."

"Them?" Harp chuckled uneasily. "I don't guess I could do it that good he'd come for it."

"Don't *do* it, Harp!"

"All right, hon." Her eyes were closed, her head drooping back. "Don't git nerved up so."

I started wondering whether a man still seeming sane could dream up such a horror for the unconscious purpose of tormenting a woman too young for him, a woman he could never imagine he owned. If he told her a fox bark wasn't right for a fox, she'd believe him. I said, "We shouldn't talk about it if it upsets her."

He glanced at me like a man floating up from under water. Leda said in a small, aching voice: "I wish to *God* we could move to Boston."

The granite face closed in defensiveness. "Led', we been all over that. Nothing is going to drive me off of my land. I got no time for the city at my age. What the Jesus would I do? Night watchman? Sweep out somebody's back room, b' Jesus Christ? Savings'd be gone in no time. We been all over it. We ain't moving nowhere."

"I could find work." For Harp of course that was the worst thing she could have said. She probably knew it from his stricken silence. She said clumsily, "I forgot something upstairs." She snatched up her mending and she was gone.

We talked no more of it the rest of the day. I followed through the milking and other chores, lending a hand where I could, and we made everything as secure as we could against storm and other enemies. The long-toothed furry thing was the spectral guest at dinner, but we cut him, on Leda's account, or so we pretended. Supper would have been awkward anyway. They weren't in the habit of putting up guests, and Leda was a rather deadly cook because she cared nothing about it. A Darkfield girl, I suppose she had the usual 20th-Century mishmash of television dreams until some impulse or maybe false signs of pregnancy tricked her into marrying a man out of the 19th. We had venison treated like beef and overdone vegetables. I don't like venison even when it's treated right.

At six Harp turned on his battery radio and sat stone-faced through the day's bad news and the weather forecast—"a blizzard which may prove the worst in 42 years. Since 3:00 PM, 18 inches have fallen at Bangor, 21 at Boston. Precipitation is not expected to end until tomorrow. Winds will increase during the night with gusts up to 70 miles per hour." Harp shut it off, with finality. On other evenings I had spent there he let Leda play it after supper only kind of soft, so there had been a continuous muted bleat and blatter all evening. Tonight Harp meant to listen for other sounds. Leda washed the dishes, said an early good night, and fled upstairs.

Harp didn't talk, except as politeness obliged him to answer some blah of mine. We sat and listened to the snow and the lunatic wind. An hour of it was enough for me; I said I was beat and wanted to turn in early. Harp saw me to my bed in the parlor and placed a new chunk of rock maple in the pot-bellied stove. He produced a difficult granite smile, maybe using up his allowance for the week, and pulled out a bottle from a cabinet that had stood for many years below a parlor print—George Washington, I think, concluding a treaty with some offbeat sufferer from hepatitis who may have been General Cornwallis if the latter had two left feet. The bottle contained a brand of rye that Harp sincerely believed to be drinkable, having charred his gullet forty-odd years trying to prove it. While my throat healed Harp said, "Shouldn't've bothered you with all this crap, Ben. Hope it ain't going to spoil your sleep." He got me his spare flashlight, then let me be, and closed the door.

I heard him drop back into his kitchen armchair. Under too many covers, lamp out, I heard the cruel whisper of the snow. The stove muttered, a friend, making me a cocoon of living heat in a waste of outer cold. Later I heard Leda at the head of the stairs, her voice timid, tired, and sweet with invitation: "You comin' up to bed, Harp?" The stairs creaked under him.

I remembered something Adelaide Simmons had told me about this house, where I had not gone upstairs since Harp and I were boys. Adelaide, one of the very few women in Darkfield who never spoke unkindly of Leda, said that the tiny west room across from Harp's and Leda's bedroom was fixed up for a nursery, and Harp wouldn't allow anything in there but baby furniture. Had been so since they were married seven years before.

Another hour dragged on, in my exasperations of sleeplessness.

Then I heard Longtooth.

The noise came from the west side, beyond the snow-hidden vegetable garden. When it snatched me from the edge of sleep, I tried to think it was a fox barking, the ringing, metallic shriek the little red beast can belch dragon-like from his throat. But wide awake, I knew it had been much deeper, chestier. Horned owl?—no. A sound that belonged to ancient times when men relied on chipped stone weapons and had full reason to fear the dark.

The cracks in the stove gave me firelight for groping back into my clothes. The wind had not calmed at all. I stumbled to the west window, buttoning up, and found it a white blank. Snow had drifted above the lower sash. On tiptoe I could just see over it. A light appeared, dimly illuminating the snowfield beyond. That would be coming from a lamp in the Ryders' bedroom, shining through the nursery room and so out, weak and diffused, into the blizzard chaos.

Yaaarrhh!

Now it had drawn horribly near. From the north windows of the parlor I saw black nothing. Harp squeaked down to my door. "'Wake, Ben?"

"Yes. Come look at the west window."

He had left no night light burning in the kitchen, and only a scant glow came down to the landing from the bedroom. He murmured behind me, "Ayah, snow's up some. Must be over three foot on the level by now."

Yaaarrhh!

The voice had shouted on the south side, the blinder side of the house, overlooked only by one kitchen window and a small one in the pantry where the hand pump stood. The view from the pantry window was mostly blocked by a great maple that overtopped the house. I heard the wind shrilling across the tree's winter bones.

"Ben, you want to git your boots on? Up to you—can't ask it. I might have to go out." Harp spoke in an undertone as if the beast might understand him through the tight walls.

"Of course." I got into my knee boots and caught up my parka as I followed him into the kitchen. A .30-caliber rifle and his heavy shotgun hung on deerhorn over the door to the woodshed. He found them in the dark.

What courage I possessed that night came from being shamed into action, from fearing to show a poor face to an old friend in trouble. I went through the Normandy invasion. I have camped out alone, when I was younger and healthier, and slept nicely. But that noise of Longtooth stole courage. It ached along the channel of the spine.

I had the spare flashlight, but knew Harp didn't want me to use it here. I could make out the furniture, and Harp reaching for the gun rack. He already had on his boots, fur cap, and mackinaw. "You take this'n," he said, and put the ten-gauge in my hands. "Both barrels loaded. Ain't my way to do that, ain't right, but since this thing started—"

Yaaarrhh!

"Where's he got to now?" Harp was by the south window. "Round this side?"

"I thought so . . . Where's Droopy?"

Harp chuckled thinly. "She come upstairs at the first sound of him and went under the bed. I told Led' to stay upstairs. She'd want a light down here. Wouldn't make sense."

Then, apparently from the east side of the hen-loft and high, booming off some resonating surface: *Yaaarrhh!*

"He can't! Jesus, that's twelve foot off the ground!" But Harp plunged out into the shed, and I followed. "Keep your light on the floor, Ben." He ran up the narrow stairway. "Don't shine it on the birds, they'll act up."

So far the chickens, stupid and virtually blind in the dark, were making only a peevish tut-tutting of alarm. But something was clinging to the outside of the barricaded east window, snarling, chattering teeth, pounding on the two-by-fours. With a fist?—it sounded like nothing else. Harp snapped, "Get your light on the window!" And he fired through the glass.

We heard no outcry. Any noise outside was covered by the storm and the squawks of the hens scandalized by the shot. The glass was dirty from their continual disturbance of the litter; I couldn't see through it. The bullet had drilled the pane without shattering it, and passed between the two-by-fours, but the beast could have dropped before he fired. "I got to go out there. You stay, Ben." Back in the kitchen he exchanged rifle for shotgun. "Might not have no chance to aim. You remember this piece, don't y'?—eight in the clip."

"I remember it."

"Good. Keep your ears open. Harp ran out through the door that gave on a small paved area by the woodshed. To get around under the east loft window he would have to push through the snow behind the barn, since he had blocked all the rear openings. He could have circled the house instead, but only by bucking the west wind and fighting deeper drifts. I saw his big shadow melt out of sight.

Leda's voice quavered down to me: "He—get it?"

"Don't know. He's gone to see. Sit tight . . . "

I heard that infernal bark once again before Harp returned, and again it sounded high off the ground; it must have come from the big maple. And then moments later—I was still trying to pierce the dark, watching for Harp—a vast smash of broken glass and wood, and the violent bang of the door upstairs. One small wheezing shriek cut short, and one scream such as no human being should ever hear. I can still hear it.

I think I lost some seconds in shock. Then I was groping up the narrow stairway, clumsy with the rifle and flashlight. Wind roared at the opening of the kitchen door, and Harp was crowding past me, thrusting me aside. But I was close behind him when he flung the bedroom door open. The blast from the broken window that had slammed the door had also blown out the lamp. But our flashlights said at once that Leda was not there. Nothing was, nothing living.

Droopy lay in a mess of glass splinters and broken window sash, dead from a crushed neck—something had stamped on her. The bedspread had been pulled almost to the window—maybe Leda's hand had clenched on it. I saw blood on some of the glass fragments, and on the splintered sash, a patch of reddish fur.

Harp ran back downstairs. I lingered a few seconds. The arrow of fear was deep in me, but at the moment it made me numb. My light touched up an ugly photograph on the wall, Harp's mother at fifty or so, petrified and acid-faced before the camera, a puritan deity with shallow, haunted eyes. I remembered her.

Harp had kicked over the traces when his father died, and quit going to church. Mrs. Ryder "disowned" him. The farm was his; she left him with it and went to live with a widowed sister in Lohman, and died soon, unreconciled. Harp lived on as a bachelor, crank, recluse, until his strange marriage in his fifties. Now here was Ma still watchful, pucker-faced, unforgiving. In my dullness of shock I thought: Oh, they probably always made love with the lights out.

But now Leda wasn't there.

I hurried after Harp, who had left the kitchen door to bang in the wind. I got out there with rifle and flashlight, and over across the road I saw his torch. No other light, just his small gleam and mine.

I knew as soon as I had forced myself beyond the corner of the house and into the fantastic embrace of the storm that I could never make it. The west wind ground needles into my face. The snow was up beyond the middle of my thighs. With weak lungs and maybe an imperfect heart, I could do nothing out here except die quickly to no purpose. In a moment Harp would be starting down the slope of the woods. His trail was already disappearing under my beam. I drove myself a little further, and an instant's lull in the storm allowed me to shout: "Harp! I can't follow!"

He heard. He cupped his mouth and yelled back: "Don't try! Git back to the house! Telephone!" I waved to acknowledge the message and struggled back.

I only just made it. Inside the kitchen doorway I fell flat, gun and flashlight clattering off somewhere, and there I stayed until I won back enough breath to keep myself living. My face and hands were ice-blocks, then fires. While I worked at the task of getting air into my body, one thought continued, an inner necessity: *There must be a rational cause. I do not abandon the rational cause.* At length I hauled myself up and stumbled to the telephone. The line was dead.

I found the flashlight and reeled upstairs with it. I stepped past poor Droopy's body and over the broken glass to look through the window space. I could see that snow had been pushed off the shed roof near the bedroom window; the house sheltered that area from the full drive of the west wind, so some evidence remained. I guessed that whatever came must have jumped to the house roof from the maple, then down to the shed roof and then hurled itself through the closed window without regard for it as an obstacle. Losing a little blood and a little fur.

I glanced around and could not find that fur now. Wind must have pushed it out of sight. I forced the door shut. Downstairs, I lit the table lamps in kitchen and parlor. Harp might need those beacons—if he came back. I refreshed the fires, and gave myself a dose of Harp's horrible whiskey. It was nearly one in the morning. If he never came back?

It might be days before they could plow out the road. When the storm let up I could use Harp's snowshoes, maybe . . .

Harp came back at 1:20, bent and staggering. He let me support him to the armchair. When he could speak he said, "No trail. No trail." He took the bottle from my hands and pulled on it. "Christ Jesus! What can I do, Ben . . . ? I got to go to the village, get help. If they got any help to give."

"Do you have an extra pair of snowshoes?"

He stared toward me, battling confusion. "Hah? No, I ain't. Better you stay anyhow. I'll bring yours from your house if you want, if I can git there." He drank again and slammed in the cork with the heel of his hand. "I'll leave you the ten-gauge."

He got his snowshoes from a closet. I persuaded him to wait for coffee. Haste could accomplish nothing now; we could not say to each other that we knew Leda was dead. When he was ready to go, I stepped outside with him into the mad wind. "Anything you want me to do before you get back?" He tried to think about it.

"I guess not, Ben . . . God, ain't I *lived* right? No, that don't make sense? God? That's a laugh." He swung away. Two or three great strides and the storm took him.

That was about two o'clock. For four hours I was alone in the house. Warmth returned, with the bedroom door closed and fires working hard. I carried the kitchen lamp into the parlor, and then huddled in the nearly total dark of the kitchen with my back to the wall, watching all the windows, the ten-gauge near my hand, but I did not expect a return of the beast, and there was none.

The night grew quieter, perhaps because the house was so drifted in that snow muted the sounds. I was cut off from the battle, buried alive.

Harp would get back. The seasons would follow their natural way, and somehow we would learn what had happened to Leda. I supposed the beast would have to be something in the human pattern—mad, deformed, gone wild, but still human.

After a time I wondered why we had heard no excitement in the stable. I forced myself to take up gun and flashlight and go look. I groped through the woodshed, big with the jumping shadows of Harp's cordwood, and into the barn. The cows were peacefully drowsing. In the center alley I dared to send my weak beam swooping and glimmering through the ghastly distances of the hayloft. Quiet, just quiet; natural rustling of mice. Then to the stable, where Ned whickered and let me rub his brown cheek, and Jerry rolled a humorous eye. I suppose no smell had reached them to touch off panic, and perhaps they had heard the barking often enough so that it no longer disturbed them. I went back to my post, and the hours crawled along a ridge between the pits of terror and exhaustion. Maybe I slept.

No color of sunrise that day, but I felt paleness and change; even a blizzard will not hide the fact of dayshine somewhere. I breakfasted on bacon and eggs, fed the hens, forked down hay and carried water for the cows and horses. The one cow in milk, a jumpy Ayrshire, refused to concede that I meant to be useful. I'd done no milking since I was a boy, the knack was gone from my hands, and relief seemed less important to her than kicking over the pail; she was getting more amusement than discomfort out of it, so for the moment I let it go. I made myself busy-work shoveling a clear space by the kitchen door. The wind was down, the snowfall persistent but almost peaceful. I pushed out beyond the house and learned that the stuff was up over my hips.

Out of that, as I turned back, came Harp in his long, snowshoe stride, and down the road three others. I recognized Sheriff Robart, overfed but powerful; and Bill Hastings, wry and ageless, a cousin of Harp's and one of his few friends; and last, Curt Davidson, perhaps a friend to Sheriff Robart but certainly not to Harp.

I'd known Curt as a thickwitted loudmouth when he was a kid; growing to man's years hadn't done much for him. And when I saw him I thought, irrationally perhaps: Not good for our side. A kind of absurdity, and yet Harp and I were joined against the world simply because we had experienced together what others were going to call impossible, were going to interpret in harsh, even damnable ways; and no help for it.

I saw the white thin blur of the sun, the strength of it growing. Nowhere in all the white expanse had the wind and the new snow allowed us any mark of the visitation of the night.

The men reached my cleared space and shook off snow. I opened the woodshed. Harp gave me one hopeless glance of inquiry and I shook my head.

"Having a little trouble?" That was Robart, taking off his snowshoes.

Harp ignored him. "I got to look after my chores." I told him I'd done it except for that damn cow. "Oh, Bess, ayah, she's nervy. I'll see to her." He gave me my snowshoes that he had strapped to his back. "Adelaide, she wanted to know about your groceries. Said I figured they was in the ca'."

"Good as an icebox," says Robart, real friendly.

Curt had to have his pleasures, too. "Ben, you sure you got hold of old Bess by the right end, where the tits was?" Curt giggles at his own jokes, so nobody else is obliged to. Bill Hastings spat in the snow.

"Okay if I go in?" Robart asked. It wasn't a simple inquiry: he was present officially and meant to have it known. Harp looked him up and down.

"Nobody stopping you. Didn't bring you here to stand around, I suppose."

"Harp," said Robart pleasantly enough, "don't give me a hard time. You come tell me certain things happened, I got to look into it is all." But Harp was already striding down the woodshed to the barn entrance. The others came into the house with me, and I put on water for fresh coffee. "Must be your ca' down the rud a piece, Ben? Heard you kind of went into a ditch. All's you can see now is a hump in the snow. Deep freeze might be good for her, likely you've tried everything else." But I wasn't feeling comic, and never had been on those terms with Robart. I grunted, and his face shed mirth as one slips off a sweater. "Okay, what's the score? Harp's gone and told me a story I couldn't feed to the dogs, so what about it? Where's Mrs. Ryder?"

Davidson giggled again. It's a nasty little sound to come out of all that beef. I don't think Robart had much enthusiasm for him either, but it seems he had sworn in the fellow as deputy before they set out. "Yes, sir," said Curt, "that was *really* a story, that was."

"Where's Mrs. Ryder?"

"Not here," I told him. "We think she's dead."

He glowered, rubbing cold out of his hands. "Seen that window. Looks like the frame is smashed."

"Yes, from the outside. When Harp gets back you'd better look. I closed the door on that room and haven't opened it. There'll be more snow, but you'll see about what we saw when we got up there."

"Let's look right now," said Curt.

Bill Hastings said, "Curt, ain't you a mite busy for a dep'ty? Mr. Dane said when Harp gets back." Bill and I are friends; normally he wouldn't mister me. I think he was trying to give me some flavor of authority.

I acknowledged the alliance by asking: "You a deputy too, Bill?" Giving him an opportunity to spit in the stove, replace the lid gently, and reply: "Hell no."

Harp returned and carried the milk pail to the pantry. Then he was looking us over. "Bill, I got to try the woods again. You want to come along?"

"Sure, Harp. I didn't bring no gun."

"Take my ten-gauge."

"Curt here'll go along," said Robart. "Real good man on snowshoes. Interested in wild life."

Harp said, "That's funny, Robart. I guess that's the funniest thing I heard since Cutler's little girl fell under the tractor. You joining us too?"

"Fact is, Harp, I kind of pulled a muscle in my back coming up here. Not getting no younger neither. I believe I'll just look around here a little. Trust you got no objection? To me looking around a little?"

"Coffee's dripped," I said.

"Thing of it is, if I'd 've thought you had any objection, I'd 've been obliged to get me a warrant."

"Thanks, Ben." Harp gulped the coffee scalding. "Why, if looking around the house is the best you can do, Sher'f, I got no objection. Ben, I shouldn't be keeping you away from your affairs, but would you stay? Kind of keep him company? Not that I got much in the house, but still—you know—"

"I'll stay." I wished I could tell him to drop that manner; it only got him deeper in the mud.

Robart handed Davidson his gun belt and holster. "Better have it, Curt, so to be in style."

Harp and Bill were outside getting on their snowshoes; I half heard some remark of Harp's about the sheriff's aching back. They took off. The snow had almost ceased. They passed out of sight down the slope to the north, and Curt went plowing after them. Behind me Robart said, "You'd think Harp believed it himself."

"That's how it's to be? You make us both liars before you've even done any looking?"

"I got to try to make sense of it is all." I followed him up to the bedroom. It was cruelly cold. He touched Droopy's stiff corpse with his foot. "Hard to figure a man killing his own dog."

"We get nowhere with that kind of idea."

"Ben, you got to see this thing like it looks to other people. And keep out of my hair."

"That's what scares me, Jack. Something unreasonable did happen, and Harp and I were the only ones to experience it—except Mrs. Ryder."

"You claim you saw this—animal?"

"I didn't say that. I heard her scream. When we got upstairs this room was the way you see it." I looked around, and again couldn't find that scrap of fur, but I spoke of it, and I give Robart credit for searching. He shook out the bedspread and blankets, examined the floor and the closet. He studied the window space, leaned out for a look at the house wall and the shed roof. His big feet avoided the broken glass, and he squatted for a long gaze at the pieces of window sash. Then he bore down on me, all policeman personified, a massive, rather intelligent, conventionally honest man with no patience for imagination, no time for any fact not already in the books. "Piece of fur, huh?" He made it sound as if I'd described a Jabberwock with eyes of flame. "Okay, we're done up here." He motioned me downstairs—all policemen who'd ever faced a crowd's dangerous stupidity with their own.

As I retreated I said, "Hope you won't be too busy to have a chemist test the blood on that sash."

"We'll do that." He made move-along motions with his slab hands. "Going to be a pleasure to do that little thing for you and your friend."

Then he searched the entire house, shed, barn, and stable. I had never before watched anyone on police business; I had to admire his zeal. I got involved in the farce of holding the flashlight for him while he rooted in the cellar. In the shed I suggested that if he wanted to restack twenty-odd cords of wood he'd better wait till Harp could help him; he wasn't amused. He wasn't happy in the barn loft either. Shifting tons of hay to find a hypothetical corpse was not a one-man job. I knew he was capable of returning with a crew and machinery to do exactly that. And by his lights it was what he ought to do. Then we were back in the kitchen, Robart giving himself a manicure with his jackknife, and I down to my last cigarette, almost the last of my endurance.

Robart was not unsubtle. I answered his questions as temperately as I could—even, for instance: "Wasn't you a mite sweet on Leda yourself?" I didn't answer any of them with flat silence; to do that right you need an accompanying act like spitting in the stove, and I'm not a chewer. From the north window he said: "Comin' back. It figures." They had been out a little over an hour.

Harp stood by the stove with me to warm his hands. He spoke as if alone with me: "No trail, Ben." What followed came in an undertone: "Ben, you told me about a friend of yours, scientist or something, professor—"

"Professor Malcolm?" I remembered mentioning him to Harp a long while before; I was astonished at his recalling it. Johnny Malcolm is a professor of biology who has avoided too much specialization. Not really a close friend. Harp was watching me out of a granite despair as if he had asked me to appeal to some higher court. I thought of another acquaintance in Boston too, whom I might consult—Dr. Kahn, a psychiatrist who had once seen my wife Helen through a difficult time...

"Harp," said Robart, "I got to ask you a couple, three things. I sent word to Dick Hammond to get that goddamned plow of his into this road as quick as he can. Believe he'll try. Whiles we wait on him, we might 's well talk. You know I don't like to get tough."

"Talk away," said Harp, "only Ben here he's got to get home without waiting on no Dick Hammond."

"That a fact, Ben?"

"Yes. I'll keep in touch."

"Do that," said Robart, dismissing me. As I left he was beginning a fresh manicure, and Harp waited rigidly for the ordeal to continue. I felt morbidly that I was abandoning him.

Still—corpus delicti—nothing much more would happen until Leda Ryder was found. Then if her body were found dead by violence, with no acceptable evidence of Longtooth's existence—well, what then?

I don't think Robart would have let me go if he'd known my first act would be to call Short's brother Mike and ask him to drive me in to Lohman where I could get a bus for Boston.

Johnny Malcolm said, "I can see this is distressing you, and you wouldn't lie to me. But, Ben, as biology it won't do. Ain't no such animile. You know that."

He wasn't being stuffy. We were having dinner at a quiet restaurant, and I had of course enjoyed the roast duckling too much. Johnny is a rock-ribbed beanpole who can eat like a walking famine with no regrets. "Suppose," I said, "just for argument and because it's not biologically inconceivable, that there's a basis for the Yeti legend."

"Not inconceivable. I'll give you that. So long as any poorly known corners of the world are left—the Himalayan uplands, jungles, tropic swamps, the tundra—legends will persist and some of them will have little gleams of truth. You know what I think about moon flights and all that?" He smiled; privately I was hearing Leda scream. "One of our strongest reasons for them, and for the biggest flights we'll make if we don't kill civilization first, is a hunt for new legends. We've used up our best ones, and that's dangerous."

"Why don't we look at the countries inside us?" But Johnny wasn't listening much.

"Men can't stand it not to have closed doors and a chance to push at them. Oh, about your Yeti—he might exist. Shaggy anthropoid able to endure severe cold, so rare and clever the explorers haven't tripped over him yet. Wouldn't have to be a carnivore to have big ugly canines—look at the baboons. But if he was active in a Himalayan winter, he'd have to be able to use meat, I think. Mind you, I don't believe any of this, but you can have it as a biological not-impossible. How'd he get to Maine?"

"Strayed? Tibet—Mongolia—Arctic ice."

"Maybe." Johnny had begun to enjoy the hypothesis as something to play with during dinner. Soon he was helping along the brute's passage across the continents, and having fun till I grumbled something about alternatives, extraterrestrials. He wouldn't buy that, and got cross. Still hearing Leda scream, I assured him I wasn't watching for little green men.

"Ben, how much do you know about this—Harp?"

"We grew up along different lines, but he's a friend. Dinosaur, if you like, but a friend."

"Hardshell Maine bachelor picks up dizzy young wife—"

"She's not dizzy. Wasn't. Sexy, but not dizzy."

"All right. Bachelor stewing in his own juices for years. Sure he didn't get up on that roof himself?"

"Nuts. Unless all my senses were more paralyzed than I think, there wasn't time."

"Unless they were more paralyzed than you think."

"Come off it! I'm not senile yet .... What's he supposed to have done with her? Tossed her into the snow?"

"Mph," said Johnny, and finished his coffee. "All right. Some human freak with abnormal strength and the endurance to fossick around in a Maine blizzard stealing women. I liked the Yeti better. You say you suggested a madman to Ryder yourself. Pity if you had to come all the way here just so I could repeat your own guesswork. To make amends, want to take in a bawdy movie?"

"Love it."

The following day Dr. Kahn made time to see me at the end of the afternoon, so polite and patient that I felt certain I was keeping him from his dinner. He seemed undecided whether to be concerned with the traumas of Harp Ryder's history or those of mine. Mine were already somewhat known to him. "I wish you had time to talk all this out to me. You've given me a nice summary of what the physical events appear to have been, but—"

"Doctor," I said, "it *happened.* I heard the animal. The window *was* smashed—ask the sheriff. Leda Ryder did scream, and when Harp and I got up there together, the dog had been killed and Leda was gone."

"And yet, if it was all as clear as that, I wonder why you thought of consulting me at all, Ben. I wasn't there. I'm just a head-shrinker."

"I wanted . . . Is there any way a delusion could take hold of Harp *and* me, disturb our senses in the same way? Oh, just saying it makes it ridiculous."

Dr. Kahn smiled. "Let's say, difficult."

"Is it possible Harp could have killed her, thrown her out through the window of the *west* bedroom—the snow must have drifted six feet or higher on that side—and then my mind distorted my time sense? So I might've stood there in the dark kitchen all the time it went on, a matter of minutes instead of seconds? Then he jumped down by the shed roof, came back into the house the normal way while I was stumbling upstairs? Oh, hell."

Dr. Kahn had drawn a diagram of the house from my description, and peered at it with placid interest. "Benign" was a word Helen had used for him. He said, " Such a distortion of the time sense would be—unusual . . . Are you feeling guilty about anything?"

"About standing there and doing nothing? I can't seriously believe it was more than a few seconds. Anyway that would make Harp a monster out of a detective story. He's not that. How could he count on me to freeze in panic? Absurd. I'd 've heard the struggle, steps, the window of the west room going up. Could he have killed her and I known all about it at the time, even witnessed it, and then suffered amnesia for that one event?"

He still looked so patient I wished I hadn't come. "I won't say any trick of the mind is impossible, but I might call that one highly improbable. Academically, however, considering your emotional involvement—"

"I'm not emotionally involved!" I yelled that. He smiled, looking much more interested. I laughed at myself. That was better than poking him in the eye. "I'm upset, Doctor, because the whole thing goes against reason. If you start out knowing nobody's going to believe you, it's all messed up before you open your mouth."

He nodded kindly. He's a good joe. I think he'd stopped listening for what I didn't say long enough to hear a little of what I did say. "You're not unstable, Ben. Don't worry about amnesia. The explanation, perhaps some human intruder, will turn out to be within the human norm. The norm of possibility does include such things as lycanthropic delusions, maniacal behavior, and so on. Your police up there will carry on a good search for the poor woman. They won't overlook that snowdrift. Don't underestimate them, and don't worry about your own mind, Ben."

"Ever see our Maine woods?"

"No, I go away to the Cape."

"Try it some time. Take a patch of it, say about fifty miles by fifty, that's twenty-five hundred square miles. Drop some eager policemen into it, tell 'em to hunt for something they never saw before and don't want to see, that doesn't want to be found."

"But if your beast is human, human beings leave traces. Bodies aren't easy to hide, Ben."

"In those woods? A body taken by a carnivorous animal? Why not?" Well, our minds didn't touch. I thanked him for his patience and got up. "The maniac responsible," I said. "But whatever we call him, Doctor, he was *there*."

Mike Short picked me up at the Lohman bus station, and told me something of a ferment in Darkfield. I shouldn't have been surprised. "They're all scared, Mr. Dane. They want to hurt somebody." Mike is Jim Short's younger brother. He scrapes up a living with his taxi service and occasional odd jobs at the garage. There's a droop in his shaggy ringlets, and I believe thirty is staring him in the face. "Like old Harp he wants to tell it like it happened and nobody buys. That's sad, man. You been away what, three days? The fuzz was pissed off. You better connect with Mister Sheriff Robart like soon. He climbed all over my ass just for driving you to the bus that day, like I should've known you shouldn't."

"I'll pacify him. They haven't found Mrs. Ryder?"

Mike spat out the car window, which was rolled down for the mild air. "Old Harp he never got such a job of snow-shoveling done in all his days. By the c'munity, for free. No, they won't find her." In that there was plenty of I-want-to-be-asked, and something more, a hint of the mythology of Mike's generation.

"So what's your opinion, Mike?"

He maneuvered a fresh cigarette against the stub of the last and drove on through tiresome silence. The road was winding between ridged mountains of plowed, rotting snow. I had the window down on my side too for the genial afternoon sun, and imagined a tang of spring. At last Mike said, "You prob'ly don't go along... Jim got your ca' out, by the way. It's at your place ... Well, you'll hear 'em talking it all to pieces. Some claim Harp's telling the truth. Some say he killed her himself. They don't say how he made her disappear. Ain't heard any talk against you, Mr. Dane, nothing that counts. The sheriff's peeved, but that's just on account you took off without asking." His vague, large eyes watched the melting landscape, the ambiguous messages of spring. "Well, I think, like, a demon took her, Mr. Dane. She was one of his own, see? You got to remember, I knew that chick. Okay, you can say it ain't scientific, only there is a science to these things, I read a book about it. You can laugh if you want."

I wasn't laughing. It wasn't my first glimpse of the contemporary medievalism and won't be my last if I survive another year or two. I wasn't laughing, and I said nothing. Mike sat smoking, expertly driving his 20th-Century artifact while I suppose his thoughts were in the 17th, sniffing after the wonders of the invisible world, and I recalled what Johnny Malcolm had said about the need for legends. Mike and I had no more talk.

Adelaide Simmons was dourly glad to see me. From her I learned that the sheriff and state police had swarmed all over Harp's place and the surrounding countryside, and were still at it. Result, zero. Harp had repeatedly told our story and was refusing to tell it any more. "Does the chores and sets there drinking," she said, "or staring off. Was up to see him yesterday, Mr. Dane—felt I should. Couple days they didn't let him alone a minute, maybe now they've eased off some. He asked me real sharp, was you back yet. Well, I redd up his place, made some bread, least I could do."

When I told her I was going there, she prepared a basket, while I sat in the kitchen and listened. "Some say she busted that window herself, jumped down and run off in the snow, out of her mind. Any sense in that?"

"Nope."

"And some claim she deserted him. Earlier. Which'd make you a liar. And they say whichever way it was, Harp's made up this crazy story because he can't stand the truth." Her clever hands slapped sandwiches into shape. "They claim Harp got you to go along with it, they don't say how."

"Hypnotized me, likely. Adelaide, it all happened the way Harp told it. I heard the thing too. If Harp is ready for the squirrels, so am I."

She stared hard, and sighed. She likes to talk, but her mill often shuts off suddenly, because of a quality of hers which I find good as well as rare: I mean that when she has no more to say she doesn't go on talking.

I got up to Ryder's Ridge about suppertime. Bill Hastings was there. The road was plowed slick between the snow ridges, and I wondered how much of the litter of tracks and crumpled paper and spent cigarette packages had been left by sight-seers. Ground frost had not yet yielded to the mud season, which would soon make normal driving impossible for a few weeks. Bill let me in, with the look people wear for serious illness. But Harp heaved himself out of that armchair, not sick in body at least. "Ben, I heard him last night. Late."

"What direction?"

"North."

"You hear it, Bill?" I set down the basket.

My pint-size friend shook his head. "Wasn't here." I couldn't guess how much Bill accepted of the tale.

Harp said, "What's the basket?—oh. Obliged. Adelaide's a nice woman." But his mind was remote. "It was north, Ben, a long way, but I think I know about where it would be. I wouldn't 've heard it except the night was so still, like everything had quieted for me. You know, they been a-deviling me night and day. Robart, state cops, mess of smart little buggers from the papers. I couldn't sleep, I stepped outside like I was called. Why, he might've been the other side of the stars, the sky so full of 'em and nothing stirring. Cold . . . You went to Boston, Ben?"

"Yes. Waste of time. They want it to be something human, anyhow something that fits the books."

Whittling, Bill said neutrally, "Always a man for the books yourself, wasn't you, Ben?"

I had to agree. Harp asked, "Hadn't no ideas?"

"Just gave me back my own thoughts in their language. We have to find it, Harp. Of course some wouldn't take it for true even if you had photographs."

Harp said, "Photographs be goddamned."

"I guess you got to go," said Bill Hastings. "We been talking about it, Ben. Maybe I'd feel the same if it was me . . . I better be on my way or supper'll be cold and the old woman raising hell-fire." He tossed his stick back in the woodbox.

"Bill," said Harp, "you won't mind feeding the stock couple, three days?"

"I don't mind. Be up tomorrow."

"Do the same for you some time. I wouldn't want it mentioned anyplace."

"Harp, you know me better'n that. See you, Ben."

"Snow's going fast," said Harp when Bill had driven off. "Be in the woods a long time yet, though."

"You wouldn't start this late."

He was at the window, his lean bulk shutting off much light from the time-seasoned kitchen where most of his indoor life had been passed. "Morning, early. Tonight I got to listen."

"Be needing sleep, I'd think."

"I don't always get what I need," said Harp.

"I'll bring my snowshoes. About six? And my carbine—I'm best with a gun I know."

He stared at me a while. "All right, Ben. You understand, though, you might have to come back alone. I ain't coming back till I get him, Ben. Not this time."

At sunup I found him with Ned and Jerry in the stable. He had lived eight or ten years with that team. He gave Ned's neck a final pat as he turned to me and took up our conversation as if night had not intervened. "Not till I get him. Ben, I don't want you drug into this ag'inst your inclination."

"Did you hear it again last night?"

"I heard it. North."

The sun was at the point of rising when we left on our snowshoes, like morning ghosts ourselves. Harp strode ahead down the slope to the woods without haste, perhaps with some reluctance. Near the trees he halted, gazing to his right where a red blaze was burning the edge of the sky curtain; I scolded myself for thinking that he was saying goodbye to the sun.

The snow was crusted, sometimes slippery even for our web feet. We entered the woods along a tangle of tracks, including the fat tire-marks of a snow-scooter. "Guy from Lohman," said Harp. "Hired the goddamn thing out to the state cops and hisself with it. Goes pootin' around all over hell, fit to scare everything inside eight, ten miles." He cut himself a fresh plug to last the morning. "I b'lieve the thing is a mite further off than that. They'll be messing around again today." His fingers dug into my arm. "See how it is, don't y'? They ain't looking for what we are. Looking for a dead body to hang onto my neck. And if they was to find her the way I found—the way I found—"

"Harp, you needn't borrow trouble."

"I know how they think," he said. "Was I to walk down the road beyond Darkfield, they'd pick me up. They ain't got me in shackles because they got no—no body, Ben. Nobody needs to tell me about the law. They got to have a body. Only reason they didn't leave a man here overnight, they figure I can't go nowhere. They think a man couldn't travel in three, four feet of snow ... Ben, I mean to find that thing and shoot it down ... We better slant off thisaway."

He set out at a wide angle from those tracks, and we soon had them out of sight. On the firm crust our snowshoes left no mark. After a while we heard a grumble of motors far back, on the road. Harp chuckled viciously. "Bright and early like yesterday." He stared back the way we had come. "They'll never pick that up, without dogs. That son of a bitch Robart did talk about borrying a hound somewhere, to sniff Leda's clothes. More likely give 'em a sniff of mine, now."

We had already come so far that I didn't know the way back. Harp would know it. He could never be lost in any woods, but I have no mental compass such as his. So I followed him blindly, and trying to memorize our trail. It was a region of uniform old growth, mostly hemlock, no recent lumbering, few landmarks. The monotony wore down native patience to a numbness, and our snowshoes left no more impression than our thoughts.

An hour passed, or more; after that sound of motors faded. Now and then I heard the wind move peacefully overhead. Few bird calls, for most of our singers had not yet returned. "Been in this part before, Harp?"

"Not with snow on the ground, not lately." His voice was hushed and careful. "Summers. About a mile now, and the trees thin out some. Stretch of slash where they was taking out pine four, five years back and left everything a Christly pile like they always do."

No, Harp wouldn't get lost here, but I was well lost, tired, sorry I had come. Would he turn back if I collapsed? I didn't think he could, now, for any reason. My pack with blanket roll and provisions had become infernal. He had said we ought to have enough for three or four days. Only a few years earlier I had carried heavier camping loads than this without trouble, but now I was blown, a stitch beginning in my side. My wrist watch said only nine o'clock.

The trees thinned out as he had promised, and here the land rose in a long slope to the north. I looked up across a tract of eight or ten acres where the devastation of stupid lumbering might be healed if the hurt region could be let alone for sixty years. The deep snow, blinding out here where only scrub growth interfered with the sunlight, covered the worst of the wreckage. "Good place for wild ras'berries," Harp said quietly. "Been time for 'em to grow back. Guess it was nearer seven years ago when they cut here and left this mess. Last summer I couldn't hardly find their logging road. Off to the left—"

He stopped, pointing with a slow arm to a blurred gray line that wandered up from the left to disappear over the rise of ground. The nearest part of that gray curve must have been four hundred feet away, and to my eyes it might have been a shadow cast by an irregularity of the snow surface; Harp knew better. Something had passed there, heavy enough to break the crust. "You want to rest a mite, Ben? Once over that rise I might not want to stop again."

I let myself down on the butt of an old log that lay tilted toward us, cut because it had happened to be in the way, left to rot because they happened to be taking pine. "Can you really make anything out of that?"

"Not enough," said Harp. "But it could be him." He did not sit by me but stood relaxed with his load, snowshoes spaced so he could spit between them. "About half a mile over that rise," he said, "there's a kind of gorge. Must've been a good brook, former times, still a stream along the bottom in summer. Tangle of elders and stuff. Couple, three caves in the bank at one spot. I guess it's three summers since I been there. Gloomy goddamn place. There was foxes into one of them caves. Natural caves, I b'lieve. I didn't go too near, not then."

I sat in the warming light, wondering whether there was any way I could talk to Harp about the beast—if it existed, if we weren't merely a pair of aging men with disordered minds. Any way to tell him the creature was important to the world outside our dim little village? That it ought somehow to be kept alive, not just shot down and shoveled aside? How could I say this to a man without science, who had lost his wife and also the trust of his fellow-men?

Take away that trust and you take away the world.

Could I ask him to shoot it in the legs, get it back alive? Why, to my own self, irrationally, that appeared wrong, horrible, as well as beyond our powers. Better if he shot to kill. Or if I did. So in the end I said nothing, but shrugged my pack into place and told him I was ready to go on.

With the crust uncertain under that stronger sunshine, we picked our way slowly up the rise, and when we came at length to that line of tracks, Harp said matter-of-factly, "Now you've seen his mark. It's him."

Sun and overnight freezing had worked on the trail. Harp estimated it had been made early the day before. But wherever the weight of Longtooth had broken through, the shape of his foot showed clearly down there in its pocket of snow, a foot the size of a man's but broader, shorter. The prints were spaced for the stride of a short-legged person. The arch of the foot was low, but the beast was not actually flat-footed. Beast or man. I said, "This is a man's print, Harp. Isn't it?"

He spoke without heat. "No. You're forgetting, Ben. I seen him."

"Anyhow there's only one."

He said slowly, "Only one set of tracks."

"What d' you mean?"

Harp shrugged. "It's heavy. He could've been carrying something. Keep your voice down. That crust yesterday, it would've held me without no web feet, but he went through, and he ain't as big as me." Harp checked his rifle and released the safety. "Half a mile to them caves. B'lieve that's where he is, Ben. Don't talk unless you got to, and take it slow."

I followed him. We topped the rise, encountering more of that lumberman's desolation on the other side. The trail crossed it, directly approaching a wall of undamaged trees that marked the limit of the cutting. Here forest took over once more, and where it began, Longtooth's trail ended. "Now you seen how it goes," Harp said. "Any place where he can travel above ground he does. He don't scramble up the trunks, seems like. Look here—he must've got aholt of that branch and swung hisself up. Knocked off some snow, but the wind knocks off so much too you can't tell nothing. See, Ben, he—he figures it out. He knows about trails. He'll have come down out of these trees far enough from where we are now so there ain't no chance of us seeing the place from here. Could be anywhere in a halfcircle, and draw it as big as you please."

"Thinking like a man."

"But he ain't a man," said Harp. "There's things he don't know. How a man feels, acts. I'm going on to them caves." From necessity, I followed him . . .

I ought to end this quickly. Prematurely I am an old man, incapacitated by the effects of a stroke and a damaged heart. I keep improving a little—sensible diet, no smoking, Adelaide's care. I expect several years of tolerable health on the way downhill. But I find, as Harp did, that it is even more crippling to lose the trust of others. I will write here once more, and not again, that my word is good.

It was noon when we reached the gorge. In that place some melancholy part of night must always remain. Down the center of the ravine between tangles of alder, water murmured under ice and rotting snow, which here and there had fallen in to reveal the dark brilliance. Harp did not enter the gorge itself but moved slowly through tree-cover along the left edge, eyes flickering for danger. I tried to imitate his caution. We went a hundred yards or more in that inching advance, maybe two hundred. I heard only the occasional wind of spring.

He turned to look at me, with a sickly triumph, a grimace of disgust and of justification, too. He touched his nose and then I got it also, a rankness from down ahead of us, a musky foulness with an ammoniacal tang and some smell of decay. Then on the other side of the gorge, off in the woods but not far, I heard Longtooth.

A bark, not loud. Throaty, like talk.

Harp suppressed an answering growl. He moved on until he could point down to a black cave-mouth on the opposite side. The breeze blew the stench across to us. Harp whispered, "See, he's got a path. Jumps down to that flat rock, then to the cave. We'll see him in a minute." Yes, there were sounds in the brush. "You keep back." His left palm lightly stroked the underside of his rifle barrel.

So intent was he on the opening where Longtooth would appear, I may have been first to see the other who came then to the cave mouth and stared up at us with animal eyes. Longtooth had called again, a rather gentle sound. The woman wrapped in filthy hides may have been drawn by that call or by the noise of our approach.

Then Harp saw her.

He knew her. In spite of the tangled hair, scratched face, dirt, and the shapeless deer-pelt she clutched around herself against the cold, I am sure he knew her. I don't think she knew him, or me. An inner blindness, a look of a beast wholly centered on its own needs. I think human memories had drained away. She knew Longtooth was coming. I think she wanted his warmth and protection, but there were no words in the whimper she made before Harp's bullet took her between the eyes.

Longtooth shoved through the bushes. He dropped the rabbit he was carrying and jumped down to that flat rock snarling, glancing sidelong at the dead woman who was still twitching. If he understood the fact of death, he had no time for it. I saw the massive overdevelopment of thigh and leg muscles, their springy motions of preparation. The distance from the flat rock to the place where Harp stood must have been fifteen feet. One spear of sunlight touched him in that blue-green shade, touched his thick red fur and his fearful face.

Harp could have shot him. Twenty seconds for it, maybe more. But he flung his rifle aside and drew out his hunting knife, his own long tooth, and had it waiting when the enemy jumped.

So could I have shot him. No one needs to tell me I ought to have done so.

Longtooth launched himself, clawed fingers out, fangs exposed. I felt the meeting as if the impact had struck my own flesh. They tumbled roaring into the gorge, and I was cold, detached, an instrument for watching.

It ended soon. The heavy brownish teeth clenched in at the base of Harp's neck. He made no more motion except the thrust that sent his blade into Longtooth's left side. Then they were quiet in that embrace, quiet all three. I heard the water flowing under the ice.

I remember a roaring in my ears, and I was moving with slow care, one difficult step after another, along the lip of the gorge and through mighty corridors of white and green. With my hardwon detached amusement I supposed this might be the region where I had recently followed poor Harp Ryder to some destination or other, but not (I thought) one of those we talked about when we were boys. A band of iron had closed around my forehead, and breathing was an enterprise needing great effort and caution, in order not to worsen the indecent pain that clung as another band around my diaphragm. I leaned against a tree for thirty seconds or thirty minutes, I don't know where. I knew I mustn't take off my pack in spite of the pain, because it carried provisions for three days. I said once: "Ben, you are lost."

I had my carbine, a golden bough, staff of life, and I recall the shrewd management and planning that enabled me to send three shots into the air. Twice.

It seems I did not want to die, and so hung on the cliff-edge of death with a mad stubbornness. They tell me it could not have been the second day that I fired the second burst, the one that was heard and answered—because, they say a man can't suffer the kind of attack I was having and then survive a whole night of exposure. They say that when a search party reached me from Wyndham Village (18 miles from Darkfield), I made some garbled speech and fell flat on my face.

I woke immobilized, without power of speech or any motion except for a little life in my left hand, and for a long time memory was only a jarring of irrelevancies. When that cleared I still couldn't talk for another long deadly while. I recall someone saying with exasperated admiration that with cerebral hemorrhage on top of coronary infarction, I had no damn right to be alive; this was the first sound that gave me any pleasure. I remember recognizing Adelaide and being unable to thank her for her presence. None of this matters to the story, except the fact that for months I had no bridge of communication with the world; and yet I loved the world and did not want to leave it.

One can always ask: What will happen next?

Some time in what they said was June my memory was (I think) clear. I scrawled a little, with the nurse supporting the deadened part of my arm. But in response to what I wrote, the doctor, the nurses, Sheriff Robart, even Adelaide Simmons and Bill Hastings, looked—sympathetic. I was not believed. I am not believed now, in the most important part of what I wish I might say: that there are things in our world that we do not understand, and that this ignorance ought to generate humility. People find this obvious, bromidic—oh, they always have!—and therefore they do not listen, retaining the pride of their ignorance intact.

Remnants of the three bodies were found in late August, small thanks to my efforts, for I had no notion what compass direction we took after the cut-over area, and there are so many such areas of desolation I couldn't tell them where to look. Forest scavengers, including a pack of dogs, had found the bodies first. Water had moved them too, for the last of the big snow melted suddenly, and for a couple of days at least there must have been a small river raging through that gorge. The head of what they are calling the "lunatic" got rolled downstream, bashed against rocks, partly buried in silt. Dogs had chewed and scattered what they speak of as "the man's fur coat."

It will remain a lunatic in a fur coat, for they won't have it any other way. So far as I know, no scientist ever got a look at the wreckage, unless you glorify the coroner by that title. I believe he was a good vet before he got the job. When my speech was more or less regained, I was already through trying to talk about it. A statement of mine was read at the inquest—that was before I could talk or leave the hospital. At this ceremony society officially decided that Harper Harrison Ryder, of this township, shot to death his wife Leda and an individual, male, of unknown identity, while himself temporarily of unsound mind, and died of knife injuries received in a struggle with the said individual of unknown, and so forth.

I don't talk about it because that only makes people more sorry for me, to think a man's mind should fail so, and he not yet sixty.

I cannot even ask them: "What is truth?" They would only look more saddened, and I suppose shocked, and perhaps find reasons for not coming to see me again.

They are kind. They will do anything for me, except think about it.

Stephen King

ONE FOR
THE ROAD

IT WAS QUARTER past ten and Herb Tooklander was thinking of
closing for the night when the man in the fancy overcoat and the white,
staring face burst into Tookey's Bar, which lies in the northern part of
Falmouth. It was the tenth of January, just about the time most folks are
learning to live comfortably with all the New Year's resolutions they
broke, and there was one hell of a northeaster blowing outside. Six inches
had come down before dark and it had been going hard and heavy since
then. Twice we had seen Billy Larribee go by high in the cab of the town
plow, and the second time Tookey ran him out a beer—an act of pure
charity my mother would have called it, and my God knows she put down
enough of Tookey's beer in her time. Billy told him they were keeping
ahead of it on the main road, but the side ones were closed and apt to stay
that way until next morning. The radio in Portland was forecasting
another foot and a forty-mile-an-hour wind to pile up the drifts.

There was just Tookey and me in the bar, listening to the wind howl
around the eaves and watching it dance the fire around on the hearth.
"Have one for the road, Booth," Tookey says, "I'm gonna shut her down."

He poured me one and himself one and that's when the door cracked
open and this stranger staggered in, snow up to his shoulders and in his
hair, like he had rolled around in confectioner's sugar. The wind billowed
a sand-fine sheet of snow in after him.

"Close the door!" Tookey roars at him. "Was you born in a barn?"

I've never seen a man who looked that scared. He was like a horse that's
spent an afternoon eating fire nettles. His eyes rolled toward Tookey and
he said, "My wife—my daughter—" and he collapsed on the floor in a dead
faint.

"Holy Joe," Tookey says. "Close the door, Booth, would you?"

I went and shut it, and pushing it against the wind was something of a
chore. Tookey was down on one knee holding the fellow's head up and
patting his cheeks. I got over to him and saw right off that it was nasty.
His face was fiery red, but there were gray blotches here and there, and
when you've lived through winters in Maine since the time Woodrow

Wilson was President, as I have, you know those gray blotches mean frostbite.

"Fainted," Tookey said. "Get the brandy off the backbar, will you?"

I got it and came back. Tookey had opened the fellow's coat. He had come around a little; his eyes were half open and he was muttering something too low to catch.

"Pour a capful," Tookey says.

"Just a cap?" I asks him.

"That stuff's dynamite," Tookey says. "No sense overloading his carb."

I poured it down. It was a remarkable thing to watch. The man trembled all over and began to cough. His face got redder. His eyelids, which had been at half-mast, flew up like window shades. I was a bit alarmed, but Tookey only sat him up like a big baby and clapped him on the back.

The man started to retch, and Tookey clapped him again.

"Hold onto it," he says, "that brandy comes dear."

The man coughed some more, but it was diminishing now. I got my first good look at him. City fellow, all right, and from somewhere south of Boston, at a guess. He was wearing kid gloves, expensive but thin. There were probably some more of those grayish-white patches on his hands, and he would be lucky not to lose a finger or two. His coat was fancy, all right; a three-hundred-dollar job if ever I'd seen one. He was wearing tiny little boots that hardly came up over his ankles, and I began to wonder about his toes.

"Better," he said.

"All right," Tookey said. "Can you come over to the fire?"

"My wife and my daughter," he said. "They're out there ... in the storm."

"From the way you came in, I didn't figure they were at home watching the TV," Tookey said. "You can tell us by the fire as easy as here on the floor. Hook on, Booth."

He got to his feet, but a little groan came out of him and his mouth twisted down in pain. I wondered about his toes again, and I wondered why God felt he had to make fools from New York City who would try driving around in southern Maine at the height of a northeast blizzard. And I wondered if his wife and his little girl were dressed any warmer than him.

We hiked him across to the fireplace and got him sat down in a rocker that used to be Missus Tookey's favorite until she passed on in '74. It was Missus Tookey that was responsible for most of the place, which had been written up in *Down East* and the *Sunday Telegram* and even once in the Sunday supplement of the Boston *Globe*. It's really more of a public house than a bar, with its big wooden floor, pegged together rather than nailed, the maple bar, the old barn-raftered ceiling, and the monstrous big fieldstone hearth. Missus Tookey started to get some ideas in her head after the *Down East* article came out, wanted to start calling the place Tookey's Inn or Tookey's Rest, and I admit it has sort of a Colonial ring to it, but I prefer plain old Tookey's Bar. It's one thing to get uppish in the summer, when the state's full of tourists, another thing altogether in the winter, when you and your neighbors have to trade together. And there had been plenty of winter nights, like this one, that Tookey and I had spent all alone together, drinking scotch and water or just a few beers. My own Victoria passed on in '73, and Tookey's was a place to go where there were enough voices to mute the steady ticking of the deathwatch beetle—even if there was just Tookey and me, it was enough. I wouldn't have felt the same about it if the place had been Tookey's Rest. It's crazy but it's true.

We got this fellow in front of the fire and he got the shakes harder than ever. He hugged onto his knees and his teeth clattered together and a few drops of clear mucus spilled off the end of his nose. I think he was starting to realize that another fifteen minutes out there might have been enough to kill him. It's not the snow, it's the wind-chill factor. It steals your heat.

"Where did you go off the road?" Tookey asked him.

"S-six miles s-south of h-here," he said.

Tookey and I stared at each other, and all of a sudden I felt cold. Cold all over.

"You sure?" Tookey demanded. "You came six miles through the snow?"

He nodded. "I checked the odometer when we came through t-town. I was following directions . . . going to see my wife's s-sister . . . in Cumberland . . . never been there before . . . we're from New Jersey . . ."

New Jersey. If there's anyone more purely foolish than a New Yorker it's a fellow from New Jersey.

"Six miles, you're sure?" Tookey demanded.

"Pretty sure, yeah. I found the turnoff but it was drifted in . . . it was . . ."

Tookey grabbed him. In the shifting glow of the fire his face looked pale and strained, older than his sixty-six years by ten. "You made a right turn?"

"Right turn, yeah. My wife—"

"Did you see a sign?"

"Sign?" He looked up at Tookey blankly and wiped the end of his nose. "Of course I did. It was on my instructions. Take Jointer Avenue through Jerusalem's Lot to the 295 entrance ramp." He looked from Tookey to me and back to Tookey again. Outside, the wind whistled and howled and moaned through the eaves. "Wasn't that right, mister?"

"The Lot," Tookey said, almost too soft to hear. "Oh my God."

"What's wrong?" the man said. His voice was rising. "Wasn't that right? I mean, the road looked drifted in, but I thought . . . if there's a town there, the plows will be out and . . . and then I . . ."

He just sort of tailed off.

"Booth," Tookey said to me, low. "Get on the phone. Call the sheriff."

"Sure," this fool from New Jersey says, "that's right. What's wrong with you guys, anyway? You look like you saw a ghost."

Tookey said, "No ghosts in the Lot, mister. Did you tell them to stay in the car?"

"Sure I did," he said, sounding injured. "I'm not crazy."

Well, you couldn't have proved it by me.

"What's your name?" I asked him. "For the sheriff."

"Lumley," he says. "Gerard Lumley."

He started in with Tookey again, and I went across to the telephone. I picked it up and heard nothing but dead silence. I hit the cutoff buttons a couple of times. Still nothing.

I came back. Tookey had poured Gerard Lumley another tot of brandy, and this one was going down him a lot smoother.

"Was he out?" Tookey asked.

"Phone's dead."

"Hot damn," Tookey says, and we look at each other. Outside the wind gusted up, throwing snow against the windows.

Lumley looked from Tookey to me and back again.

"Well, haven't either of you got a car?" he asked. The anxiety was back in his voice. "They've got to run the engine to run the heater. I only had about a quarter of a tank of gas, and it took me an hour and a half to . . . Look, will you *answer* me?" He stood up and grabbed Tookey's shirt.

"Mister," Tookey says, "I think your hand just ran away from your brains there."

Lumley looked at his hand, at Tookey, then dropped it. "Maine," he hissed. He made it sound like a dirty word about somebody's mother. "All right," he said. "Where's the nearest gas station? They must have a tow truck—"

"Nearest gas station is Falmouth Center," I said. "That's three miles down the road from here."

"Thanks," he said, a bit sarcastic, and headed for the door, buttoning his coat.

"Won't be open, though," I added.

He turned back slowly and looked at us.

"What are you talking about, old man?"

"He's trying to tell you that the station in the Center belongs to Billy Larribee and Billy's out driving the plow, you damn fool," Tookey says patiently. "Now why don't you come back here and sit down, before you bust a gut?"

He came back, looking dazed and frightened. "Are you telling me you can't . . . that there isn't . . . "

"I ain't telling you nothing," Tookey says. "You're doing all the telling, and if you stopped for a minute, we could think this over."

"What's this town, Jerusalem's Lot?" he asked. "Why was the road drifted in? And no lights on anywhere?"

I said, "Jerusalem's Lot burned out two years back."

"And they never rebuilt?" He looked like he didn't believe it.

"It appears that way," I said, and looked at Tookey. "What are we going to do about this?"

"Can't leave them out there," he said.

I got closer to him. Lumley had wandered away to look out the window into the snowy night.

"What if they've been got at?" I asked.

"That may be," he said. "But we don't know it for sure. I've got my Bible on the shelf. You still wear your Pope's medal?"

I pulled the crucifix out of my shirt and showed him. I was born and raised Congregational, but most folks who live around the Lot wear something—crucifix, St. Christopher's medal, rosary, something. Because two years ago, in the span of one dark October month, the Lot went bad. Sometimes, late at night, when there were just a few regulars drawn up around Tookey's fire, people would talk it over. Talk around it is more like the truth. You see, people in the Lot started to disappear. First a few, then a few more, then a whole slew. The schools closed. The town stood empty for most of a year. Oh, a few people moved in—mostly damn fools from out of state like this fine specimen here—drawn by the low property values, I suppose. But they didn't last. A lot of them moved out a month or two after they'd moved in. The others . . . well, they disappeared. Then the town burned flat. It was at the end of a long dry fall. They figure it started up by the Marsten House on the hill that overlooked Jointner Avenue, but no one knows how it started, not to this day. It burned out of control for three days. After that, for a time, things were better. And then they started again.

I only heard the word "vampires" mentioned once. A crazy pulp truck driver named Richie Messina from over Freeport way was in Tookey's that night, pretty well liquored up. "Jesus Christ," this stampeder roars, standing up about nine feet tall in his wool pants and his plaid shirt and his leather-topped boots. "Are you all so damn afraid to say it out? Vampires! That's what you're all thinking, ain't it? Jesus-jumped-up-Christ in a chariot-driven sidecar! Just like a bunch of kids scared of the movies! You know what there is down there in 'Salem's Lot? Want me to tell you?"

"Do tell, Richie," Tookey says. It had got real quiet in the bar. You could hear the fire popping, and outside the soft drift of November rain coming down in the dark. "You got the floor."

"What you got over there is your basic wild dog pack," Richie Messina tells us. "That's what you got. That and a lot of old women who love a good spook story. Why, for eighty bucks I'd go up there and spend the night in what's left of that haunted house you're all so worried about. Well, what about it? Anyone want to put it up?"

But nobody would. Richie was a loudmouth and a mean drunk and no one was going to shed any tears at his wake, but none of us were willing to see him go into 'Salem's Lot after dark.

"Be screwed to the bunch of you," Richie says. "I got my four-ten in the trunk of my Chevy, and that'll stop anything in Falmouth, Cumberland, or Jerusalem's Lot. And that's where I'm goin'."

He slammed out of the bar and no one said a word for a while. Then Lamont Henry says, real quiet, "That's the last time anyone's gonna see Richie Messina. Holy God." And Lamont, raised to be a Methodist from his mother's knee, crossed himself.

"He'll sober off and change his mind," Tookey said, but he sounded uneasy. "He'll be back by closin' time, makin' out it was all a joke."

But Lamont had the right of that one, because no one ever saw Richie again. His wife told the state cops she thought he'd gone to Florida to beat a collection agency, but you could see the truth of the thing in her eyes— sick, scared eyes. Not long after, she moved away to Rhode Island. Maybe she thought Richie was going to come after her some dark night. And I'm not the man to say he might not have done.

Now Tookey was looking at me and I was looking at Tookey as I stuffed my crucifix back into my shirt. I never felt so old or so scared in my life.

Tookey said again, "We can't just leave them out there, Booth."

"Yeah. I know."

We looked at each other for a moment longer, and then he reached out and gripped my shoulder. "You're a good man, Booth." That was enough to buck me up some. It seems like when you pass seventy, people start forgetting that you are a man, or that you ever were.

Tookey walked over to Lumley and said, "I've got a four-wheel-drive Scout. I'll get it out."

"For God's sake, man, why didn't you say so before?" He had whirled around from the window and was staring angrily at Tookey. "Why'd you have to spend ten minutes beating around the bush?"

Tookey said, very softly, "Mister, you shut your jaw. And if you get urge to open it, you remember who made that turn onto an unplowed road in the middle of a goddamned blizzard."

He started to say something, and then shut his mouth. Thick color had risen up in his cheeks. Tookey went out to get his Scout out of the garage. I felt around under the bar for his chrome flask and filled it full of brandy. Figured we might need it before this night was over.

Maine blizzard—ever been out in one?

The snow comes flying so thick and fine that it looks like sand and sounds like that, beating up on the sides of your car or pickup. You don't want to use your high beams because they reflect off the snow and you can't see ten feet in front of you. With the low beams on, you can see maybe fifteen feet. But I can live with the snow. It's the wind I don't like, when it picks up and begins to howl, driving the snow into a hundred weird flying shapes and sounding like all the hate and pain and fear in the world. There's death in the throat of a snowstorm wind, white death—and maybe something beyond death. That's no sound to hear when you're tucked up all cozy in your own bed with the shutters bolted and the doors locked. It's that much worse if you're driving. And we were driving smack into 'Salem's Lot.

"Hurry up a little, can't you?" Lumley asked.

I said, "For a man who came in half frozen, you're in one hell of a hurry to end up walking again."

He gave me a resentful, baffled look and didn't say anything else. We were moving up the highway at a steady twenty-five miles an hour. It was hard to believe that Billy Larribee had just plowed this stretch an hour ago; another two inches had covered it, and it was drifting in. The strongest gusts of wind rocked the Scout on her springs. The headlights showed a swirling white nothing up ahead of us. We hadn't met a single car.

About ten minutes later Lumley gasps: "Hey! What's that?"

He was pointing out my side of the car; I'd been looking dead ahead. I turned, but it was a shade too late. I thought I could see some sort of slumped form fading back from the car, back into the snow, but that could have been imagination.

"What was it? A deer?" I asked.

"I guess so," he says, sounding shaky. "But its eyes—they looked red." He looked at me. "Is that how a deer's eyes look at night?" He sounded almost as if he were pleading.

"They can look like anything," I says, thinking that might be true, but I've seen a lot of deer at night from a lot of cars, and never saw any set of eyes reflect back red.

Tookey didn't say anything.

About fifteen minutes later, we came to a place where the snowbank on the right of the road wasn't so high because the plows are supposed to raise their blades a little when they go through an intersection.

"This looks like where we turned," Lumley said, not sounding too sure about it. "I don't see the sign—"

"This is it," Tookey answered. He didn't sound like himself at all. "You can just see the top of the signpost."

"Oh. Sure." Lumley sounded relieved. "Listen, Mr. Tooklander, I'm sorry about being so short back there. I was cold and worried and calling myself two hundred kinds of fool. And I want to thank you both—"

"Don't thank Booth and me until we've got them in this car," Tookey said. He put the Scout in four-wheel drive and slammed his way through the snowbank and onto Jointner Avenue, which goes through the Lot and out to 295. Snow flew up from the mudguards. The rear end tried to break a little bit, but Tookey's been driving through snow since Hector was a pup. He jockeyed it a bit, talked to it, and on we went. The headlights picked out the bare indication of other tire tracks from time to time, the ones made by Lumley's car, and then they would disappear again. Lumley was leaning forward, looking for his car. And all at once Tookey said, "Mr. Lumley."

"What?" He looked around at Tookey.

"People around these parts are kind of superstitious about 'Salem's Lot," Tookey says, sounding easy enough—but I could see the deep lines of strain around his mouth, and the way his eyes kept moving from side to side. "If your people are in the car, why, that's fine. We'll pack them up, go back to my place, and tomorrow, when the storm's over, Billy will be glad to yank your car out of the snowbank. But if they're not in the car—"

"Not in the car?" Lumley broke in sharply. "Why wouldn't they be in the car?"

"If they're not in the car," Tookey goes on, not answering, "we're going to turn around and drive back to Falmouth Center and whistle for the sheriff. Makes no sense to go wallowing around at night in a snowstorm anyway, does it?"

"They'll be in the car. Where else would they be?"

I said, "One other thing, Mr. Lumley. If we should see anybody, we're not going to talk to them. Not even if they talk to us. You understand that?"

Very slow, Lumley says, "Just what are these superstitions?"

Before we could say anything—God alone knows what I would have said—Tookey broke in. "We're there."

We were coming up on the back end of a big Mercedes. The whole hood of the thing was buried in a snowdrift, and another drift had socked in the whole left side of the car. But the taillights were on and we could see exhaust drifting out of the tailpipe.

"They didn't run out of gas, anyway," Lumley said.

Tookey pulled up and pulled on the Scout's emergency brake. "You remember what Booth told you, Lumley."

"Sure, sure." But he wasn't thinking about anything but his wife and daughter. I don't see how anybody could blame him, either.

"Ready, Booth?" Tookey asked me. His eyes held on mine, grim and gray in the dashboard lights.

"I guess I am," I said.

We all got out and the wind grabbed us, throwing snow in our faces. Lumley was first, bending into the wind, his fancy topcoat billowing out behind him like a sail. He cast two shadows, one from Tookey's headlights, the other from his own taillights. I was behind him, and Tookey was a step behind me. When I got to the trunk of the Mercedes, Tookey grabbed me.

"Let him go," he said.

"Janey! Francie!" Lumley yelled. "Everything okay?" He pulled open the driver's side door and leaned in. "Everything—"

He froze to a dead stop. The wind ripped the heavy door right out of his hand and pushed it all the way open.

"Holy God, Booth," Tookey said, just below the scream of the wind. "I think it's happened again."

Lumley turned back toward us. His face was scared and bewildered, his eyes wide. All of a sudden he lunged toward us through the snow, slipping and almost falling. He brushed me away like I was nothing and grabbed Tookey.

"How did you know?" he roared. "Where are they? What the hell is going on here?"

Tookey broke his grip and shoved past him. He and I looked into the Mercedes together. Warm as toast it was, but it wasn't going to be for much longer. The little amber low-fuel light was glowing. The big car was empty. There was a child's Barbie doll on the passenger's floormat. And a child's ski parka was crumpled over the seatback.

Tookey put his hands over his face . . . and then he was gone. Lumley had grabbed him and shoved him right back into the snowbank. His face was pale and wild. His mouth was working as if he had chewed down on

some bitter stuff he couldn't yet unpucker enough to spit out. He reached in and grabbed the parka.

"Francie's coat?" he kind of whispered. And then loud, bellowing: "*Francie's coat!*" He turned around, holding it in front of him by the little fur-trimmed hood. He looked at me, blank and unbelieving. "She can't be out without her coat on, Mr. Booth. Why ... why ... she'll freeze to death."

"Mr. Lumley—"

He blundered past me, still holding the parka, shouting: "*Francie! Janey! Where are you? Where are youuu?*"

I gave Tookey my hand and pulled him onto his feet. "Are you all—"

"Never mind me," he says. "We've got to get hold of him, Booth."

We went after him as fast as we could, which wasn't very fast with the snow hip-deep in some places. But then he stopped and we caught up to him.

"Mr. Lumley—" Tookey started, laying a hand on his shoulder.

"This way," Lumley said. "This is the way they went. Look!"

We looked down. We were in a kind of dip here, and most of the wind went right over our heads. And you could see two sets of tracks, one large and one small, just filling up with snow. If we had been five minutes later, they would have been gone.

He started to walk away, his head down, and Tookey grabbed him back. "No! No, Lumley!"

Lumley turned his wild face up to Tookey's and made a fist. He drew it back ... but something in Tookey's face made him falter. He looked from Tookey to me and then back again.

"She'll freeze," he said as if we were a couple of stupid kids. "Don't you get it? She doesn't have her jacket on and she's only seven years old—"

"They could be anywhere," Tookey said. "You can't follow those tracks. They'll be gone in the next drift."

"What do you suggest?" Lumley yells, his voice high and hysterical. "If we go back to get the police, she'll freeze to death! Francie *and* my wife!"

"They may be frozen already," Tookey said. His eyes caught Lumley's. "Frozen, or something worse."

"What do you mean?" Lumley whispered. "Get it straight, goddamn it! Tell me!"

"Mr. Lumley," Tookey says, "there's something in the Lot—"

But I was the one who came out with it finally, and the word I never expected to say. "Vampires, Mr. Lumley. Jerusalem's Lot is full of vampires. I expect that's hard for you to swallow—"

He was staring at me as if I'd gone green. "Loonies," he whispers. "You're a couple of loonies." Then he turned away, cupped his hands around his mouth, and bellowed, "*FRANCIE! JANEY!*" He started floundering off again. The snow was up to the hem of his fancy coat.

I looked at Tookey. "What do we do now?"

"Follow him," Tookey says. His hair was plastered with snow, and he *did* look a little bit loony. "I can't just leave him out here, Booth. Can you?"

"No," I says. "Guess not."

So we started to wade through the snow after Lumley as best we could. But he kept getting further and further ahead. He had his youth to spend, you see. He was breaking the trail, going through the snow like a bull. My arthritis began to bother me something terrible, and I started to look down at my legs, telling myself: A little further, just a little further, keep goin', damn it, keep goin' . . .

I piled right into Tookey, who was standing spread-legged in a drift. His head was hanging and both of his hands were pressed to his chest.

"Tookey," I says, "you okay?"

"I'm all right," he said, taking his hands away. "We'll stick with him, Booth, and when he fags out he'll see reason."

We topped a rise and there was Lumley at the bottom, looking desperately for more tracks. Poor man, there wasn't a chance he was going to find them. The wind blew straight across down there where he was, and any tracks would have been rubbed out three minutes after they was made, let alone a couple of hours.

He raised his head and screamed into the night: *"FRANCIE! JANEY! FOR GOD'S SAKE!"* And you could hear the desperation in his voice, the terror, and pity him for it. The only answer he got was the freight-train wail of the wind. It seemed to be laughin' at him, saying: *I took them Mister New Jersey with your fancy car and camel's-hair top-coat. I took them and I rubbed out their tracks and by morning I'll have them just as neat and frozen as two strawberries in a deepfreeze . . .*

"Lumley!" Tookey bawled over the wind. "Listen, you never mind vampires or boogies or nothing like that, but you mind this! You're just making it worse for them! We got to get the—"

And then there *was* an answer, a voice coming out of the dark like little tinkling silver bells, and my heart turned cold as ice in a cistern.

"Jerry . . . Jerry, is that you?"

Lumley wheeled at the sound. And then *she* came, drifting out of the dark shadows of a little copse of trees like a ghost. She was a city woman, all right, and right then she seemed like the most beautiful woman I had ever seen. I felt like I wanted to go to her and tell her how glad I was she was safe after all. She was wearing a heavy green pullover sort of thing, a poncho, I believe they're called. It floated all around her, and her dark hair streamed out in the wild wind like water in a December creek, just before the winter freeze stills it and locks it in.

Maybe I did take a step toward her, because I felt Tookey's hand on my shoulder, rough and warm. And still—how can I say it?—I *yearned* after

her, so dark and beautiful with that green poncho floating around her neck and shoulders, so exotic and strange as to make you think of some beautiful woman from a Walter de la Mare poem.

"Janey!" Lumley cried. *"Janey!"* He began to struggle through the snow toward her, his arms outstretched.

"No!" Tookey cried. *"No, Lumley!"*

He never even looked . . . but she did. She looked up at us and grinned. And when she did, I felt my longing, my yearning turn to horror as cold as the grave, as white and silent as bones in a shroud. Even from the rise we could see the sullen red glare in those eyes. They were less human than a wolf's eyes. And when she grinned you could see how long her teeth had become. She wasn't human anymore. She was a dead thing somehow come back to life in this black howling storm.

Tookey made the sign of the cross at her. She flinched back . . . and then grinned at us again. We were too far away, and maybe too scared.

"Stop it!" I whispered. "Can't we stop it?"

"Too late, Booth!" Tookey says grimly.

Lumley had reached her. He looked like a ghost himself, coated in snow like he was. He reached for her . . . and then he began to scream. I'll hear that sound in my dreams, that man screaming like a child in a nightmare. He tried to back away from her, but her arms, long and bare and as white as the snow, snaked out and pulled him to her. I could see her cock her head and then thrust it forward—

"Booth!" Tookey said hoarsely. "We've got to get out of here!"

And so we ran. Ran like rats, I suppose some would say, but those who would weren't there that night. We fled back down along our own back-trail, falling down, getting up again, slipping and sliding. I kept looking back over my shoulder to see if that woman was coming back at us, grinning that grin and watching us with those red eyes.

We got back to the Scout and Tookey doubled over, holding his chest. "Tookey!" I said, badly scared. "What—"

"Ticker," he said. "Been bad for five years or more. Get me around in the shotgun seat, Booth, and then get us the hell out of here."

I hooked an arm under his coat and dragged him around and somehow boosted him up and in. He leaned his head back and shut his eyes. His skin was waxy-looking and yellow.

I went back around the hood of the truck at a trot, and I damned near ran into the little girl. She was just standing there beside the driver's-side door, her hair in pigtails, wearing nothing but a little bit of a yellow dress.

"Mister," she said in a high, clear voice, as sweet as morning mist, "won't you help me find my mother? She's gone and I'm so cold—"

"Honey," I said, "honey, you better get in the truck. Your mother's—"

I broke off, and if there was ever a time in my life I was close to swooning, that was the moment. She was standing there, you see, but she was standing *on top* of the snow and there were no tracks, not in any direction.

She looked up at me then, Lumley's daughter Francie. She was no more than seven years old, and she was going to be seven for an eternity of nights. Her little face was a ghastly corpse white, her eyes a red and silver that you could fall into. And below her jaw I could see two small punctures like pinpricks, their edges horribly mangled.

She held out her arms at me and smiled. "Pick me up, mister," she said softly. "I want to give you a kiss. Then you can take me to my mommy."

I didn't want to, but there was nothing I could do. I was leaning forward, my arms outstretched. I could see her mouth opening. I could see the little fangs inside the pink ring of her lips. Something slipped down her chin, bright and silvery, and with a dim, distant, faraway horror, I realized she was drooling.

Her small hands clasped themselves around my neck and I was thinking: Well, maybe it won't be so bad, not so bad, maybe it won't be so awful after a while—when something black flew out of the Scout and struck her on the chest. There was a puff of strange-smelling smoke, a flashing glow that was gone an instant later, and then she was backing away, hissing. Her face was twisted into a vulpine mask of rage, hate, and pain. She turned sideways and then . . . and then she was gone. One moment she was there and the next there was a twisting knot of snow that looked a little bit like a human shape. Then the wind tattered it away across the fields.

"Booth!" Tookey whispered. "Be quick, now!"

And I was. But not so quick that I didn't have time to pick up what he had thrown at that little girl from hell. His mother's Douay Bible.

*   *   *

That was some time ago. I'm a sight older now, and I was no chicken then. Herb Tooklander passed on two years ago. He went peaceful, in the night. The bar is still there, some man and his wife from Waterville bought it, nice people, and they've kept it pretty much the same. But I don't go by much. It's different somehow with Tookey gone.

Things in the Lot go on pretty much as they always have. The sheriff found that fellow Lumley's car the next day, out of gas, the battery dead. Neither Tookey nor I said anything about it. What would have been the point? And every now and then a hitchhiker or a camper will disappear around here someplace, up on Schoolyard Hill or out near the Harmony Hill cemetery. They'll turn up the fellow's packsack or a paperback book all swollen and bleached out by the rain or snow, or some such. But never the people.

I still have bad dreams about that stormy night we went out there. Not about the woman so much as the little girl, and the way she smiled when she held her arms up so I could pick her up. So she could give me a kiss. But I'm an old man and the time comes when dreams are done.

You may have an occasion to be traveling in southern Maine yourself one of these days. Pretty part of the countryside. You may even stop by Tookey's Bar for a drink. Nice place. They kept the name just the same. So have your drink, and then my advice is to keep on moving north. Whatever you do, don't go up that road to Jerusalem's Lot.

Especially not after dark.

There's a little girl somewhere out there. And I think she's still waiting for her good-night kiss.

Ruth Sawyer

FOUR DREAMS OF GRAM PERKINS

GRAM PERKINS WAS not my grandmother. I had good reason to believe that she had died and received Christian burial a half century before I first set foot in Haddock harbour. Neither were the dreams of my dreaming; so my connection with her was always remote and impersonal. Nevertheless, I came to know through her all the horror and the fascination of a perturbed spirit.

For those who may not know the harbour, let me explain that it bites into the northern stretch of Maine coast. Summer resorters are still in the minority, and peace and beauty serve as perpetual handmaidens to those few exhausted, nerve-racked city folk who have found refuge there. I was there only a few days when the immortal essence of Gram Perkins confronted me. Perkins is a prevailing name at the harbour. A Perkins peddles fish on Tuesdays and Fridays. A Perkins keeps the village store in whose windows are displayed those amazing knickknacks somebody or other creates out of sweet grass, beads, birch bark, and sealing wax. A Perkins is framed daily in the general delivery window of the post office, and his brother drives the one village jitney.

It was Cal Perkins of tender years who indirectly introduced me to the mysterious dreamer of the dreams. Cal took me on my first scaling of the blueberry ledges. Standing like Balboa on the Peak of Darien he swept a hand inland and said: "Somewhars, over thar, lives Zeb Perkins. Hain't never laid eyes on him myself, but Pa says you doan't never want to hear him tell of them four dreams he's had of Grandmother Perkins. Woan't sleep ag'in fur a month ef you do." It was not long before I discovered those dreams were as firm a tradition at the harbour as the "Three Hairs of Grandfather Knowital" are in Eastern Europe—only with a difference. Natives in the Balkans pass on their story for the asking; whereas in Haddock harbour they evade all questions leading to Gram Perkins, while their tongues travel to their cheeks.

One day Cal took me to the cemetery and showed me the Perkins monument. It was a splendid affair in two shades of marble with a wrought-iron fence and gateway, and all about it were the headstones

93

marking the graves of the separate members of the Perkins family. I read the inscription on Gram Perkins's stone:

Sara Amanda Perkins
Beloved wife of Benjamin Perkins, Sea Captain
1791-1863
May she rest in perfect peace!

"Wall, she didn't!" Cal hurled the words at me as he catapulted through the gate, shaking all over like the aspen back of the lot. I caught a final mumbling: "Never aim to stop nigh *her*. Pa says I might git to dreamin', too."

Here was distinctly unpleasant food for thought. Already she had a firm grip on my waking hours, and there was no relish to the idea of her haunting my sleeping ones. The manner in which she possessed the town was astounding. She lurked wherever one went, popping out with the most casual remark when one was buying a pound of butter or a pint of clams. And yet, for all the daily allusions and innuendoes, one never got at the heart of the matter; one never rightly understood why Gram Perkins was and yet was not five feet below the sod. As for the dreamer of the dreams, one never found him clothed in anything more solid than words.

I questioned Peddling Perkins one Friday when he came to our house with the makings of a chowder. "Tell me," I began, "where does Zeb Perkins live and what relation is he to you?"

He paused in his weighing. The scales hung from a rafter in his cart and worked somewhat mysteriously. He might have been weighing out the exact amount of relationship he cared to claim. "Fur as I can make out he's sort of a third cousin."

"Did he ever tell you about those dreams?"

"No, ma'am!" He fixed me with a fore-warning eye. "What's more, he hain't never goin' to. I seen Scip Perkins—time he told him. Scairt! Never seen a feller so shook up in his life. Didn't take off his clothes and lay good abed fur a week. No, ma'am!"

I questioned the post-office Perkins one day: "Do you happen to know what Zeb Perkins dreamed about his grandmother?"

"Dreamed! Gosh, what didn't he dream? Think of anything a sensible woman, dead and buried fifty years, stands liable to do and you wouldn't have the half of it." He finished snapping his teeth together to signify that he had gone as far with those dreams as he intended to go—for the present, anyway.

A few days later I took the matter to the village store. I even bought a chain and earrings of sealing wax to make my going seem less mercenary.

"Those dreams," I ventured, "how did they happen and do they belong entirely to Zeb?"

"They do, God be praised!" Whereupon the storekeeper retired behind the necklace for a good two minutes, and then partially emerged to whisper, "No one's layin' any claim at all to those dreams but Zeb. And I've always thought myself if he hadn't had them, no knowing what he mightn't have had."

II

For two recurring summers I stayed fixed at this point. And then came a spring when I slipped off early to the harbour for trout. The Perkins who drives the jitney met me at the wharf as I stepped from the Boston boat. "Hain't a summer resorter nor a bluejay here yit," was his greeting. "Weather's right smart—nips ye considerable." And it did. The water in the brooks was so cold my fingers remained stiff and blue all day. But the fishing was good, and in the end I caught something more than trout.

A morning came with a southeast wind. Up to that I had lost almost no flies, so I started out with little extra tackle. The middle of the morning found me a mile deep in an alder swamp, bog on one side and piled-up brush on the other. It was what you would call dirty fishing, and in half an hour I had lost every fly and leader I had with me. There was nothing to do but put up my rod and go back. In an effort to strike higher ground I came into what was new country to me. A trail led up toward where I judged the blueberry ledges would be, and climbing for a mile or so I suddenly broke through into a clearing and a wagon road. A grayish house stood beside the road. A thin spiral of smoke curled out of the chimney. On a split stake, even with the road, teetered a sign reading:

HAND MADE TROUT FLIES FOR SALE HERE

I attacked the door without mercy. A moment's knocking brought the sound of stirring from within, and the door finally creaked open, displaying the oddest cut of a little man in a wheelchair. He blinked at me like some great nocturnal bird, and soon there was an intelligent wag of the head—more at my clothes than at me.

"Come in. Doan't gin'rally get lady fishermen. Hearn tell they git 'em down to the harbour lookin' jes' as he-ish as the men." He rolled his chair backward from the door, beckoning me to follow. I could hear him repeating the last of his words under his breath as if by way of confirmation: "Yes, sir, lookin' jes' as he-ish as the men."

He led me into a room that might have been identified even in the uttermost corner of the world as having been conceived and delivered in the State of Maine. An airtight stove centred it, and on its pinnacle stood a nickel-plated moose at bay. There were a half a dozen pulled-in rugs; fruit pulled in; red, yellow and purple roses pulled in; a rooster pulled in; and other things that defied the imagination. The two window sills were gay with geraniums and begonias. Crayon portraits panelled the walls, and between each portrait hung a hair wreath. Fronting the door was a shower of coffin plates, strung together with a fish line. A large coloured print of a clipper hung over the mantel, while all about hung trophies of the South Seas—strings of shells and beads and corals. But the most amazing exhibit was the feathers: peacock, egret, flamingo, pheasant, turkey, and cock tails, yellowhammer and bluejay wings, breasts, crests and whatnot. The work bench was littered with tiny feathers, partridge and guinea fowl, and spools of bright silk. He brushed all these aside and reached underneath to a drawer, bringing out a handful of trout flies. It took no close scrutiny to tell their exquisite workmanship.

"Pick out what ye want. Swamp back yonder jes' eats 'em up, doan't it?" And he smiled an ingratiating, toothless smile.

I made my selections slowly, studying the little man more than the flies. His head was as bald and pink as a baby's. His lips were tremulous, and his eyes showed that pale blue opacity of the very old or very young. It was his hands that held me confounded. They were twisted like bird claws. How they could have ever taken wisps of feather and fine lengths of silk and wound them into the perfect semblance of tiny aerial creatures was more than I could conceive. He caught at my wondering and with a burst of crowing laughter he held the claws closer for inspection. "Handsome, hain't they? Cal'ate I work 'em steady as most folks work a good pair. Can't stand wet nor cold, no better 'n Gram Perkins could in hern. Good days she was the smartest knitter in the county."

So here was another Perkins. I aimed my habitual question at him, expecting no better results. "Tell me, do you know anything about those four dreams?"

He sat a moment, motionless, in what one might have termed a vainglorious silence. He sucked his lips in and out over those vacant gums as if he found them full of flavour; then he suddenly burst into the triumphant crow of a chanticleer. "Yes, ma'am! Cal'ate I do know them dreams—seein' I dreamed 'em. I be Zeb Perkins!" He said it with as sweet an unction as if he had announced himself King of the Hejaz. In a flash the room stood revealed anew. It spoke aloud of Sara Amanda Perkins, beloved wife of Benjamin Perkins, sea captain; of his clipper, of the relics of his voyages, of her handiwork in rugs and wreaths. The very begonias might be slip grandchildren of the ones she had planted. Here, indeed, was a stage set for those dreams. Here sat Zeb Perkins, playwright and stage manager, picking excitedly at his pink head, eternally ready to ring up his curtain. He caught my eye on the wreaths.

"Them little tow-headed fergit-me-nots belonged to her first son as died a baby. She set a terrible store by him. The black in them susans come from her sister Ida, my great-aunt Perkins. See them coffin plates. Ye'll see every one of them was copper, nickled over, every one but Gram's. Hers was solid."

There was a wealth of information conveyed in that last word. I had been standing until now. One of Zeb's claws waved itself away from the coffin plates to a chair: "Set, woan't ye? Ye'll see them rockers under ye are worn as flat as sledge runners. That was Gram's chair; and we wore them rockers off luggin' her 'round. She was all crippled up, Gram was, same as me; only in them days there warn't no wheelchairs."

The chair was all Zeb claimed. There was no more rock to it than to a dray sledge. From the chair his eyes flew to the crayon portraits. "Look at them! Look at Marm—then look at Gram. Why, there was nary a thing Gram couldn't do, for all her crippled-upness. Bake a pie, fry a batch o' doughnuts, clean up the butt'ry. But Marm seems like she was born fretty and tired. Made ye tired jest to watch her travel from the sink to the cook stove. She'd handle a batch o' biscuits like she never expected to live to see 'em baked. Jes' lookin' at 'em, can' ye make out a difference?"

I did and I could. In spite of everything the artist had done to obliterate all human expression he had mastered the single point of difference. One face sagged utterly, the other looked out with sharp alert eyes on a world that interested her immensely. There was a grim humour about the mouth, and a firmness that spoke a challenge even at the end of a century.

"I tell ye," Zeb's eulogy was gathering momentum. "We boys set a terrible store by Gram. She was cuter and smarter tied to that chair than Marm was on two good legs—hands to match 'em. Golly! How sick boys git bein' whined at. Didn't make no odds what we done—good or bad— Marm al'ays whined, but Gram—she stood by like she'd been a boy herself. She'd beg us off hoin' fer circus and fair days and slip us dimes for this or that. Cal'ate she's slipped us enough nickels and dimes to stretch clean to the upper pasture. Pasture! Golly! When we was up thar, hot days, hayin', she'd al'ays mix us a pitcher o' somethin' cool—cream o' tartar water or lemon and m'lasses. When she had it ready she'd take a stick and tick-tack on the wind'y. She could whistle, too; whistle through them crooked fingers o' hern like a yallerhammer. She'd whistle whenever she wanted to be fetched anywhars; then one of us boys would come runnin' and heave her to whersomever she aimed to go—kitchen to butt'ry— butt'ry to settin' room—settin' room to shed."

Zeb stopped here and illustrated. He put two of his crooked fingers to his mouth and shrilled out a thin, wailing note as eery as a banshee's.

"That's the way she done it," he continued. "And Marm would fuss and fret and say she didn't see why the Lord 'lowed a little crippled-up body like Gram's to stay so chuck full o' spunk. Some days she git sort o' vengeful, Marm would, and tell Gram she'd better quiet down decent, or more'n likely she'd never rest quiet in her grave after she died."

III

A hush fell on the room. There was a baleful light shimmering through Zeb's dull eyes, his claws began a nervous intertwining. "Wall . . ." he broke the silence at last. "Gram died. Night afore she died seems like she got scairt. She grabbed us boys one after another and made us all promise we wouldn't bury her twell we were good and sure she was dead. 'Keep me five days—promise me that,' she kept a'sayin'. And we promised. Recollect it didn't seem to me then as how Gram could die—so full of smartness and spunk. Even after old Doc Coombs come and pronounced her, seemed like she'd open her eyes any minute and ask us boys to lug her somewhars. 'Stead o' that she lay so quiet, seemed like I could hear Doomsday strike."

The air about us became suddenly supercharged with something. Was it that ravenous desire for life that must have consumed Gram Perkins? Under their glass domes the hair wreaths seemed to move as if fanned by a breath. The feathers about us swayed. The rooster in the pulled-in rug seemed to pulse with a life and a desire to crow. A crowing shook the room, but it came from Zeb.

"Hot! Golly, Gram died in the sizzlingest spell, middle of August, folks can remember. Didn't embalm in them days, so 'twas ice or nothing. We drew lots for shifts—us boys. Ben and Ellery drew day; Sam and me night. Mebbe we didn't work! Lugged in hunks from the ice house to the shed; thar we cracked and lugged in dish pans to the settin' room. Crack—lug—mop—lug—crack. Five days! It's been a powerful sight o' comfort sence to know we kept Gram's promise. Then come the funeral—smart one. Slathers o' flowers and mourners and hacks. Cal'ate you've seen the lot whar we buried her?"

At the mention of burial a sense of enormity made me shudder. I was beginning to realize that the further Zeb progressed in the matter of the obsequies of Gram Perkins the more alive she became. At that moment she possessed the house—every crack and cranny in it. She possessed Zeb, and she possessed me. I found myself straining my ears for the rattle of dishes in the butt'ry or the sharp thin note of a whistle. Zeb's ear was cocked as well as mine.

"Them dreams," he said, pulling himself together. "First one come fifteen years after Gram died. All was gone from the harbour by that time but me. Ben took the pneumony and died quick. Ellery got liver complaint, turned yaller as arnicy and thinned out to a straw. Sort o' blew away he did. Sam—he got trampled on by a horse. That left jes' me. Night after I buried Marm I come back here and had my first dream. I was young ag'in. Boys back, Marm back, all of us settin' thar at Gram's funeral. Parson was a-prayin'—had been fur a considerable time. I could hear Nate French fumblin' fur his tunin' fork, so's to lead the departin' hymn when plain as daylight I heard a whistle. Yes, ma'am. Then I heard a tick-tack—like Gram was knockin' on some wind'y. Kept hopin' she'd quiet down when out shot another whistle—clear above the parson's prayin'. Nobody but me seemed to notice, so I got up gingerly and tiptoed over to the coffin and raised the lid.

"Thar she was—fixin' fur to tick-tack ag'in. I grabbed her fingers quick and shoved 'em back whar they belonged. Then I leaned over and whispered, loud as I durst, 'Lay still, Gram. Parson's nigh through and we'll be movin' along shortly. Folks 'll be passin' 'round in a moment to view the remains. Fur the Lord's sake, close your eyes and act sensible.' Wall . . . that fixed her. She give me a wink so'd I know she'd act right, and I tiptoed back to my place. They was all still a-prayin'—kept right on a-prayin' twell I woke up. Three years later, come November, I had the second."

Zeb shivered, and so did I. I wanted that second dream and yet I did not want it. Had I chosen I could no more have stayed it than one could have held back the second act of a Greek tragedy.

"We was on our way to the cemetery," Zeb's voice lifted me free of all choice in the matter. "I was ridin' outside the first hack, bein' the youngest, and I was thinkin' what a fine day it was fur that time o' year. Sort o' funny, too, fur Gram died in August and here it was November and we was jes' gittin' to bury her. I was lookin' at the hearse when it happened. Hearses was different in them days, black urns at the four top corners with black plumes stickin' out and a pair o' solid wooden doors behind. Above the poundin' of the horses' hoofs I heard a hammerin' on them solid doors. Bang . . . bang . . . plain as daylight. Old Jared Sims was drivin' and I didn't want he should hear so I sung out, 'Cal'ate they're shinglin' the Coomb's barn.' He turned 'round in his seat to look, and jes' that minute thar come a regular whale of a hammerin' and the doors of the hearse bust open. Thar was Gram—top of her own coffin, peekin' down low at me and beckonin' fur me to come and git her.

"Mad! I was as mad as a hornet. I went back to that wink she'd given me in t'other dream and seemed like she'd gone back on her word— something Gram had never done livin'. I was off the seat of that hack in a jiffy, runnin' aside the hearse. When the goin' slowed up I stuck my head inside and hollered, 'Ye git straight back whar ye b'long! And what's more ye stay thar!' Then I begun to whimper like I couldn't stand my feelin's another minute. 'Gram,' says I, 'hain't ye got any heart? Do ye want to disgrace us boys? How'll ye cal'ate we'll feel to have the neighbours thinkin' we're tryin' to bury ye ag'in your will? We give ye them five days like we promised—can't ye lay down decent and proper now?'

"That settled her. She turned, meek as a cow, climbed back into her coffin and closed the lid down. I went back to the hack and climbed up. We was still a'goin' when I woke up."

IV

An interlude followed. I tried to bring back my mind to the reality of life as I knew it to be. I fingered my trout flies and did my best to image the still, deep pool below the swamp where I had been on the point of casting just as my last leader broke. Half an hour more I could be back there, casting again. But the pool and the trout faded into oblivion beside the sterner reality of Gram Perkins. I was on the hack with young Zeb, my eyes fastened in growing perturbation on a pair of solid black doors.

"Jes' started on our January thaw when the next dream took me," broke in Zeb. "We'd reached the cemetery. Grave dug, coffin lowered, folks standin' 'round fur a final prayer. To all appearances everything was goin' first rate. But the sexton hadn't more than picked up his shovel, easy-like, when out comes a whistle, clear as a fog horn. I opened my eyes quick and looked down. Thar was Gram, poppin' out like a jack-in-the-box, lid swung wide open and both hands reachin' fur the dirt the sexton was shovellin' in. Yes, ma'am! Ye never saw dirt fly in all your born days the way Gram made it fly. At the rate she was goin', I knew we'd be standin' thar twell Doomsday, gittin' her buried.

"Everybody else was prayin' hard along with the parson, and he was 'most to the Resurrection. I knew somethin' had to be done quick, so in I jumped. I slapped the dirt out of her hands hard like you would with a child and says I, 'Land 'o goodness, Gram, what ails ye? We've fetched ye along to what the Bible calls your last restin' place. All we boys is askin' of ye now is to keep quiet and rest twell Jedgment Day.'

"The words warn't more'n out afore I knew I'd said the wrong thing. She didn't lay any more store 'bout this eternal restin' than what ye would, settin' thar fingerin' them flies. She give me the most pitiful look ye ever saw on a human face. It said, plain as daylight, 'Zeb, lug me back home and let me git to work ag'in.'

"Wall. . . I took to whimperin' like a two-year-old. 'Ef ye woan't do it fur the Bible,' says I, 'do it fur us boys. Ye've al'ays been terrible proud of us— al'ays wanted we should have jes' what we wanted, and thar's nothin' in the whole o' creation we want so much this minute as to see ye restin' peaceful. Git back in. Close your eyes, fold your hands, git that listen fur the last trumpet look on your face. Hurry, woan't ye? The sexton's shovellin' like sixty.'

"She give me another of them pitiful looks—nigh broke me all up—and she sort o' slid back and slammed the lid down on her fur all the world like one of those cuckoo clocks. I lit out and landed side o' the parson jes' as he said, 'Amen.'... 'Amen,' says I, thankful-like. 'Amen,' says the sexton.... 'Amen,' says the mourners in a roarin' chorus like the sea. And then I swear to ye that way under the dirt I heard Gram sing out Amen! Tell ye I woke in a sweat!"

"Cold sweat?" I asked. It was all I could think of.

"Cold as a clam, dripped with it."

"That makes three."

"Three!" Zeb tolled it out like a passing bell. "All bad enough—the fourth, worst of all. Ye wait."

I waited.

"Three years I lived comfortable in my mind. Seemed like that last Amen had settled things. Then May come along. I'd been slippin' some of them geraniums to take up to the cemetery Memorial Day. I could still walk some—slowly, but git about—and I went to bed mighty real happy at the idea o' fixin' up Gram's grave. Right on top o' that came the fourth dream!

"I was swingin' up the road toward the cemetery, and in one hand I carried a pot with the slips in, and t'other held my stick I walked with. Jes' about reached the lot when up comes a jedge from Boston—nice feller— and I asked him to come along and see the view from our place. 'Most famous in the State,' says I. 'Clear days we can see 'most anything.'

"I fetched him through the iron gates and stood him up close to the monument and begun pointin' places out. 'Thar's Mount Washington,' says I. 'Some days ye can see the whole Presidential Range.... Thar's Katahdin...thar's...' But I stopped thar dead. I'd caught something move in the grass by Gram's headstone. The next minute out come a whistle, loudest I ever heard. I swung the jedge clear 'round and pointed out to sea. 'Thar's Mount Desert,' says I, and 'thar's Isle au Haut. That's the Rockland boat ye hear whistlin'—consarn it!"

"I looked at Gram. She'd got her head and shoulders clear and she was whistlin' ag'in fur dear life. Then she took her fingers out of her mouth and nodded her head toward out back. Seemed like she was askin' me fur the last time to take her home. The jedge seemed lost in the scenery, and I stepped up to Gram and showed her the geranium slips. 'Look at them,' says I. 'Fetched 'em all the way over to decorate your grave, and here ye be, bustin' loose and cuttin' up. Hain't ye ever goin' to give in and rest in peace?'

"Wall, she never said a word, jes' kept working herself further and further out. I was terrible scairt the jedge would turn round any second and ketch her. Stood thar on pins and needles watchin' Gram rise from her grave. 'Have a heart, Gram,' I begun coaxin' ag'in. 'How'd ye like a city feller like that jedge to ketch a Perkins turnin' ghost like?' . . . Never finished what I set out to say. She looked so queer and upset—so like she wanted to tell me something and didn't know how. I stood thar, geraniums in one hand, stick in t'other, tryin' to make out what it was Gram wanted to tell me. Then it come over me, all of a flash. 'Twasn't she that wanted to git out; 'twas that smart, spunky body o' hern. It was drivin' the sperrit same as a strong wind drives a cloud afore it. She was ready to rest if that doggoned crippled-up, pie-bakin', doughnut-fryin' body would have let her be. But it wouldn't. It was draggin' her out of her coffin, out of her grave, turnin' her loose about the county like no decent sperrit could stand.

"'I'll fix it,' says I, droppin' the geraniums and grabbin' the stick with both hands, 'I'll fix it so it'll let ye rest quiet twell Doomsday,' and with that I laid on Gram with that stick. I beat her up twell thar warn't nothin' left but a scatterin' of dust on the spring sod. Yes, ma'am! I reduced Gram to dust and ashes like the Bible said had to be."

A long sigh swept the stillness of the room. The face of Zeb Perkins underwent a sequence of changes. Triumph had been there, but it dwindled out and sorrow took its place; and then a fear, a tremulous commiseration and, finally, bewilderment. He now looked straight at me. His eyes were dull, fearful. "They doan't understand, them Perkins to the harbour. They doan't think I ever ought to have done that to Gram."

I gathered up my flies and was halfway to the door before Zeb spoke again. His voice had now grown querulous: "Wall—what do ye think?"

I gave my answer as I slipped out of doors, into the wide spaces again. "I think the trout are going to bite," said I.

Harriet Prescott Spofford

CIRCUMSTANCE

SHE HAD REMAINED, all that day, with a sick neighbor—those eastern wilds of Maine in that epoch making neighbors and miles synonymous—and so busy had she been that she did not at first observe the approaching night. But finally the level rays threw their gleam upon the wall, and, hastily donning cloak and hood, she bade her friend farewell and sallied forth. Home lay some three miles distant, across a copse, a meadow, and a piece of woods—the woods being a fringe of the great forests that stretch far away into the North. Home was one of a dozen log-houses lying a few furlongs apart, with half-cleared demesnes separating them at the rear from wilderness untrodden save by stealthy native or deadly panther tribes.

She was in a nowise exalted frame of spirit—on the contrary, rather depressed by the pain she had witnessed and the fatigue she had endured; but in certain temperaments such a condition throws open the mental pores and renders one receptive of every influence. Through the little copse she walked slowly, with her cloak folded about her; the sunset filtered purple through the mist of woven spray and twig. Just on the edge of the evening she emerged and began to cross the meadowland. At one hand lay the forest to which her path wound; at the other the evening star hung over a tide of failing orange that slowly slipped down the earth's broad side. Walking rapidly now, and with her eyes wide-open, she distinctly saw in the air before her a winding sheet—cold, white, and ghastly, waved by the likeness of four wan hands, while a voice, spectral and melancholy, sighed, "The Lord have mercy on the people! The Lord have mercy on the people!" Three times the sheet with its corpse-covering outline waved beneath the pale hands, and the voice, awful in its solemn and mysterious depth, sighed, "The Lord have mercy on the people!" Then all was gone, the place was clear again; she looked about her, shook her shoulders decidedly, and, pulling on her hood, went forward once more.

She might have been frightened by such an apparition if she had led a life of less reality than frontier settlers are apt to lead; but dealing with hard fact does not engender a flimsy habit of mind. She did not even believe herself subject to an hallucination, but smiled simply, a little vexed that her thought could have framed such a glamour from the day's occurrences, and not sorry to lift the bough of the warder of the woods and enter the path. If she had been imaginative, she would have hesitated; but I suppose that the thought of a little child at home would conquer that propensity in the most habituated. So, biting a bit of spicy birch, she went along. Suddenly, a swift shadow, like the fabulous flying-dragon, writhed through the air before her, and she felt herself instantly seized and borne aloft. It was that wild beast—the most savage and subtle and fearless of our latitudes—known as the Indian Devil, and he held her in his clutches on the broad floor of a swinging fir-bough. His long sharp claws were caught in her clothing, he worried them a little, then, finding that ineffectual to free them, he commenced licking her bare arm with his rasping tongue and pouring over her wide streams of hot, fetid breath. So quick had this flashing action been that the woman had had no time for alarm, moreover, she was not of the screaming kind; but now, as she felt him endeavoring to disentangle his claws, and the horrid sense of her fate smote her, and she saw instinctively the fierce plunge of those weapons, the long strips of living flesh torn from her bones, the agony, while by her side and holding her in his great lithe embrace the monster crouched, his white tusks whetting and gnashing, his eyes glaring through the darkness like balls of fire—a shriek that startled every winter-housed thing tore through her lips. The beast left the arm, once white, now crimson, and looked up alertly.

She did not think at this instant to call upon God. She called upon her husband. It seemed to her that she had but one friend in the world—that was he; and again the cry echoed through the woods. It was not the shriek that disturbed the creature; he was not born in the woods to be scared of an owl. It must have been the echo, most musical, most resonant, repeated and yet repeated, dying with long sighs of sweet sound, vibrated from rock to river and back again. Her thought flew after it; she knew that, even if her husband heard, he could not reach her in time; she saw that while the beast listened he would not gnaw—and this she *felt* directly, when the rough, sharp, and multiplied stings of his tongue retouched her arm. Again her lips opened by instinct, but the sound that issued came by reason. She had heard that music charmed wild beasts— this point between life and death intensified every faculty—and when she opened her lips the third time it was not for shrieking, but for singing.

A little thread of melody stole out; it was the cradlesong with which she rocked her baby. Then she remembered the baby sleeping on the long settee before the fire; the father cleaning his gun, with one foot on the green wooden rundle; the merry light from the chimney dancing out through the room and lingering on the baby, with his fringed gentian eyes, his chubby fists, and his fine hair. All this struck her, and made a sob of her breath, and she ceased.

Immediately the long red tongue was thrust forth again. A song sprang to her lips, a wild sea-song, such as some sailor might be singing far out on blue water that night—a song with the wind in its burden and the spray in its chorus. The monster raised his head, then fretted the imprisoned claws a moment and was quiet; only the breath like the vapor from some hell-pit still swathed her. Her voice, at first faint and fearful, gradually lost its quaver, grew under her control; it rose on long swells, it fell in subtle cadences, now and then pealed out like bells from distant belfries on fresh sonorous mornings. She sung the song through, and, wondering if he would detect her, she repeated it. Once or twice the beast stirred uneasily, turned, and made the bough sway at his movement. As she ended, he snapped his jaws together, and tore away the fettered member, curling it under him with a snarl—when she burst into the gayest reel that ever answered a fiddle bow. How many a time she had heard her husband play it on the homely fiddle; how many a time she had seen it danced on the floor of their one room; how many a time she had danced it herself? Did she not remember once, as they joined clasps for right-hands-round, how it had lent its gay, bright measure to her life? And here she was singing it alone, in the forest, at midnight, to a wild beast! As she sent her voice trilling up and down, the creature who grasped her uncurled his paw and scratched the bark from the bough; she must vary the spell, and her voice spun leaping along the projecting points of a hornpipe. She felt herself twisted about with a low growl and a lifting of the red lip from the glittering teeth; she broke the hornpipe's thread, and commenced unraveling a lighter, livelier thing, an Irish jig. Up and down and round about her flew, the beast threw back his head so that the diabolical face fronted hers, and the torrent of his breath prepared her for his feast as the anaconda slimes his prey. Frantically she darted from tune to tune; his restless movements followed her. She tired herself with dancing and vivid national airs, growing feverish and singing spasmodically as she felt her horrid tomb yawning wider. The beast moved again, but only to lay the disengaged paw across her with heavy satisfaction. She did not dare to pause; through the clear, cold air, the frosty starlight, she sang. If there were yet any tremor in the tone, it was not fear—she had learned the secret of sound at last; nor could it be chill—far too high a fervor throbbed her pulses; it was nothing but the thought of the log house and of what might be passing within it. She fancied the baby stirring in his sleep and moving his pretty lips—her husband rising and opening the door, looking out after her, and wondering at her absence. She fancied the light pouring through the chink and then shut in again with all the safety and comfort and joy, her husband taking down the fiddle and playing lightly with his head inclined, playing while she sang, while she sang for her life to an Indian Devil.

Suddenly she woke with the daggered tooth penetrating her flesh—dreaming of safety, had ceased singing and lost it. The beast had regained the use of all his limbs, and now, standing and raising his back, bristling and foaming, with sounds that would have been like hisses but for their deep and fearful sonority, he withdrew step by step toward the trunk of the tree. She was free, on one end of the bough, twenty feet from the ground. She did not measure the distance, but rose to drop herself down, careless of any death, so that it were not this. Instantly, as if he scanned her thoughts, the creature bounded forward with a yell and caught her again in his dreadful hold. It might be that he was not greatly famished; for, as she suddenly flung up her voice again, he settled himself composedly on the bough, still clasping her to his rough, ravenous breast, and listening in a fascination to the sad, strange U-la-lu that now moaned forth in loud, hollow tones above him. He half closed his eyes, and sleepily reopened and shut them again.

What rending pains were close at hand! Death! And what a death! Worse than any other is that to be named! Water, be it cold or warm, kisses as it kills, and draws you down gently through darkening fathoms to its heart. Death at the sword is the festival of trumpet and bugle and banner, with glory ringing out around you. No gnawing disease can bring such hideous end as this; for that is a fiend bred of your own flesh. What dread comes with the thought of perishing in flames! But fire, as it devours, arouses neither hatred nor disgust; does not drop our blood into our faces from foaming mouth nor snarl above us with vitality. Let us be ended by wild beasts, and the base, cursed thing howls with us forever through the forest. All this she felt as she calmed him, and what force it lent to her song God knows. If her voice should fail! If the damp and cold should give her any fatal hoarseness! If all the silent powers of the forest did not conspire to help her! The dark, hollow night rose indifferently over her; the wide cold air breathed rudely past her, lifted her wet hair and blew it down again; the great boughs swung with a ponderous strength, now and then clashed their iron lengths together and shook off a sparkle of icy spears or some long-lain weight of snow from their heavy shadows. The green depths were utterly cold and silent and stern. These beautiful haunts that all the summer were hers and rejoiced to share with her their bounty, all these friends of three moons ago forgot her now and knew her no longer.

Feeling her desolation, wild, melancholy, forsaken songs rose thereon from that frightful aerie—weeping, wailing tunes, that overflow with unexpressed sadness, and that rise and fall like the wind and tide—sailor songs, to be heard only in lone mid-watches beneath the moon and stars.

Still the beast lay with closed eyes, yet never relaxing his grasp. Once a half-whine of enjoyment escaped him—he fawned his fearful head upon her; once he scored her cheek with his tongue: savage caresses that hurt like wounds. How weary she was! and yet how terribly awake! How fuller and fuller of dismay grew the knowledge that she was only prolonging her anguish and playing with death! How appalling the thought that with her voice ceased her existence! Yet she could not sing forever; her throat was dry and hard, her very breath was a pain, her mouth was hotter than any desert-worn pilgrim's—if she could but drop upon her burning tongue one atom of the ice that glittered about her!—but both of her arms were pinioned in the giant's vise. She remembered the winding-sheet, and for the first time in her life shivered with spiritual fear. Was it hers? She asked herself, as she sang, what sins she had committed, what life she had led, to find her punishment so soon and in these pangs, and then she sought eagerly for some reason why her husband was not up and abroad to find her. He failed her—her one sole hope in life—and without being aware of it her voice forsook the songs of suffering and sorrow for old Covenanting hymns—hymns with which her mother had lulled her—grand and sweet Methodist hymns, brimming with melody and fantastic involutions of tune to suit that ecstatic worship, hymns full of the beauty of holiness, sanctified by the salvation had lent to those in worse extremity than hers, for they had found themselves in the grasp of hell, while she was but in the jaws of death. Out of this strange music, peculiar to one character of faith, her voice soared into the glorified chants of churches. What to her was death by cold or famine or wild beasts? "Though He slay me, yet will I trust in Him," she sang. High and clear through the night, the moonbeams splintering in the wood, those sacred anthems rose as a hope from despair. Was she not in God's hands? Did not the world swing at His will? If this were in His great plan of Providence, was it not best, and should she not accept it?

"He is the Lord our God; His judgments are in all the earth."

Never ceasing in the rhythm of her thoughts, articulated in music as they thronged, the memory of her first communion flashed over her. Again she was in that distant place on that sweet spring morning. Again the congregation rustled out, and the few remained, and she trembled to find herself among them. How well she remembered the devout, quiet faces, the snowy linen at the altar, the silver vessels slowly and silently shifting as the cup approached. She had seemed, looking up through the windows where the sky soared blue in constant freshness, to feel all heaven's balms dripping from the portals, and to scent the lilies of eternal peace! "And does it need the walls of a church to renew my communion?" she asked. "Does not every moment stand a temple four-square to God?

And in that morning, with its buoyant sunlight, was I any dearer to the Heart of the World than now?" "My beloved is mine, and I am his," she sang over and over again, with all varied inflection and profuse tune. How gently all the winter-wrapt things bent toward her then! Into what relation with her had they grown! How this common dependence was the spell of their intimacy! How at one with Nature had she become! How all the night and the silence and the forest seemed to hold its breath, and to send its soul up to God in her singing! It was no longer despondency, that singing. It was neither prayer nor petition. She had left imploring "How long wilt Thou forget me, O Lord?" She cried rather, "Yea, though I walk through the valley of the shadow of death, I will fear no evil, for Thou art with me; Thy rod and Thy staff, they comfort me"; and lingered, and repeated, and sang again, "I shall be satisfied when I awake, with Thy likeness."

She had no comfort or consolation such as sustained the Christian martyrs in the amphitheatre. She was not dying for her faith, there were no palms in heaven for her to wave—but how many a time had she declared, "I had rather be a doorkeeper in the house of my God, than to dwell in the tents of wickedness!" As the broad rays here and there broke through the dense covert of shade and lay in rivers of lustre on crystal sheathing and frozen fretting of trunk and limb, she sang "And there shall be no night there, for the Lord God giveth them light."

How the night was passing! And still the beast crouched upon the bough, changing only the posture of his head that again he might command her with those charmed eyes. Half their fire was gone—she could almost have released herself from his custody—yet, had she stirred, no one knows what malevolent instinct might have dominated anew. But of that she did not dream; long ago stripped of any expectation, she was experiencing in her divine rapture how mystically true it is that "he that dwelleth in the secret place of the Most High shall abide under the shadow of the Almighty."

Slow clarion cries now wound from the distance as the cocks caught the intelligence of the day and reechoed it faintly from farm to farm. Still she chanted on. A remote crash of brushwood told of some other beast, or some night-belated traveller groping his way through the narrow path. Still she chanted on. The far, faint echoes of the chanticleers died into distance, the crashing of the branches grew nearer. No wild beast that, but a man's step, a man's form in the moonlight, stalwart and strong, on one arm slept a little child, in the other hand he held his gun. Still she chanted on.

Perhaps, when her husband last looked forth, he was half ashamed to find what a fear he felt for her. He knew she would never leave the child so long but for some direct need—and yet he may have laughed at

himself, as he lifted and wrapped it with awkward care, and, loading his gun and strapping on his horn, opened the door again and closed it behind him, plunging into the darkness and dangers of the forest. He was more alarmed than he would have been willing to acknowledge; as he sat with his bow hovering over the strings, he half believed to hear her voice mingling gayly with the instrument, till he paused and listened if she were not about to lift the latch and enter. As he drew nearer the heart of the forest, that intimation of melody seemed to grow more actual, to take body and breath, to come and go on long swells and ebbs of the night-breeze, to increase with tune and words, till a strange, shrill singing grew ever clearer, and, as he stepped into an open space of moonbeams, far up in the branches, rocked by the wind, and singing, he saw his wife—his wife—but great God in heaven! how? Some mad exclamation escaped him, but without diverting her. The child knew the singing voice, though never heard before in that unearthly key, and tuned toward it through the veiling dreams. With a celerity almost instantaneous, it lay, in the twinkling of an eye, on the ground at the father's feet, while his gun was raised to his shoulder and levelled at the monster covering his wife with shaggy form and flaming gaze—his wife so ghastly white, so rigid, so stained with blood, her eyes so fixedly bent above, and her lips, the chiselled pallor of marble, parted only with that flood of song.

I do not know if it were the mother-instinct that for a moment lowered her eyes—those eyes, so lately riveted on heaven, now suddenly seeing all lifelong bliss possible. A thrill of joy pierced and shivered through her like a weapon, her voice trembled in its course, her glance lost its steady strength, fever-flushes chased each other over her face, yet she never once ceased chanting. She was quite aware that if her husband shot now the ball must pierce her body before reaching any vital part of the beast—and yet better death, by his hand, than the other. But her husband remained motionless, just covering the creature with the sight. He dared not fire lest some wound not mortal should break the spell exercised by her voice, and the beast, enraged with pain, should rend her in atoms; moreover, the light was too uncertain for his aim. So he waited. Now and then he examined his gun to see if the damp were injuring its charge, now and then he wiped the great drops from his forehead. Again the cocks crowed with the passing hour—the last time they were heard on that night. Cheerful home sound then, how full of safety and all comfort and rest it seemed. What sweet morning incidents of sparkling fire and sunshine, of gay household bustle and cooing baby, of steaming cattle in the yard, and brimming milk-pails at the door! What pleasant voices, what laughter, what security! And here . . .

Now as she sang on in the slow, endless, infinite moments, the fervent vision of God's peace was gone. Just as the grave had lost its sting, she was snatched back again into the arms of earthly hope. Her eyes trembled on her husband's, and she could think only of him, and of the child, and of happiness that yet might be. But what a dreadful gulf of doubt between! She shuddered now in the suspense; all calm forsook her; her face contracted, growing small and pinched; her voice was hoarse and sharp—every tone cut like a knife—the notes became heavy to lift—impossible. One gasp, a convulsive effort, and there was silence—she had lost her voice.

The beast made a sluggish movement—stretched and fawned like one awakening—then, as if he would have yet more of the enchantment, stirred her slightly with his muzzle. As he did so a sidelong hint of the man standing below with the raised gun smote him; he sprung round furiously, and, seizing his prey, was about to leap into some unknown airy den of the topmost branches now waving to the slow dawn. The woman, suspended in mid-air an instant, cast only one agonized glance beneath, but across and through it, ere the lids could fall, shot a withering sheet of flame—a rifle-crack was lost in the terrible yell of desperation that bounded after it, and in the wide arc of some eternal descent she was falling—but the beast fell under her.

I think that the moment following must have been too sacred for us, and perhaps the three have no special interest again till they issue from the shadows of the wilderness upon the white hills that skirt their home.

The father carries the child hushed into slumber, the mother follows with no such feeble step as might be anticipated; and as they slowly climb the steep under the clear gray sky and the paling morning star, she stops to gather a spray of the red-rose berries or a feathery tuft of dead grasses for the chimney piece of the log-house—and of these quiet, happy folk you would scarcely dream how lately they had stolen from under the banner and encampment of the great King Death. The husband proceeds a step or two in advance; the wife lingers over a footprint in the snow, stoops and examines it, then looks up with a hurried word. Her husband stands alone on the hill, his arms folded across the babe, his gun fallen— stands defined against the pallid sky like a bronze. What is there in their home, lying below, to fix him with such a stare? She springs to his side. There is no home. The log-house, the barns, the neighboring farms, the fences, are all blotted out and mingled in one smoking ruin. Desolation and death were indeed there, and beneficence and life in the forest. Toma-hawk and scalping-knife, descending during that night, had left behind them only this and one subtle footprint in the snow.

For the rest—the world was all before them where to choose.

Edward Page Mitchell

THE LAST CRUISE OF THE JUDAS ISCARIOT

"SHE FORMERLY SHOWED the name *Flying Sprite* on her starn moldin'," said Captain Trumbull Cram, "but I had thet gouged out and planed off, and *Judas Iscariot* in gilt sot thar instid."

"That was an extraordinary name," said I.

"'Strornary craft," replied the captain, as he absorbed another inch and a half of niggerhead. "I'm neither a profane man or an irreverend; but sink my jig if I don't believe the sperrit of Judas possessed thet schooner. Hey, Ammi?"

The young man addressed as Ammi was seated upon a mackerel barrel. He deliberately removed from his lips a black brierwood and shook his head with great gravity.

"The cap'n," said Ammi, "is neither a profane or an irreverend. What he says he mostly knows; but when he sinks his jig, he's allers to be depended on."

Fortified with this neighborly estimate of character, Captain Cram proceeded. "You larf at the idea of a schooner's soul? Perhaps you hev sailed 'em forty-odd year up and down this here coast, an' 'quainted yourself with their dispositions an' habits of mind. Hey, Ammi?"

"The cap'n," explained the gentleman on the mackerel keg, "hez coasted an' hez fished for forty-six year. He's lumbered and he's iced. When the cap'n sees fit for to talk about schooners he understands the subjeck."

"My friend," said the captain, "a schooner has a soul like a human being, but considerably broader of beam, whether for good or for evil. I ain't a goin' to deny thet I prayed for the *Judas* in Tuesday 'n' Thursday evenin' meetin', week arter week an' month arter month. I ain't a goin' to deny thet I interested Deacon Plympton in the 'rastle for her redemption. It was no use, my friend; even the deacon's powerful p'titions were clear waste."

I ventured to inquire in what manner this vessel had manifested its depravity. The narrative which I heard was the story of a demon of treachery with three masts and a jib boom.

The *Flying Sprite* was the first three-master ever built at Newaggen, and the last. People shook their heads over the experiment. "No good can come of sech a critter," they said. "It's contrairy to natur. Two masts is masts enough." The *Flying Sprite* began its career of base improbity at the very moment of its birth. Instead of launching decently into the element for which it was designed, the three-masted schooner slumped through the ways into the mud and stuck there for three weeks, causing great expense to the owners, of whom Captain Trumbull Cram was one to the extent of an undivided third. The oracles of Newaggen were confirmed in their forebodings. "Two masts is masts enough to sail the sea," they said; "the third is the Devil's hitchin' post."

On the first voyage of the *Flying Sprite,* Captain Cram started her for Philadelphia, loaded with ice belonging to himself and Lawyer Swanton; cargo uninsured. Ice was worth six dollars a ton in Philadelphia; this particular ice had cost Captain Cram and Lawyer Swanton eighty-five cents a ton shipped, including sawdust. They were happy over the prospect. The *Fying Sprite* cleared the port in beautiful shape, and then suddenly and silently went to the bottom in Fiddler's Reach, in eleven feet of salt water. It required only six days to float her and pump her out, but owing to a certain incompatibility between the ice and salt water, the salvage consisted exclusively of sawdust.

On her next trip the schooner carried a deckload of lumber from the St. Croix River. It was in some sense a consecrated cargo, for the lumber was intended for a new Baptist meetinghouse in southern New Jersey. If the prayerful hopes of the navigators, combined with the prayerful expectations of the consignees had availed, this voyage, at least, would have been successfully made. But about sixty miles southeast of Nantucket the *Flying Sprite* encountered a mild September gale. She ought to have weathered it with perfect ease, but she behaved so abominably that the church timber was scattered over the surface of the Atlantic Ocean from about latitude 40^0 15' to about latitude 43^0 50'. A month or two later she contrived to go on her beam ends under a gentle land breeze, dumping a lot of expensively carved granite from the Fox Island quarries into a deep hole in Long Island Sound. On the very next trip she turned deliberately out of her course in order to smash into the starboard bow of a Norwegian brig, and was consequently libeled for heavy damages.

It was after a few experiences of this sort that Captain Cram erased the old name from the schooner's stern and from her quarter, and substituted that of *Judas Iscariot.* He could discover no designation that expressed so well his contemptuous opinion of her moral qualities. She seemed animate with the spirit of purposeless malice, of malignant perfidy. She was a floating tub of cussedness.

A board of nautical experts sat upon the *Judas Iscariot,* but could find nothing the matter with her, physically. The lines of her hull were all right, she was properly planked and ceiled and calked, her spars were of good Oregon pine, she was rigged taut and trustworthy, and her canvas had been cut and stitched by a God-fearing sailmaker. According to all theory, she ought to have been perfectly responsible as to her keel. In practice, she was frightfully cranky. Sailing the *Judas Iscariot* was like driving a horse with more vices than hairs in his tail. She always did the unexpected thing, except when bad behavior was expected of her on general principles. If the idea was to luff, she would invariably fall off; if to jibe, she would come round dead in the wind and hang there like Mohammed's coffin. Sending a man to haul the jib sheet to windward was sending a man on a forlorn hope; the jib habitually picked up the venturesome navigator, and, after shaking him viciously in the air for a second or two, tossed him overboard. A boom never crossed the deck without breaking somebody's head. Start on whatever course she might, the schooner was certain to run before long into one of three things, namely, some other vessel, a fog bank, or the bottom. From the day on which she was launched her scent for a good, sticky mud bottom was unerring. In the clearest weather fog followed and enveloped her as misfortune follows wickedness. Her presence on the Banks was enough to drive every codfish to the coast of Ireland. The mackerel and porgies were always where the *Judas Iscariot* was not. It was impossible to circumvent the schooner's fixed purposes to ruin everybody who chartered her. If chartered to carry a deckload, she spilled it; if loaded between decks, she dived and spoiled the cargo. She was like one of the trick mules which, if they cannot otherwise dislodge the rider, get down and roll over and over. In short, the *Judas Iscariot* was known from Marblehead to the Bay of Chaleur as the consummate schooneration of malevolence, turpitude, and treachery.

After commanding the *Judas Iscariot* for five or six years, Captain Cram looked fully twenty years older. It was in vain that he had attempted to sell her at a sacrifice. No man on the coast of Maine, Massachusetts, or the British provinces would have taken the schooner as a gift. The belief in her demoniac obsession was as firm as it was universal.

Nearly at the end of a season, when the wretched craft had been even more unprofitable than usual a conference of the owners was held in the Congregational vestry one evening after the monthly missionary meeting. No outsider knows exactly what happened, but it is rumored that in the two hours during which these capitalists were closeted certain arithmetical computations were effected which led to significant results and to a singular decision.

On the forenoon of the next Friday there was a general suspension of business at Newaggen. The *Judas Iscariot*, with her deck scoured and her spars scraped till they shone in the sun like yellow amber, lay at the wharf by Captain Cram's fish house. Since Monday the captain and his three boys and Andrew Jackson's son Tobias from Mackerel Cove had been busy loading the schooner deep. This time her cargo was an extraordinary one. It consisted of nearly a quarter of a mile of stone wall from the boundaries of the captain's shore pasture. "I calklet," remarked the commander of the *Judas Iscariot,* as he saw the last boulder disappearing down the main hatch, "thar's nigh two hundud'n fifty ton of stone fence aboard thet schoon'r."

Conjecture was wasted over this unnecessary amount of ballast. The owners of the *Judas Iscariot* stood up well under the consolidated wit of the village; they returned witticism for witticism, and kept their secret. "Ef you must know, I'll tell ye," said the captain. "I hear thar's a stone-wall famine over Machias way. I'm goin' to take mine over'n peddle it out by the yard." On this fine sunshiny Friday morning, while the luckless schooner lay on one side of the wharf, looking as bright and trim and prosperous as if she were the best-paying maritime investment in the world, the tug *Pug* of Portland lay under the other side, with steam up. She had come down the night before in response to a telegram from the owners of the *Judas Iscariot.* A good land breeze was blowing, with the promise of freshening as the day grew older.

At half past seven o'clock the schooner put off from the landing, carrying not only the captain's pasture wall, but also a large number of his neighbors and friends, including some of the solidest citizens of

Newaggen. Curiosity was stronger than fear. "You know what the critter," the captain had said, in reply to numerous applications for passage. "Ef you're a mind to resk her antics, come along, an' welcome." Captain Cram put on a white shirt and a holiday suit for the occasion. As he stood at the wheel shouting directions to his boys and Andrew Jackson's son Tobias at the halyards, his guests gathered around him—a fair representation of the respectability, the business enterprise, and the piety of Newaggen Harbor. Never had the *Judas Iscariot* carried such a load. She seemed suddenly struck with a sense of decency and responsibility, for she came around into the wind without balking, dived her nose playfully into the brine, and skipped off on the short hitch to clear Tumbler Island, all in the properest fashion. The *Pug* steamed after her.

The crowd on the wharf and the boys in the small boats cheered this unexpectedly orthodox behavior, and they now saw for the first time that Captain Cram had painted on the side of the vessel in conspicuous white letters, each three or four feet long, the following legend:

THIS IS THE SCHOONER *JUDAS ISCARIOT*
N.B.—GIVE HER A WIDE BERTH!!

Hour after hour the schooner bounded along before the northwest wind, holding to her course as straight as an arrow. The weather continued fine. Every time the captain threw the log he looked more perplexed. Eight, nine, nine and a half knots! He shook his head as he whispered to Deacon Plympton: "She's meditatin' mischief o' some natur or other." But the *Judas* led the *Pug* a wonderful chase, and by half past two in the afternoon, before the demijohn which Andrew Jackson's son Tobias had smuggled on board was three quarters empty, and before Lawyer Swanton had more than three quarters finished his celebrated story about Governor Purington's cork leg, the schooner and the tug were between fifty and sixty miles from land.

Suddenly Captain Cram gave a grunt of intelligence. He pointed ahead, where a blue line just above the horizon marked a distant fog bank. "She smelt it an' she run for it," he remarked, sententiously. "Time for business."

Then ensued a singular ceremony. First Captain Cram brought the schooner to, and transferred all his passengers to the tug. The wind had shifted to the southeast, and the fog was rapidly approaching. The sails of the *Judas Iscariot* flapped as she lay head to the wind; her bows rose and fell gently under the influence of the long swell. The *Pug* bobbed up and down half a hawser's length away.

Having put his guests and crew aboard the tug, Captain Cram proceeded to make everything shipshape on the decks of the schooner.

He even picked up and threw overboard the stopper of Andrew Jackson's son Tobias' demijohn. His face wore an expression of unusual solemnity. The people on the tug watched his movements eagerly, but silently. Next he tied one end of a short rope to the wheel and attached the other end loosely by means of a running bowline to a cleat upon the rail. Then he was seen to take up an ax, and to disappear down the companionway. Those on the tug distinctly heard several crashing blows. In a moment the captain reappeared on deck, walked deliberately to the wheel, brought the schooner around so that her sails filled, pulled the running bowline taut, and fastened the rope with several half hitches around the cleat, thus lashing the helm, jumped into a dory, and sculled over to the tug.

Left entirely to herself, the schooner rolled once or twice, tossed a few bucketfuls of water over her dancing bows, and started off toward the South Atlantic. But Captain Trumbull Cram, standing in the bow of the tugboat, raised his hand to command silence and pronounced the following farewell speech, being sentence, death warrant, and funeral oration, all in one:

"I ain't advancin' no theory to 'count for her cussedness. You all know the *Judas*. Mebbe thar was too much fore an' aff to her. Mebbe the inickerty of a vessel's in the fore an' aff, and the vartue in the squar' riggin'. Mebbe two masts *was* masts enough. Let that go; bygones is bygones. Yonder she goes, carryin' all sail on top, two hundred'n-odd ton o' stone fence in her holt, an' a hole good two foot acrost stove in her belly. The way of the transgressor is hard. Don't you see her settlin'? It should be a lesson, my friends, for us to profit by; there's an end to the long-sufferin'est mercy, and unless—Oh, yer makin' straight for the fog, are ye? Well, it's your last fog bank. The bottom of the sea's the fust port you'll fetch, you critter, you! Git, and be d——d to ye!"

This, the only occasion on which Captain Cram was ever known to say such a word, was afterward considered by a committee of discipline of the Congregational Church at Newaggen; and the committee, after pondering all the circumstances under which the word was uttered, voted unanimously to take no action.

Meanwhile, the fog had shut in around the tug, and the *Judas Iscariot* was lost to view. The tug was put about and headed for home. The damp wind chilled everybody through and through. Little was said. The contents of the demijohn had long been exhausted. From a distance to the south was heard at intervals the hoarse whistling of an ocean steamer.

"I hope that feller's well underwrit," said the captain grimly, "for the *Judas*'ll never go down afore she's sarched him out'n sunk him."

"And was the abandoned schooner ever heard of?" I asked, when my informant had reached this point in the narrative.

The captain took me by the arm and led me out of the grocery store down to the rocks. Across the mouth of the small cove back of his house, blocking the entrance to his wharf and fishhouse, was stretched a skeleton wreck.

"Thar she lays," he said, pointing to the blackened ribs. "That's the *Judas*. Did yer suppose she'd sink in deep water, where she could do no more damage? No, sir, not if all the rocks on the coast of Maine was piled onto her, and her hull bottom knocked clean out. She come home to roost. She come sixty mile in the teeth of the wind. When the tug got back next mornin' thar lay the *Judas Iscariot* acrost my cove, with her jib boom stuck through my kitchen winder. I say schooners has souls."

Carlos Baker

THE PREVARICATOR

HIS WATCH SAID ten past ten when the Sea Sled whipped into sight around the wind-lashed corner of East Point and went roaring past the Spindle. Its blunt nose was better than a yard out of water, and behind it the powerful propellers hurled a thick white feather of spray high into the air. From where he stood on the wide veranda, he could see the hull slapping every second ground swell with what he knew must sound like pistol shots.

He could not hear the sound because of the nearer one that the wind was making, howling around the corners of the house. The flag on the pole beside the Coast Guard Station streamed out straight. On the rocky beach big combers still clawed at the pebbles and over all the visible sea were heaving blankets of foam and seaweed. Tons of white water were still pouring and sloshing over the top of the red granite rock they called Elephant's Back. Even the air was thick with salt spume, and shreds of hurrying cloud, the last remnants of the first big storm of the season, blew like battle smoke all across the proscenium arch of sky between East Point and South Point.

He raised the binoculars for a closer look at the plunging Sea Sled. Its course was due south through the deep water just beyond Beach and Rock Islands, and he picked them up as they cleared the highest bulk of Beach Island, two heads crouched in the cockpit close together.

Then a strange thing happened. The whole craft seemed to gather itself like a hooked and angry swordfish, leaping clear of the water almost the way those racing boats in the Everglades take a low hurdle. For a second or two it lurched wildly, veering out to sea, but whoever was steering yanked her back on course, the plume of spray dropped down, and for another few seconds she bobbled like a broken toy in the scramble of waves. Then he saw the nose coming up and around, the tail plume feathering aloft once more, and in astonishment he lowered the binoculars to watch that crazy pair of idiots ramming her right across the dangerous water of the shoals inside Rock Island, heading like an arrow for the Coast Guard cove.

He slid the glasses into the leather pouch beside the front door, vaulted the veranda railing to the lawn, splashed through the mud puddles in the road, and ran for the cove, the tough sea grass whipping against his bare legs and feet. Up in the window of the Coast Guard watchtower he could see Red Horsfield's mop of hair, and he cupped his hands and yelled, pointing at the sled. Red stuck out his head, then his shoulders and half his torso, his mouth opening in a black O as he yelled something in reply, but the wind ripped and scattered whatever it was he was saying.

Griff could hear the engine now, plosive as a distant drumbeat. From the water's edge where he stood the oncoming bow looked enormous. Two hundred yards offshore the steersman swerved to clear the rocking covey of the Coast Guardsmen's skiffs and dories, and now he could see both faces—wind-reddened blobs under sailor hats pulled down around their ears. He waited for them to shut off power and drift in the rest of the way, but there was no break in the pounding roar and in amazement Griff leaped aside out of their path. At the last possible moment the driver cut the engine, the plume slapped down, and the whole forward part of the sled crunched heavily on the egg-sized stones of the beach.

One of the men was over the side like a monkey. His khaki pants and the heavy shawl-collared navy blue sweater were soaked and he wore red and white deck shoes. He had pulled off the sailor hat and was stuffing it into his hip pocket. The breakers curled around his knees as he waded ashore and squatted down beside the bow. "Look at that," he said. "For Christ's sakes will you look at that?"

Just aft of the prow was a gaping hole in the sled bottom. Daylight showed through. Torn splinters of wood hung dripping around the edges.

"By God, look at that," the short man said again.

The man at the wheel was easing one long leg stiffly over the gunwale. With evident distaste, he swung down into the water and moved slowly toward where Griff was standing, throwing him a kind of ironic salute. "Morning, Cap," he said in a booming bass. "Can't you do something to warm up this Maine water?"

Griff grinned back at him. "It'll warm up in August," he said.

"So I've heard tell," the limping man said, "and do in part believe. But it sure isn't warm in July."

His yellow oilskin parka dripped with moisture and Griff saw that there was a slash of blood on his left cheek. He sat down stiffly on the stones and began to rub one of his knees tenderly.

"The thing I can't figure out," he said, partly to Griff and partly to the other man, "is *what* we hit." He fixed Griff with a blue-eyed stare. "What *did* we hit, Cap? Can you tell me that?" He waved his unoccupied hand vaguely seaward.

"Nothing out there but water," Griff said. Anton Staples, the Coast

Guard captain, was picking his way over the wall of kelp that the storm had washed up. "Deep water, too. The chart shows fifteen fathoms."

"Except for that goddam rock in the middle of it," the short man said. He was still hunkered down under the bow, fingering the jagged splinters.

"No rocks there," said Griff quietly. "Here's the captain. You can ask the captain."

Anton came up puffing, his cap askew as always, each of his chins separately quivering. "Something wrong, boys?" he said in his high-pitched voice.

The man under the bow spoke again. "Nothing but half the bottom tore out."

"How come you came in full throttle?" asked Anton.

"Keep the nose up," the little man said shortly. He found a blue rag in the pocket of his sweater and mopped his face with it. "Bow tore out, you got to keep the nose up or else drown."

Anton chewed his morning cud slowly. His small observant eyes swept the craft. "Likely it was them ground swells," he said. "You come down from Portland?"

"Boothbay," the older man said.

"You hit a lot of ground swells between Boothbay and here," Anton said. "One plank loosens up and you hit a ground swell just so and you're a goner. Ain't that right, Swiv?"

Griff winced at the old nickname, his bugbear since childhood. Swiv or Swiveon, short for the Swivel-Tongued One, invented ten years ago by his professor-uncle, boiled down to Swiveon by his mother, who said it was a very poetic name, and cut to Swiv by his father, who still sometimes used it to get his goat. It did, too, because it stayed in his mind as the badge of that time, the really bad time, when he was fighting to be believed, when they would all look askance and grin quizzically at each other the minute he opened his mouth to tell them about anything that had happened to him. "The ring-tailed roarer," the professor-uncle said. "The supreme prevaricator. The vendor of Bologna."

Griff would leap up in a rage and go storming out of the house because they would not believe the things he wanted to tell them. Even the true stories that he told with such care to replace the kid stories that he had only half-believed himself. How long would it take for them to forget all that and bury the hated nickname for all time?

He cleared his throat. "It's rough enough out there today," he said to Captain Staples. "Coming from Boothbay all that pounding could have loosened the boards."

The tall man arose from the stones and limped over to shake hands with Anton. "Name's Williamson," he said in the booming bass voice. "That's Pete Mapes in the wet britches."

"Cap'm Staples," Anton said with dignity. "This here's Swiv Axton. Like he says, nothing out there past the island but a lot of rough water."

Pete Mapes stood like a pint-sized athlete, blunt red hands on his hips, doubt in his pale eyes. "Could be a dory tore loose from somewheres," he said.

Anton placed a large right hand on his whitish shirtfront to hold the black service tie in place and leaned forward to spit. "Could be the *Lucy Tanya*," he said with a lopsided grin. He turned towards the watchtower where Red Horsfield still leaned from the window. "Hey, Red," he called. "You want to take that glass and glom her over out there where they say they hit something. Could be they hit some floating objick. See what you can see."

The bronze snout of the telescope appeared in the window, moving slowly back and forth. Then it withdrew and the red head replaced it. "Too rough yet," Horsfield called. "All riled up. Can't make out nothing."

"It's a nothing that is something," Williamson boomed. "Hoisted us clean out. You could hear it smack."

Anton pursed his lips as if he were going to spit. "We got a shorthanded crew here right now," he said, "or we'd take a little run out there and have a look-see. Could be driftwood. Could be a log come down the Saco."

"Could be Moby Dick the white whale," said Williamson.

"Tell you what," Anton said. "I'll get the cutter on the phone, see'f they'll take a run down here. Might be a powerboat capsized and bottom-up. That would do it. Something like that counts as a mare-time hazard. You boys come on in, get warmed up. Come on, Swiv, time for a coffee break."

"Griff," the boy muttered, but a gust of wind blew out the word like a match flame.

II

Eating lunch alone in the Axton kitchen he wondered again for the thousand and first time how long it took to get rid of a liar's reputation. For years now it had stuck with him like a cockleburr, made him turn laconic, made him choose every word with care, never uttering a sentence that was anything but the truth. And nobody seemed to notice.

All around him every day there were people talking, yarning, telling anecdotes that they refurbished to make them sound better, to dramatize them, stories that only grazed the truth if they came anywhere near it. Red Horsfield for one, telling how he had lied—yes, lied—about his age and got into the army at fifteen. He said it was his seventeenth birthday when they went in on Casablanca, and he could go on for an hour or more any time about the back streets and alleys and Arabian babes in every North African city from Casablanca to Bizerte. Lies, most of them. Or take Anton Staples for another, sagged back in the captain's rocker, chewing his quid, as swivel-tongued and smooth-talking as they came, and nobody contradicted him or seemed to question anything he said.

But let Griff Axton get out the first sentence of a truth he knew and the old doubting-Thomas look began to show on all the faces—even Red's, even Anton's—and the room would fall so quiet that his voice would drop and trail off and he would begin clearing his throat with embarrassment in the atmosphere of disbelief and after a decent interval Anton would shift his quid into one cheek and start again, "Swiv, I ever tell you about the feller that—"

Griff stopped chewing and tossed the sandwich aside with distaste. The name was a habit by now, and habits dissolved slowly. There was nothing to do but call them on it each time, saying *Griff* firmly as soon as they said *Swiv*, just as he had done with Anton that morning. He scraped the rest of the lunch off the plate into the garbage pail, slammed down the lid, found the old red swimming trunks and a pair of battered sneakers, and went down to bail out his skiff.

The wind had dropped now and the sea was flat, though the air remained as sticky as ever. The station flag hung limp, a tri-colored splash against the monochrome of hazy blue. In the wide inlet directly in front of the house, the skiff pulled placidly at its rope. He saw that the storm had left it half full of water and weed.

Downshore in the station cove the Sea Sled still lay where they had slammed it full throttle through the morning breakers, but the ebbing tide had left it high and dry. For the first couple of hours, all the curious had come from miles around to marvel at the ripped floorboards, theorizing about the cause. In the end they had fallen silent, gazed speculatively out to sea, and departed. Mapes and Williamson had gone off, too—ignominiously enough—on the noon bus to Portland. Everything was silent now, like an empty room.

He picked up an old jam tin from the jetsam on the shore and waded out to his skiff. The cold water bit at his ankles. Up in the station watchtower he could see Poquelin's bald head, standing the watch from noon to four because they were shorthanded now, with Sikes's ruptured appendix and Hank Simons off on liberty. Later, he knew, the captain would puff his way up the stairs to relieve Poquelin while he cooked supper. Red Horsfield would come yawning out of his dormitory sack to sniff the steam of the kettles on the stove, insult Poquelin's cooking, eat it swiftly and noisily, pick his teeth while he listened to the six o'clock newscast, go outside to haul down and stow the station flag, and get squared away for the eight to midnight watch in the tower.

It occurred to him to beach the skiff and dump the water all at once. But it was pleasant to stand out there beside it, watching it buoy up slowly as he bailed it out, canful by canful. When it was nearly empty he got in and sat in the stern. The captive water gurgled cool around his feet as he bailed steadily—*slup, slosh, slup, slosh*—so absorbed in the rhythm that he barely heard his name being called.

"Swiv. Swiv Axton." It was Red Horsfield's voice from the shore. He did not break the rhythm of his bailing or turn his head.

"Hey, Griff."

So it had worked this time. He turned and waved with the bailing can. Red stood near the water's edge, the white gob's hat on the back of his flaming mop of hair.

"It's your bedtime," Griff said. "You're supposed to be in the sack."

"Couldn't get to sleep," Horsfield said. "Too muggy, like a darned oven up there. Kep' thinking about that Sea Sled. They swore up and down they hit something big. Short man says it was huge."

"What did he think it was?"

"Going too fast to tell," Horsfield said. "Says they leapfrogged. Says the darn sled took off in the air for twenty or thirty feet. Says if they'd have held out their arms they'd be airborne yet."

There was a tall tale for you, and Red Horsfield telling it like gospel truth. Griff slipped the painter, unshipped the oars, and pulled ashore.

"Let's go out there and check the spot," he said.

"Who's rowing, Swiv, you or me?" asked Red.

"Me. And the name is *Griff.*"

"Okay, let me just slip off my Sunday shoes." He left them with his socks at the edge of the sea grass and came limping back over the stones. "I swear I don't know which hurts the worst, barefoot or Sunday shoes," he said, climbing in. He began to roll up the legs of his pants. "You row out and I'll row back," he said, and then, like an afterthought, "Griff."

Griff rowed steadily and expertly along the route they always took, following the edge of the wide trench that made in past the southern tip of Beach Island like a submarine avenue. The Gut, they called it locally. Ordinarily you could read the dimensions of the trench by the bobbling line of lobster buoys that led in a long curve to the gap between Beach and Rock Islands. But not today. The storm had ripped everything loose, tossed the buoys and even some of the traps ashore. Or almost all. He grazed one of the buoys with an oar going past. It was painted green and white to show that it belonged to Harry Phillips, the English-born lobster man.

"Where's your folks, Swiv?" asked Red.

Griff ignored the question, rowing rhythmically.

"I ain't seen 'em around today, have I?"

"Gone up to Seal Harbor," Griff said shortly. In the thick humidity he was beginning to sweat. "Back tomorrow night."

As they neared the island, all the gulls and terns leaped aloft, mewing and bleating, afraid you would come ashore and step on the eggs they had laid on the dry patches of seaweed among the stones. Griff pulled on past to where the ground swells, huge and slow, swept majestically under the skiff. Over Red's shoulders he could see the line of cottages along the shore—Phillips, Fletcher, Axton, and then the break where the Coast Guard property began, then the red-roofed, white-painted bulk of the station itself. He took a rough bearing on his own front porch, the watchtower, and the southern tip of the island, and then paused, letting the oars trail in the water.

"Just about here," he said.

"I'd said they was a little more south," Horsfield said.

"We'll look around," Griff said, beginning to row again.

Red shaded his eyes with both hands, peering out on either side. "Course we don't stand no chance," he said. "Whatever they hit, if they hit a log or even a dory, we ain't going to find it."

"The wind dropped down fast once it dropped," Griff said. "Anything really big couldn't have drifted far."

"No harm looking," said Red, yawning.

But they zigzagged all over the area for an hour without finding anything except acres of floating seaweed that the storm had torn from the bottom.

"Here now," said Horsfield at last. "Let me row her back. Time we get back in, supper'll be on the table."

Griff changed seats, stretching his legs in the stern, letting his hands trail in the cold water. The west-running sun was in his eyes now, and he turned his head, watching the glitter it threw on the calm surface down by South Point. It was just there that he had seen the swimming deer, late one July morning six or seven years ago, the lifted antlers black as tar in the midst of all that shimmer. That was soon after he had taken the tumble on the rocks and broken his wrist. He was still wearing the cast and standing on the high white granite rock beside the cove where Harry Phillips kept his old powerboat. Harry was transferring the morning's catch into the floating lobster car.

Griff had watched the deer for a full minute before he opened his mouth. It was a deer all right. It was swimming steadily out to sea. Dogs must have scared it in the woods and chased it and it had taken to the water to get away. Now it would drown.

"Hey, Harry," Griff yelled when he was sure of what it was. "There's a deer out there."

Harry Phillips did not pause in his work. "Out where?" he said.

"Way off South Point," Griff said. "I can see the horns. It's swimming out to sea."

"Swiv, boy, you look again," said Harry, grinning. "Likely you might change your mind. You'll see it's an old tree and them horns would be the branches."

"No, Harry," Griff yelled. "Honest to God, Harry. It's moving. I can see it swimming."

Deliberately as always, Harry closed the top of the lobster car, turned the wooden pivot that locked it shut, wiped his hands on a piece of engine waste, found the stack of Bull Durham, rolled and lighted a cigarette, and looked up to where Griff stood on the rock high above his head.

"Twelve-point buck, I'll bet," he said. "Tell me another, Swiv, old boy. I ain't heard a good one today."

High on his granite perch, Griff almost danced with frustration. It was a full four minutes before Harry would even stop grinning, his broad red face creased with seagoing wrinkles. He smoked the cigarette hungrily until it was a butt, flipped it overside, rinsed his hands in cove water, turned down the tops of his rubber boots, and at last came lumberingly up the rock to where Griff stood. He stood squinting towards the shining waters off the Point.

"Now just where was it you seen that buck?"

Griff pointed with the plaster cast, unable to speak.

"Swimming, you said. Horns sticking up."

"Yes. Yes."

"Now, Swiv boy," said Harry. "With the best will in the world I tell you I got pretty good eyes but I don't see one damn thing."

Griff peered uncertainly through the glimmer, his heart like a stone sinking in a puddle. In all that vast stretch of water there was nothing in sight. His eyes flushed hot. "You waited too long," he cried. "Now it's gone and drowned. We could have gone out there and brought him back. Now it's too late."

Harry looked uncomfortable. "Maybe so, son," he said kindly. "And *if* so, we could have brought him right back here and turned him loose. Or we could have hit him over the head and had us a nice mess of venison. *If* we could have started the motor and cast off and got out there in time. Trouble is, we couldn't. Not under twenty minutes, and it ain't but ten since you said you seen him first." Slowly, his big shoulders bent, boots clomping, Harry lifted his gear and began climbing the gravel path up the bank to his house.

"Back the same day," Red Horsfield said. "You feel all right? You ain't said a thing for ten minutes."

"Sure," said Griff distantly. "Just hungry is all."

"You got some supper at the house?"

"She left enough to feed an army."

Red shipped the oars and stretched his arms. His freckled forehead was running with sweat. "You want to tie up out there or leave her in here? Tide's starting to come."

"I guess I'll pull her up to the grass."

"Grab aholt, then," Horsfield said. "Old Cokey's putting my grub on the table right this minute."

They dragged the skiff to the edge of the sea grass. Red found his shoes but did not stop to put them on. "See you later, Swiv," he said, hurrying up the path.

"So long," Griff said absently. He was still thinking about Harry Phillips and the swimming buck.

III

Something woke him in the humid darkness of the bedroom and he rose on one elbow to read the luminous dial of his watch. Ten forty-five. Stifling still and quiet. Twelve hours ago the wind had been tearing at the shingles like a crazed animal. Now no breath of air so much as stirred the curtains and except for a sound like a far-off sigh, you would not even know that the sea was there.

He rolled free of the sticky-feeling sheet and crossed to the window. In the faint moonlight, rocks and water made a pattern in black and silver. For a moment he stood hesitant in the semi-dark by the window. Then he found the faded swim trunks on the chair, pulled them on, and let himself out of the front door. In less than a minute he was standing beside the high-and-dry skiff, feeling the cool breath of the risen ocean.

He waded in and plunged quickly, making for the flat-topped rock at the far edge of the inlet, just where the Gut swung past. He lifted himself clear and sat down dripping. A high layer of cloud half obscured the moon, and he could see the faint light in the watchtower. Red Horsfield would be sprawled in the wooden chair, readying a copy of *Field and Stream*, getting up every ten minutes to sweep the horizon for distress signals or the beaded lights of passing ships. Griff stood and plunged again, working out across the deepest part of the inlet in a slow trudgeon. A hundred yards out he came round in a slow circle, aimed for the flat rock, and ducked his head under for the leisurely return.

Better than halfway back he felt the sudden chill, like icy footsteps along his backbone. Something alive and very large was moving near him in the water.

A shark, he thought, and swam for the rock at full speed, surging out and rolling over, shaking seawater from his eyes and searching the placid gray surface for the triangular black fin. But he could see nothing and there was no sound but the *slup* of water under the rock. Imagination, he thought. Go ahead and swim in. It's close to midnight. It's cooler now and you can sleep.

Then it breached before his astonished eyes, wide and enormous in the gray light. He caught his breath and stared at the glistening black skin, whole yards of it, while the water it displaced began rolling in to break in slow waves over the edge of his rock. Shark, hell. It was as big as a whale. It must be a whale that had entered the deep trench beyond the island and would follow it out again past Elephant's Back to reach the deeper water beyond the Spindle.

As though by prearrangement the high pale moon shone through a rift in the overcast and the sea surface glittered with silver light all the way to Beach Island. The vast bulk of whatever it was still moved past the rock where he stood. As long as a freight train, he thought with wonder, and just at that instant he saw the wound, a long gouge in the leathery flesh like a scar on the flank of a mountain.

Then it lifted its head and he saw that it was not a whale, nothing like anything that he had ever seen before, the sinuous neck rising slowly from the water twenty feet away while the bulk of the body was still sliding past—and then the head, larger than the head of a horse on a heroic statue, ugly as sin, covered with short spines like a sculpin, and turning slowly from side to side as if the creature were trying to get its bearings. It was still moving north through the channel when the great head slowly descended, and the dragon-like tail that must have been its means of locomotion stirred the final waves that came sloshing over the rock where he stood. Then it was gone.

He found that he was shaking from head to foot. His mouth was dry and his sight was bleary. Not from fear. Not even with cold, but with the sudden realization that a man can reach—a scientist, a poet—when he has at last put something together that was disparate before. When he understands clearly, as now, that it could not have been a capsized boat or a huge drifting log from the mouth of the Saco that tore the bottom out of that racing Sea Sled, but an honest-to-God sea serpent that at ten o'clock of a stormy morning had blundered up from the depths to the surface, that had then sunk broodingly down to the deep sea floor to wonder, if such creatures can be said to brood or wonder, what it had been that ploughed that bloody furrow in its back, and that now, close to the middle of the night, blind, groping, puzzled, had followed the channel inshore and out again, like a slow enormous locomotive on a curving track, disappearing as majestically and inexorably as it had come.

He glanced at the shore where his skiff lay high and dry at the edge of the beach grass. It would be possible to swim in, dash up the beach, untie the rope, grab the bow, swing it around, drag it to the water, unship the oars, and set off in pursuit. But the huge beast was already gone—half a mile away by now. And what if you caught up with it? What then?

Horsfield, he thought, peering up at the watchtower where Red about now would be yawning and stretching and getting up for yet another sweep with the big telescope all around the horizon from Wood Island Light on the north to Cape Porpoise ten miles down the coast.

Red Horsfield with his tales of bloody combat in North Africa. Horsfield with his deadpan yarns about everything under the sun. Horsfield topping every tall tale you ever used to tell with another twice as incredible. And now this—a story that would beat the wildest imagination in Horsfield's repertory, yet a story that, incredibly, was absolutely true.

So what now? he thought. He saw himself dashing into the wardroom at the station, breathless from running, dripping with seawater, bursting to tell them, midnight or not, of the sight he had seen, the adventure of a lifetime. Captain Staples would be nodding in the corner. Red Horsfield just coming down from his watch in the tower. And then what? *Listen! Listen to what I saw! Not a hundred yards offshore, following the Gut.*

What was it, Swiv? Tell us about it.

I'll tell you, by God. It was a sea serpent, fifty feet long with a neck like a giraffe and a head like a nail keg and that gouge in its back from the Sea Sled this morning. That's what they hit. Don't you see how it all fits together?

Then he saw the faces—the gleam of rising doubt in Anton's beady eyes, followed by the slowly dawning tobacco-stained grin; Red Horsfield's pale eyebrows lifting like golden flags of disbelief and his big mouth widening to let out the bleat of incredulous laughter. For the love of God, now it's a sea serpent. There used to be a kid that told little ones like that one about the swimming deer off South Point that Harry Phillips said was nothing but a drifting tree root. And now here we've grown up to the biggest whopper of them all. A sea serpent, he says! Swiv, boy, it's late. Get along back home. Get yourself dried off, especially behind the ears. Roll into bed and pull up the covers and dream us up another nightmare.

It was no use. The biggest story he had ever had to tell would have to stay exactly where it was. Inside, hidden, and untold. Because there was not one single solitary soul who could ever back it up. A sea beast as long as the watchtower was high, and practically in your lap, and passing you like a slow freight, and not a chance in the world that anyone would ever believe this was so.

He turned back to gaze out across the black and silver ocean, half-expecting to see the great head and the serpentine neck rising up once again above the surface. The white breakers were lashing away as always at the lava-like rock base of East Point. Against the northeast horizon the Spindle stood up like a bare mast. Somewhere out there the huge beast was swimming, deep down now and going deeper, heading towards or even back to the aboriginal hunting grounds from which the great storm had torn or persuaded it.

He was shivering still, but now with the cold. He swam ashore rapidly, limped across the stony beach to the sea grass, and slowly picked his way down the puddled gravel of the road towards the family cottage.

Then he heard the running footsteps and the voice calling his name. A shout—"Swiv! Hey, Swiv!"

Red Horsfield, hatless for once, his white shirt looming ghostlike in the half-light, was racing down the road from the station, racing so hard that his shoes skidded on the gravel when he stopped, "What in hell was that?" he cried.

"What was what?"

"You know what I mean. That thing in the water."

"What did it look like?"

"In the telescope," Red panted. "I seen the whole thing. That black hide, acres of it. Then the damn long skinny neck and a head like a rain barrel and you on that rock right there looking at it and then the head coming down and going under and I lost it."

Griff was grinning now. "Take it easy," he said. "Just calm down. Show me. Point me out the place."

Horsfield gestured wildly. "Don't kid me, Griff. Right there in the Gut heading out for the Spindle."

"Now listen to me," Griff said. "I'm looking just where you're pointing and I've got pretty good eyes, but I tell you, Swiv Horsfield, I can't see one damn thing out there but moonshine."

Jane Yolen

ONE OLD MAN, WITH SEALS

THE DAY WAS clear and sharp and fresh when I first heard the seals. They were crying, a symphony of calls. The bulls coughed a low bass. The pups had a mewing whimper, not unlike the cry of a human child. I heard them as I ran around the lighthouse, the slippery sands making my ritual laps more exercise than I needed, more than the doctor said a seventy-five-year-old woman should indulge in. Of course he didn't say it quite like that. Doctors never do. He said: *"A woman of your age . . ."* and left it for me to fill in the blanks. It was a physician's pathetically inept attempt at tact. Any lie told then would be mine, not his.

However, as much as doctors know about blood and bones, they never do probe the secret recesses of the heart. And my heart told me that I was still twenty-five. Well, forty-five, anyway. And I had my own methods of gray liberation.

I had bought a lighthouse, abandoned as unsafe and no longer viable by the Coast Guard. (Much as I had been by the county library system. One abandoned and no longer viable children's librarian, greatly weathered and worth one gold watch, no more.) I spent a good part of my savings renovating, building bookcases and having a phone line brought in. And making sure the electricity would run my refrigerator, freezer, hi-fi, and TV set. I am a solitary, not a primitive, and my passion is the news. With in-town cable, I could have watched twenty-four hours a day. But in my lighthouse, news magazines and books of history took up the slack.

Used to a life of discipline and organization, I kept to a rigid schedule even though there was no one to impress with my dedication. But I always sang as I worked. As some obscure poet has written, "No faith can last that never sings." Up at daylight, a light breakfast while watching the morning newscasters, commercials a perfect time to scan *Newsweek* or *Time*. Then off for my morning run. Three laps seemed just right to get lungs and heart working. Then back inside to read until my nephew called. He is a classics scholar at the University and my favorite relative. I've marked him down in my will for all my books and subscriptions — and the lighthouse. The others will split the little bit of money I have left.

Since I have been a collector of fine and rare history books for over fifty years, my nephew will be well off, though he doesn't know it yet.

The phone rings between ten and eleven every morning, and it is always Mike. He wants to be sure I'm still alive and kicking. The one time I had flu and was too sick to answer the phone, he was over like a shot in that funny lobster boat of his. I could hear him pounding up the stairs and shouting my name. He even had his friend, Dr. Lil Meyer, with him. A *real* doctor, he calls her, not his kind, "all letters and no learning."

They gave me plenty of juice and spent several nights, though it meant sleeping on the floor for both of them. But they didn't seem to mind. And when I was well again, they took off in the lobster boat, waving madly and leaving a wake as broad as a city sidewalk.

For a doctor, Lil Meyer wasn't too bad. She seemed to know about the heart. She said to me, whispered so Mike wouldn't hear her, just before she left, "You're sounder than any seventy-five-year-old I've ever met, Aunt Lyssa. I don't know if it's the singing or the running or the news. But whatever it is, just keep doing it. And Mike and I will keep tabs on you."

The day I heard the seals singing, I left off my laps and went investigating. It never does to leave a mystery unsolved at my age. Curiosity alone would keep me awake, and I need my sleep. Besides, I knew that the only singing done on these shores recently was my own. Seals never came here, hadn't for at least as long as I had owned the lighthouse. And according to the records, which the Coast Guard had neglected to collect when they condemned the place, leaving me with a week-long feast of old news, there hadn't been any seals for the last 100 years. Oh, there had been plenty else—wrecks and flotsam. Wrackweed wound around the detritus of civilization: Dixie Cups, beer cans, pop bottles, and newsprint. And a small school of whales had beached themselves at the north tip of the beach in 1957 and had to be hauled off by an old whaling vessel, circa 1923, pressed into service. But no seals.

The lighthouse sits way out on a tip of land, some sixteen miles from town, and at high tide it is an island. There have been some minor skirmishes over calling it a wildlife preserve, but the closest the state has come to that has been to post some yellow signs that have weathered to the color of old mustard and are just as readable. The southeast shore is the milder shore, sheltered from the winds and battering tides. The little bay that runs between Lighthouse Point and the town of Tarryton-Across-the-Bay, as the early maps have it, is always filled with pleasure boats. By half May, the bigger yachts of the summer folk start to arrive, great white swans gliding serenely in while the smaller, colorful boats of the year-rounders squawk and gabble and gawk at them, darting about like so many squabbling mallards or grebes.

The singing of the seals came from the rougher northwest shore. So I headed that way, no longer jogging because it was a rocky run. If I slipped and fell, I might lie with a broken hip or arm for hours or days before Mike finally came out to find me. *If* he found me at all. So I picked my way carefully around the granite outcroppings.

I had only tried that northern route once or twice before. Even feeling twenty-five or forty-five, I found myself defeated by the amount of rock-climbing necessary to go the entire way. But I kept it up this time because after five minutes the seal song had become louder, more melodic, compelling. And, too, an incredible smell had found its way into my nose.

I say *found* because one of the sadder erosions of age has been a gradual loss of my sense of smell. Oh, really sharp odors eventually reach me, and I am still sensitive to the intense prickles of burned wood. But the subtle tracings of a good liqueur or the shadings of a wine's bouquet are beyond me. And recently, to my chagrin, I burned up my favorite teakettle because the whistle had failed and I didn't smell the metal melting until it was too late.

However, this must have been a powerful scent to have reached me out near the ocean, with the salt air blowing at ten miles an hour. Not a really strong wind, as coastal winds go, but strong enough.

And so I followed my ear—and my nose.

They led me around one last big rock, about the size of a small Minke whale. And it was then I saw the seals. They were bunched together and singing their snuffling hymns. Lying in their midst was an incredibly dirty bum, asleep and snoring.

I almost turned back then, but the old man let out a groan. Only then did it occur to me what a bizarre picture it was. Here was a bearded patriarch of the seals—for they were quite unafraid of him—obviously sleeping off a monumental drunk. In fact I had no idea where he had gotten and consumed his liquor or how he had ever made it to that place, sixteen miles from the nearest town by land, and a long swim by sea. There was no boat to be seen. He lay as if dropped from above, one arm flung over a large bull seal which acted like a pup, snuggling close to him and pushing at his armpit with its nose.

At that I laughed out loud and the seals, startled by the noise, fled down the shingle toward the sea, humping their way across the rocks and pebbly beach to safety in the waves. But the old man did not move.

It was then that I wondered if he were not drunk but rather injured, flung out of the sea by the tide, another bit of flotsam on my beach. So I walked closer.

The smell was stronger, and I realized it was not the seals I had been smelling. It was the old man. After years of dealing with children in libraries—from babies to young adults—I had learned to identify a variety of smells, from feces to vomit to pot. And though my sense of smell was almost defunct, my memory was not. But that old man smelled of none of the things I could easily recognize, or of anything the land had to offer. He smelled of seals and salt and water, like a wreck that had long lain on the bottom of the ocean suddenly uncovered by a freak storm. He smelled of age, incredible age. I could literally smell the centuries on him. If I was seventy-five, he had to be four, no forty times that. That was fanciful of me. Ridiculous. But it was my immediate and overwhelming thought.

I bent over him to see if I could spot an injury, something I might reasonably deal with. His gray-white, matted hair was thin and lay over his scalp like the scribbles of a mad artist. His beard was braided with seaweed, and shells lay entangled in the briery locks. His fingernails were encrusted with dirt. Even the lines of his face were deeply etched with a greenish grime. But I saw no wounds.

His clothes were an archeological dig. Around his neck were the collars of at least twenty shirts. Obviously he put on one shirt and wore it until there was nothing left but the ring, then simply donned another. His trousers were a similar ragbag of colors and weaves, and only the weakness of waistbands had kept him from having accumulated a lifetime supply. He was barefoot. The nails on his toes were as yellow as jingleshells, and so long they curled over each toe like a sheath.

He moaned again, and I touched him on the shoulder, hoping to shake him awake. But when I touched him, his shoulder burst into flames. Truly. Little fingers of fire spiked my palm. Spontaneous combustion was something I had only read about: a heap of oily rags in a hot closet leading to fire. But his rags were not oily, and the weather was a brisk 68 degrees, with a good wind blowing.

I leaped back and screamed and he opened one eye.

The flames subsided, went out. He began to snore again.

The bull seals came out of the water and began a large, irregular circle around us. So I stood up and turned to face them.

"Shoo!" I said, taking off my watch cap. I wear it to keep my ears warm when I run. "Shoo!" Flapping the cap at them and stepping briskly forward, I challenged the bulls.

They broke circle and scattered, moving about a hundred feet away in that awkward shuffling gait they have on land. Then they turned and stared at me. The younger seals and the females remained in the water, a watchful bobbing.

I went back to the old man. "Come on," I said. "I know you're awake now. Be sensible. Tell me if anything hurts or aches. I'll help you if you need help. And if not—I'll just go away."

He opened the one eye again and cleared his throat. It sounded just like a bull seal's cough. But he said nothing.

I took a step closer and he opened his other eye. They were as blue as the ocean over white sand. Clear and clean, the only clean part of him.

I bent over to touch his shoulder again, and this time the material of his shirt began to smolder under my hand.

"That's a trick," I said. "Or hypnotism. Enough of that."

He smiled. And the smoldering ceased. Instead, his shoulder seemed to tumble under my hand, like waves, like torrents, like a full high tide. My hand and sleeve were suddenly wet; sloppily, thoroughly wet.

I clenched my teeth. Mike always said that New England spinsters are so full of righteous fortitude they might be mistaken for mules. And my forebears go back seven generations in Maine. Maybe I didn't understand what was happening, but that was no excuse for lack of discipline and not holding on. I held on.

The old man sighed.

Under my hand, the shoulder changed again, the material and then the flesh wriggling and humping. A tail came from somewhere under his armpit and wrapped quickly around my wrist.

Now, as a librarian in a children's department I have had my share of snake programs, and reptiles as such do not frighten me. Spiders I am not so sanguine about. But snakes are not a phobia of mine. Except for a quick intake of breath, brought on by surprise, not fear, I did not loose my grip.

The old man gave a *humph*, a grudging sound of approval, closed his eyes and roared like a lion. I have seen movies. I have watched documentaries. I know the difference. All of Africa was in that sound.

I laughed. "All right, whoever you are, enough games," I said. "What's going on?"

He sat up slowly, opened those clean blue eyes, and said, "Wrong question, my dear." He had a slight accent I could not identify. "You are supposed to ask, 'What *will* go on?'"

Angrily, I let go of his shoulder. "Obviously you need no help. I'm leaving."

"Yes," he said. "I know." Then, incredibly, he turned over on his side. A partial stuttering snore began at once. Then a whiff of that voice came at me again. "But of course you *will* be back."

"Of course I *will* not!" I said huffily. As an exit line it lacked both dignity and punch, but it was all I could manage as I walked off. Before I had reached the big rock, the seals had settled down around him again. I know because they were singing their lullabies over the roar of his snore—and I peeked. The smell followed me most of the way back home.

Once back in the lighthouse, a peculiar lethargy claimed me. I seemed to know something I did not want to know. A story suddenly recalled. I deliberately tried to think of everything but the old man. I stared out the great windows, a sight that always delighted me. Sky greeted me, a pallid slate of sky written on by guillemots and punctuated by gulls. A phalanx of herring gulls sailed by followed by a pale ghostly shadow that I guessed might be an Iceland gull. Then nothing but sky. I don't believe I even blinked.

The phone shrilled.

I picked it up and could not even manage a hello until Mike's voice recalled me to time and place.

"Aunt Lyssa. Are you there? Are you all right? I tried to call before and there was no answer."

I snapped myself into focus. "Yes, Mike. I'm fine. Tell me a story."

There was a moment of crackling silence at the other end. Then a throat clearing. "A story? Say, are you sure you're all right?"

"I'm sure."

"Well, what do you mean—a story?"

I held on to the phone with both hands as if to coax his answer. As if I had foresight. I knew his answer already. "About an old man, with seals," I said.

Silence.

"You're the classics scholar, Mike. Tell me about Proteus."

"Try Bulfinch." He said it for a laugh. He had long ago taught me that Bulfinch was not to be trusted, for he had allowed no one to edit him, had made mistakes. "Why do you need to know?"

"A poem," I said. "A reference." No answer, but answer enough.

The phone waited a heartbeat, then spoke in Mike's voice. "One old man, with seals, coming up. One smelly old god, with seals, Aunt Lyssa. He was a shape-changer with the ability to foretell the future, only you had to hold on to him through all his changes to make him talk. Ulysses was able . . ."

"I remember," I said. "I know."

I hung up. The old man had been right. Of course I would be back. In the morning.

In the morning I gathered up pad, pencils, a sweater, and the flask of Earl Grey tea I had prepared. I stuffed them all into my old backpack. Then I started out as soon as light had bleached a line across the rocks.

Overhead a pair of Laughing gulls wrote along the wind's pages with their white-bordered wings. I could almost read their messages, so clear and forceful was the scripting. Even the rocks signed to me, the water murmured advice. It was as if the world was a storyteller, a singer of old songs. The seas along the coast, usually green-black, seemed wine-dark and full of a churning energy. I did not need to hurry. I knew he would be there. Sometimes foresight has as much to do with reason as with magic.

The whale rock signaled me, and the smell lured me on. When I saw the one, and the other found my nose, I smiled. I made the last turning, and there he was—asleep and snoring.

I climbed down carefully and watched the seals scatter before me, then I knelt by his side.

I shook my head. Here was the world's oldest, dirtiest, smelliest man. A bum vomited up by the ocean. The centuries layered on his skin. And here I was thinking he was a god.

Then I shrugged and reached out to grab his shoulder. Fire. Water. Snake. Lion. I would outwait them all.

Of course I knew the question I would *not* ask. No one my age needs to know the exact time of dying. But the other questions, the ones that deal with the days and months and years after I would surely be gone, I would ask them all. And he, being a god who cannot lie about the future, must tell me everything, everything that is going to happen in the world.

After all, I'm a stubborn old woman. And a curious one. And I have always had a passion for the news.

Donald Wismer

SAFE HARBOR

I SET UP Wave's Refuge to reflect, in various ways, my own need for separation from the oppressions of the urbania to the south. I built a baker's dozen of cabins, each out of sight of the others on the backside of a rocky dune or behind a clump of popples, just the loft windows peeking over at the sea. The wood I trucked in on flatbed truck, for I did not want to lay a chain saw on the white pine stands that were left from the last round of lumbering. A local foundation man laid concrete piers for me, and I built the frame on top of them, and insulated between the nine-inch floor joists and six-inch studs with a layer of six-mil poly stapled and taped all around the inside. I let the outside breathe through Tyvek paper and laid long, wide lapboards partly on top of one another, like shingling a room, up the cabin sides. Then I laid the roof in ceramic tile, most unusual as far down east as I was. I gave each cabin its own twenty-foot dug well and septic and gray water fields, and ran electricity in via underground cable, with some heavy-duty plastic batteries for backup.

The wood heaters presented something of a dilemma. I had to have them or the rustic flavor of the Refuge would be compromised, yet I did not want combustion within such airtight walls despite each cabin's air-to-air heat exchanger. I finally found a Danish unit that offered outside air intake coupled with a reasonably tight glass front. There were more efficient heaters, but it didn't take much to warm up those cabins, and in fact I heard some complaints when tenants had to get up in the middle of the night to let cold air in.

We, my wife and son and daughter and I, lived in the 130-year-old year-round house that had been the only structure on the acreage. It directly faced the ocean, unlike the cabins, and it was higher, on a sort of minor bluff with white pine on three sides. There was scarcely a day that we didn't hear the wind, sighing or growling or shuddering past the house, off the sea.

I advertised in the online *New Yorker*, and in a few travel bulletin boards around the eastern seaboard. In the summer I offered standard Maine fare, but I kept my rates high to discourage any casual drop-ins. In the winter I was the only open camp for fifty miles either side, and that was the unusual thing that I advertised. Solitude barely says it. I offered business people a place where they would feel truly cut off from everything outside. I offered a place with no visitors at all, no telephones, no cellular radio, no television, no interference from the outside save what the traveler might bring in on his or her own, nothing except standard satellite surveillance. Where car makers offered sexual power rather than transportation, I offered peace and quiet rather than lodging. I had had no idea if the approach would work, but it did, at least enough for us to get by, and that was our intention in the first place, and the costly piece of land was being paid for.

I was aware that Fairchild was in some way unusual almost from the first. Let me give the credit where it belongs, namely my daughter, who spotted the scar behind his ear. Fairchild was a slender, wiry sort, whiplash-strong. He came in from Bangor by human-driven chauffeured limousine, of all things, that must have cost a fortune. He had a reservation, and I had four empty cabins that week and looked forward to the money. It had been one of those snow-drought winters, and the limo had no trouble floating in on the ice glaze that lay over the dirt track that is our road, even without satlink control.

When Fairchild climbed out and looked around, I saw in him the stiffness of tension, as if he were expecting some kind of assault, from where I couldn't imagine. My daughter, Sam, was ten at the time, and was past the visitor to the back of the vehicle even before the chauffeur was. Nevertheless, she had time to see the scar with that uncanny attention for detail that she has. She didn't say anything about it then, just set herself to lifting what she could out of the hatch and laying it in a neat row along the snow-swept path.

Fairchild shook my hand and we exchanged names. His light brown eyes scarcely looked at me. Instead they cast over the wild expanse of bay that our house faced. The wind was easy that day, and even so there were whitecaps aplenty. Far across, the headland was shrouded in spray from the full force of the Atlantic, beating in from the south. The bay itself was only partly protected, and when the wind was right we felt a pounding nearly as direct as the headland itself.

Fairchild said nothing; he just looked. Just how impressed he was, I couldn't tell, but I had never yet met anyone who could look with detachment at that tossed, violent winter sea. But I was distracted then, by my daughter and the chauffeur. They were hoisting an airchair out of the back of the cab.

I had suspected a companion. Many of my clients, both men and women, brought at least one other person along, married or not I did not make it my business to know. Others came alone, though, the true partisans of solitude, and wrote books or sketched or strolled, parka-shrouded, along the beach when the wind was down. These latter were my most satisfied customers; I could have set up on the moon and offered the same thing, and they would have come back again and again.

That Fairchild had a companion had been obvious from the bulk of his luggage. The limo was not something normally found around Bangor, another sign of the cost of its trip here, and every square inch of the back must have been crammed with the things that Fairchild brought with him. That his companion was handicapped, though, was unusual. When they had the airchair set up, Sam and the cabbie moved forward to help the person out of the cab, but Fairchild waved them away and did it himself.

What he bundled out of the cab in gentle arms was a woman. She was in her mid-thirties, as far as I could tell. She had thin blond hair, cut short, and a squarish face with alert gray eyes that smiled almost all the time. Swaddled as she was in winter wear, I could see nothing abnormal about her legs, just that they hung as loose as wind socks. Moving up to her, I introduced myself and Sam, and she shook my hand with a strikingly strong grip and told us that she was Abigail Townsend, and that she was delighted to be here.

The chauffeur spun his vehicle around and sped away, the limo raising particles of snow from its cushion of air. He had shifted from manual to satellite control before he was fairly down the hill, and was already reclining his seat as the machine disappeared around the first curve.

Sam and I brought our guests to their cabin. It was a quarter-mile hike along a path beaten by our old-fashioned treaded snowmobile. Ms. Townsend handled her airchair with consummate ease, whisking ahead of us, then pivoting around as she asked with her eyes if this or that cabin was theirs. Fairchild strode along behind her. He carried a gigantic backpack. When I pressed on him that luggage delivery was one of the services of the management, he waved it away and told me that he'd carry every last item in himself. I protested, and he insisted, and being the paying guest, he won.

There was a fire going in the cabin, of course, and Ms. Townsend expressed glowing-eyed delight at everything she saw. Fairchild shucked off the pack and looked around, satisfaction on his face. Again we offered to help him, and he shooed us off as if we were panhandlers on a city street.

"He doesn't have a bug," Sam told me when we were back inside our own house.

"What?" I asked absently. We were in our large kitchen, and my attention was on the coffee that my wife was pouring out, while the baby crawled around underneath the spigot and threatened to receive a scalding drop or two.

"His bug is gone," Sam said. She was sitting on one of the barstools that we used for many of our catch-as-catch-can meals. "There's just a spider scar there. And so is hers."

My wife looked at me, and I looked at her. She was a tall, solid woman, as steady as the shore itself.

"A spider scar, like in the movies?" she said.

"Yes," my daughter said. "Maybe he's an international spy, or archfiend criminal."

I smiled. "You don't have to be an archfiend not to have a bug," I said. "I read that about half of one percent don't have them. Their bodies won't tolerate them."

"I read," said my wife, "the same article. It also said that a lot of those people bribe doctors with incredible bucks to get them to take the bugs out."

"Lots of criminals take them out," Sam said, chewing on the heel of some home-ground bread.

"But they don't have spider scars," I said. "They don't want people to know."

"Spider scars are a status symbol in some circles," my wife said. "They prove you're rich enough and independent enough and attended to enough that you don't care whether the satellite knows where you are or not."

"Not with criminals," I said.

"Suppose something happens to them," Sam went on. "Suppose they suffocate or oh-dee on drugs or something. The satellite wouldn't know. We might not find them for days."

"And suppose they really are on the run from the cops," my wife said, smiling.

"Yeah!" Sam said. My son drooled on the floor and hauled himself to his feet by my wife's pants.

Fairchild settled in easily. The second day he pointed to the stack of split ash and maple that sat outside his cabin and said: "Where do you get that?"

"I have a woodlot about a mile from here," I told him. "Mixed growth, forty acres more or less. I cut down enough every year and let them cure sitting on their own branches. Then the next fall I chain-saw them and haul them over here."

His tanned face was turned toward the sea.

"I brought an ax. Would you mind if I split some?"

Well, of course I didn't mind. The "ax" he had turned out to be a light single-headed one that any Mainer would have used only for limbing. He had a sure, savage stroke, as if he were pounding at some worry and beating it to death. I hauled up a cart full of unsplit logs and let him have them. In a few minutes he had his fur-lined coat off and was sweating freely in the fifteen-degree heat.

That seemed to hold him for a few days. I went over to the constable's office one evening, riding on the moonless cold air. Eldon Hodgdon was sitting alone in his easy chair, as he always is that time of night, watching his old color television with dull placitude. He roused himself enough to get interested about the spider scars.

"If they're illegals, we'll find out soon enough," he said, hefting himself out of the chair and moving over to his unit. He spoke to it and it looked at his retinas and let him into the police databases where I could not go. At home I had tried the social news files, but there was no Fairchild in there that made any sense, and no Abigail Townsend either.

"Nothing under those names," Eldon said after talking it over with his machine for a while. "Not necessarily illegal, though. Nothing says a man has to go by his right name all the time. You say they have a pile of money?"

"Seems like it."

Eldon scratched his chin. "Maybe if you describe them. The machine'll tell me if anyone close is wanted anywhere."

"I've got something better than that," I said, and I went to the truck and fetched the ax, which Fairchild had left sticking in the butt end of a log.

Eldon lifted the prints and ran them through the machine. A moment later he whistled.

"They're registered, all right. I never did see the like, though. The machine won't release anything on them; they're classified higher than a kite."

"Well, who are they?" I asked irritably. Foreign diplomats? CIA spies? Android robots?"

Hodgdon chuckled. "None of the above, most likely. But I get a sense from the machine that these are people to leave alone. There're a few families at the very top that you can't ever get nothing on, and by top I mean a few of the billionaires and all of the trillionaires."

The first thing that really jarred me was when Fairchild phoned me over the intercabin line that same night and asked me to shut off their electricity.

"But why?" I asked. I was almost getting used to the spider scar thing, but this was still bizarre enough to get me to wondering. "What will you use for light? How will you cook?"

"I've brought in some kerosene lamps," his uncannily calm voice came over the wire. "We've been cooking on the woodstove."

I almost said, "That's a wood heater, not a stove," but figured it wouldn't help any.

By this time my wife and Sam were hanging around me listening. The baby was in his mother's arms, nursing for dear life.

"Listen, Mr. Fairchild," I began, trying to keep the annoyance out of my voice. "I'm not sure that you realize that your cabin is superinsulated. Combustion sources are serious pollutants. If I cut off your power, you're air-to-air heat exchanger will cut out, and you won't have enough ventilation to turn a sliced apple brown."

"We've already worked that out," he said. "We've got a window cracked. Now I want the power off." It wasn't said harshly, nor angrily, nor with any emotion that I could hear, but it was as definite as bedrock and as hard.

I turned the power off.

I went over there the next day and knocked on the cabin door. It was one of the warmest days so far that winter, and for a change, nearly windless. At the house, the only heat we were needing was coming in through the windows.

Abigail Townsend opened the door. That startled me, though it shouldn't have. Again I saw that heart-stopping smile.

"Won't you come in, Mr. Deniston," she said.

"Seth," I said, and stepped inside. Her airchair, with its armrests off for inside traveling, slid aside. Fairchild looked up from some papers he was working on at the pedestal table.

"Are you folks doing all right?" I began to ask, but he cut me off.

"Your daughter was here earlier. I caught her peeking in the window. I want it stopped."

That caught me by surprise. Sam had hardly a disobedient streak in her, so it took me a moment to realize where her mind must have been. But Abigail said it first.

"I think she thinks we're international smugglers of some sort, Weston," she said. "Would you like some coffee, Mr. Deniston?"

"Seth," I said.

"Smugglers?" Fairchild said, turning his strong face toward his companion.

"I'd better explain," I said, and I told them about Sam and the spider scars, and the romantic tripe that television made of them.

Fairchild touched behind his ear.

"It is none of her business where this came from or why we're here. I hope that you'll make it clear to her," he said stiffly.

"Indeed." I was getting somewhat stiff too.

"Weston, she's just a little girl thinking and hoping she's got an adventure here," Abigail told him.

I echoed that and apologized for her. I told them that she would be over herself to make her own apology.

"There's no need," Abigail said.

"It's something she has to do," I said. "But I run this place and it's my job to ask," I continued. "I don't know much about it, but what would either of you do if you got in an accident or took sick? No one would be monitoring you. You wouldn't get help until someone else noticed what was happening."

"Do you think anyone is monitoring you?" Fairchild demanded. His gorge seemed to be rising now.

"Of course," I answered, puzzled. "If I get in physical trouble, the bug knows it and the satellite therefore knows it, and they come and get me out."

"And if you get lost in the woods or run away with someone's wife, the satellite can find you among a million trees or a million people," he sneered. Sneered. It was the first overt expression I had seen on his face.

"No one is monitoring you, Deniston. You think about it," he said. "It's some damned computer that's watching you. It's watching the sixteen billion people, and it can pay attention to each and every one because it's bigger and faster and smarter than we. Did you ever think about that?"

The spirit of the argument was rising in me now. I never could resist arguing, especially when the assumptions were something all normal people I knew shared, and the conclusions too.

"Who cares?" I said. "Virtually no one dies of a heart attack or any kind of sudden event anymore, except for accidents in remote places, like those lobstermen. We're safer, and I think we feel it and are calmer now than ever before."

"Riots in Bangladesh, food lines in Dallas, famine in the Sahara, war in Tibet. Fast service here, though," he said.

"For heaven's sake, Fairchild, I don't understand where you're coming from," I said, pushing a little. "Things are coming under control now for the first time in man's memory. The MITI computers and their network satellites just plain do a better job than we ever did ourselves."

"Coffee," Abigail said, and placed it down in front of me. I noticed that I was sitting on a barstool, hands gripping the edge of that pedestal table like two lobster claws.

"The point is that they say that people control those machines, but I don't believe it," Fairchild said, his voice subsiding toward his usual calm, seeming in inverse relationship to mine, which it probably was—the unconscious pattern of a lifetime, the damper that kept his emotionality at bay. "What I believe is that the computers themselves are in charge; wasn't that the point of the fifth generation in the first place?"

"So what?" I began, getting really heated now. "What if it's computers, and who cares if anyone admits it or not? The world is still better off than it was before. Hardly anyone talks about nuclear war anymore, for example. That's an incredible piece of progress."

"In either case, we humans have delivered our souls to those machines," Fairchild said. "Do you suppose people are, in fact, still in charge? It's just an illusion, because such people make all their decisions from information gathered, analyzed, and supplied by the machines. Either the machines are directly in control, or indirectly, and either way it's the same thing."

"Is that why you're here, fleeing the evolution of the new life form superseding the old?" I kept the sarcasm in my voice, deliberate and biting. He didn't react at all.

Abigail Townsend looked at me mutely, some kind of plea in her face. I stayed for a few minutes more, drinking the coffee and arguing, and getting nowhere.

I thought about it on the way back home. I had never had such a discussion with a tenant, and I wasn't at all sure it was a good idea. Something had come of it, though. I still didn't know who they were, but I had now a faint sense of why they were here, although I couldn't seem to reason it entirely out from their point of view. If they were after some kind of computer-free primitivism, how could they imagine that they'd find it in an exclusive camp on the coast of Maine?

I forgot how rich they probably were. One time I was in Newport, not Maine's but Rhode Island's, and walked along the renovated Cliff Walk. The great mansions of the Vanderbilts and Mellons and others were there, the incredible fifty-room palaces with their porticos and colonnades, buttresses and towers and gables and manicured lawns, one after another on land worth a million dollars a square foot.

Those mansions in Newport were their summer cottages. That was how they roughed it.

I went home and gave Sam holy hell.

The next day Fairchild came strolling by with Ms. Townsend riding on a cushion of air alongside. She gave me her usual smile that left me kind of dazed despite myself. He looked toward me, the cold pale brown of his eyes somehow inside, not paying much attention outside.

He pointed at the bay.

"I'd like to take Abigail fishing out there," he said.

"What?" exploded out of me before I could stop it. Then I caught my breath and said: "I'm sorry, Mr. Fairchild. It's just that anything smaller than a lobster boat wouldn't last a minute out there. Look at it."

The wind was up that day, and the bay had scattered chunks of ice in it that heaved up and down and sometimes ground together. The water was slate-gray, and the sky lowery. Up here on the tree-lined bluff, we could hear the sea growling, a sentient angry kind of thing, as vicious as anything on the planet.

"I see lobster pots," he said mildly, some expression coming into his eyes.

"Yes, some of the boys drag them when it's calm enough," I admitted grudgingly. "But you need years behind you to get the feel of the waves and weather; they change faster than a flea's sneeze, faster than the satellite ever knows. My rec boats are hauled out; most everyone's are, except the diehard fishermen that live on what they bring in. We always lose some of them every year, despite the bugs; you spend a few minutes in that kind of water and you're dead."

"I could hire an airboat," he said then, mostly to himself. "That would ride over the surface."

"The wind would blow it right up on shore," I said, "or if you're really unlucky, right out to sea. Of course," I needled him, "the satellite would be monitoring the boat and the Coast Guard would bring you back in."

"But that would defeat the purpose," he said, still talking to himself. Abigail Townsend was looking up at him, her smile gone for the moment.

"I beg your pardon," I said.

Ms. Townsend glanced at me and seemed about to speak, but Fairchild suddenly spun around and headed back toward their cabin. "It's something I'll put off for now," he said, again more to himself than anyone else.

I found out later that he had walked almost eleven miles a few days later, up the blunt peninsula and away from the Refuge, and asked three different lobstermen to take him and Ms. Townsend out. None of them would do it at first; they had insurance problems enough. He offered them money beyond their dreams. The first two put him off, said they'd think about it; if they were caught, it would mean the end of their life-style, and money was not necessarily enough to risk it. The third one, Hovey I think it was, had been divorced twice, and said he'd come by the first calm day, that he wouldn't chance his license if the sea was running hard. But the weather was bad that week. Fairchild had to be satisfied with that. As it happened, it was not to be.

Eight days later, the morning broke with the sky in turmoil and the sea oily and colorless. The monitor woke me up and I listened to the NOAA satellite report on mandatory. A storm was on its way, and there was a 30 percent chance it would miss us.

I thought I knew everything about what a big storm could do. Every year had its storms, but the big ones only came around once in a while, with unpredictable savagery. There had been a tremendous one in 1952, and again in 1960, 1961, 1972, and 1978, and we were overdue. In 1938 half the trees in Maine had gone down. The 1978 storm had changed parts of the coastline beyond recognition. Sometimes they were associated with hurricanes, but often they just came out of nowhere and hit too suddenly to get an official name.

If it was going to hit, it would do it in thirteen hours. I set about getting the Refuge as ready as I could.

First I sent the wife and kids inland to her sister's in Wytopitlock. Sam didn't like that; she wanted to stay with me where the action was.

At the same time I told my ten tenants what they would have to do. I had reservations inland at a motel in Hampden, and I let them know that they were being evicted from the Refuge, though of course the Hampden costs were on me.

Fairchild, by the way, took the news without the faintest flicker of expression. Abigail looked concerned, but had nothing to say, leaving it all to him.

A few hours later as I was helping the tenants climb aboard the automated airbus I had called in, I realized that the group was short. Neither Fairchild nor Abigail was with them.

I told the bus computer to stand by and ran over to the cabin. The wind was rising already, and I could hear the sea pounding savagely behind the rocks. I had seen the barometer reading a little earlier, and that, even more than the sea and the waxen sky, had scared me. And on top of it all, it was cold, five degrees Fahrenheit with an awesome windchill. I could hear that wind howling like wolves, ready to eat the land alive.

Fairchild answered the door. I saw that he had split shakes off of the logs and nailed them over the windows of the little cabin. He seemed burning from an inner fire; his hand shook just a little as he let me in the cabin.

"You've got to get out," I said. I then saw Abigail, resting on the lower cot across the room. She was leaning on one elbow, looking at me with those eyes. Even then, I saw something in their shattering grayness that I didn't think I wanted to see. And I knew that it might not be there at all.

"You've got to go," I said, addressing them both. "NOAA's best guess is that it will be at least as bad as '78, and then every building on this part of the coast was leveled flat and blown away."

Fairchild's eyes darted around the room.

"I think that you underestimate the quality you've built here," he said, his voice under that same uncanny control.

"I appreciate the compliment, but you've got to go. It's not a matter of choice anymore. The storm and high tide are going to hit at the same time. Even if the dunes stand up to it, the sea will come around and between them and flood everything in sight. You won't have a chance if that happens; your only chance is to get out now."

"If," Fairchild said. I had known the moment the word left my mouth that it was the worst thing I could have said.

"Think of Ms. Townsend," I said desperately. I turned to her. "Abigail, tell him. I don't think that airchair could fight the wind even now, and it's going to get much worse."

In some way, we had reached a crisis point. I think it was reflected in the fact that I had used her first name for the first time. Fairchild looked at her. I looked at her, and we waited. It wasn't so much that she held their lives in her hands. Instead it was Fairchild that she held there, in a figurative way, his ego and the structure of his world, built around his relationship with her and his fantasies about how the world was and how it should be. He sensed it quite directly, I think; I didn't, and I was very conscious of the muffled moan of the wind outside, and the bus full of people who were my responsibility.

"Weston and I stay, if that's his wish," she said at last.

I threw up my hands.

"I'll be back," I told them.

It took me seven hours to get the rest of them settled in Hampden, a trip that normally took an hour and a half each way. It wasn't getting there that was hard, it was getting back. I had left the airbus at the motel and taken a rental back, and the wind blew me all over the road, and five or six times I wondered if the satellite knew what it was doing. The snow was driving hard now, and I kept seeing cars off in the ditch, and I passed a number of rescue vehicles, heavy enough to resist the wind as it was so far, very busy vehicles indeed. The satlink kept warning me to get inside somewhere. At length, when the car was turning right onto the tertiary road that led to the Refuge, it ordered the car off the road to the nearest house, which it alerted to receive me. I killed the engine and went under the hood and ripped the satlink controller wires away from the car's computer box. Someday they'll find a way to seal the whole innards of a car away from knowledgeable meddlers like me, but they haven't yet. No doubt the satellite was yelling at Eldon Hodgdon about me already, but unless he was just around the corner, I had plenty of time.

I took control and drove past the last turnoff, which went fifty feet back to Quentin Harold's place behind a high hill, and headed downslope into the pocket beyond which a gradual rise would take me home.

It took me only a few minutes to pass through the low place, with salt marshes on either side, that marked the boundary of Wave's Refuge. There was a vicious crosswind at the lowest point, with no trees on either side and I thought I was going to lose her. Then it recovered and I gunned her back onto the roadbed and crossed into the Refuge.

I parked the aircar next to the garage and strode up the path to the house. I saw that some of the popples were down, but I'd expected that.

They were fast-growing trees, weak of wood and root. Around the house itself, the white pines still stood.

Then I topped the rise and the wind hit me, and I saw the sea.

God! I hope never to see it that way again, savagely beautiful and deadly as an erupting volcano.

It was a sea of white, like the foaming of a rabid dog, whitecaps breaking into scud, moving faster than I had ever seen them, hitting the shore as if they expected to go right on through. High tide was still two hours away, and even then the little that I could see told me that the water was far beyond the highest tide I had ever heard of. The wind was blowing the water into the open mouth of the bay, and, reinforced by the tides—we weren't that far from the Bay of Fundy, which has the highest tides on earth—it was piling up like sand against a cliff, only this cliff was just a low rock-and-sand coast. I looked out toward the headland across the bay, but there was no way I could see that far. The air was gray with spray, the sea white and gray, with the immense bass sound of the crashing waves underlying the howling of the wind.

I struggled against the tangible wall of wind and reached the door to the house. I fetched out the keys to the old tire-driven truck, which had been made back when manual or satellite control was still a matter of choice. I left the house door hooked open to keep the air pressure inside about the same as it was outside.

As I climbed off the bluff, heading to the garage below, I looked back, and the spray seemed to part for a moment, as if the wind were piling up somewhere waiting to burst an invisible dam. At that moment I should have been able to see the headland, but I couldn't. It was gone. There were just waves where it had been.

The rented aircar, which was a cheap subcompact, wouldn't have stood a chance, but the old truck rode on wheels, and it was a heavy machine. I pulled it out of the garage, and it stood stolidly against the wind, scarcely rocking as the gusts hit it again and again and again. I put it in park and, leaving the engine running, started out for Fairchild's cabin.

Just then, I caught a snatch of sound like another motor, and looked around and saw Eldon Hodgdon pull up. His police aircar was heavier than most, but I don't think that it could have survived if it weren't for the bluff on which the house stood. I fought the wind the other way and reached the aircar's window.

"What the hell's wrong with you?" Eldon demanded. "I got a summons on you off the satellite, and here you are taking a walk. You get yourself in that truck of yours and you follow along behind. I got lots of coast to cover and no time to screw around with you."

His beefy face was red, and it wasn't the wind. I guess he was that way with everybody.

"I've still got a tenant in one of the cabins," I said.

His face turned a shade deeper. "You don't either. The satellite says you're the only one closer than . . . Wait. You mean the folks with the spiders on them?"

We fought our way to the cabin and pounded on the door. After a moment, it opened silently and we crowded in.

"Mister, you and your lady put on them parkas and come along," Hodgdon said without preamble. He almost had to shout, the wind was so loud, even with the door shut, surrounded by six inches of superinsulation.

Fairchild was standing there, arms folded, backside leaning against the heavy pine table. I looked for Abigail, and found her again on the lower bed, propped on an elbow. Our eyes met, and I smiled slightly. She looked away.

"We're not leaving," Fairchild was saying. I noticed that his fists, at the ends of his folded arms, were clenched so tight that they were white underneath the expensive tan.

"You leave or we'll drag you out," said Hodgdon. "I've got a dozen more places to check, and the worst of it isn't here yet."

"You'll drag no one, Officer," said Fairchild. "This is a tight cabin, protected by the rock dune. We'll be perfectly safe here. You go let that satellite tell you what to do. I make the decisions here."

For the first time, Eldon hesitated. I could see that he was wanting to flatten the handsome, smug face in front of him, though I had a notion that it wouldn't be so easy to do. But Eldon was a politician, among other things. He had tried to find out about these two, and hadn't been able to, and that made him cautious.

"Listen here," he said, trying reason. "You've got a lady that can't walk, and this stretch of beach is going to get flooded out, you mark my words. I might not be able to make it back here if you get in trouble later. Deniston tells me you ripped out the cabin's radio; now, if those scars mean anything, how the hell will I know if you're in trouble or not? It's my job to get you out right now."

"We're staying," Fairchild said, his eyes as bright as agates. "If anything happens, we'll walk out."

"Don't be a fool!" I said then. "Quentin Harold's place is three miles down the road. Abigail's airchair wouldn't make it ten feet."

Fairchild looked around. The cabin, stout as it was, rattled here and there as the wind, even enervated by the dune, shook and pounded it mercilessly.

"We've got light and warmth, and food, and water," he said. You could hear the shrill satisfaction in his voice. "We need nothing and no one."

"Abigail . . ." I said, stretching a hand out to her. Hodgdon shot an odd look at me.

"No," she said.

We forced the door open against the wind and left them there.

"Damn fools," Eldon said when he was inside his vehicle. I had my head almost entirely inside his window so as to hear what he was saying. "There'll be hell to pay when this gets out."

"Why should it get out?" I asked him. "They don't have bugs. The satellite thinks we're the only ones here."

Hodgdon grunted. "You get in that truck and come along," he said. "I've got some stops to make, and I'm not waiting for you, I don't care what the damn satellite says. You get on up to Quentin's and wait there; with that big hill between him and the sea, you'll be safe enough."

He drove off then. I went back to the house and gathered together all the papers I couldn't afford to lose; the wife had taken the larger valuables with her when she left. A few more popples were down, and one of the pines, and I had thought I wouldn't make it to the house, when I felt the wind. I couldn't even see the sea now. The snow was heavy and sticking almost nowhere; instead it drove in blasting, confused gusts along with the wind, like a sandblaster.

When I came back to the truck, I looked along the path toward the cabin. It was their own damn decision, and yet I wanted to go down there and club them outside. Instead I climbed into the truck, and it clashed its gears as the satellite trundled it forward down the road. I passed the rented aircar, barely glancing at it. It was the last I would ever see of it.

Whiteout. The truck was turning into Quentin's drive when it hit. I had seen one before, such blank whiteness of snow and light that you couldn't see past a foot in front of your face. This one was intermittent. For a moment, an extra big gust of snow would rise up and you couldn't see a thing, and then it would pass and there was visibility for maybe ten feet ahead. It was getting dark, and that didn't help at all.

The satlink said that seawater was coming inland all along the coast. High tide was nearly upon us, and with it the worst of the storm. Most houses had plastic battery backup, so power outages weren't so important as they once were. But houses exposed to that wind would be in trouble.

When I reached the turnaround in front of Quentin's dark brown, vertical frame house, I just sat there as the engine turned itself off. Abigail was in my mind, of course. I felt sorry enough for Fairchild and his obsessions. But she was caught in a web. If he hadn't been there, I had no doubt that she would have come along readily enough with Eldon and me. He wouldn't have come whether she had or not.

"You all right, Seth?" the satlink suddenly relayed. I saw Quentin Harold's bearded face, peering out of his front-room window.

"Yeah," I said, and then: "I'm going back." I reached over and switched the truck to manual, and started the engine.

"Don't be crazy!" Quentin said. "What can you save, a TV or two?" Of course he didn't know about the two people, any more than the satellite did. "There're a couple of people drowned already down east. Stay here, Seth. Nothing's worth it."

But something was worth it. I would tie Fairchild up in a gunny sack if I had to. I was going to get Abigail Townsend off that beach.

When I turned onto the road, I had a lot of trouble with the whiteout. If I hadn't known the road so well, every tree and bounder on either side, I would have ended up in the woods. If I had tried the satlink, it would have tried to turn me around and head back to Quentin's. As it was, I couldn't tell the road from the ditches on either side. I couldn't decide if the truck lights were helping or hurting; I left them on. It was like crawling through a sea of white molasses.

A long time later I drove down into the pocket. I felt the truck lurch, and steered a little left. Then the view ahead of me opened up; the wind across the salt marshes was so fierce, it was driving the snow in a straight line, which gave more visibility than the confused swirling of the whiteout. I saw, and I gasped.

The road was gone. The ocean had risen over the marshes and consumed them. The road began again across thirty feet of violent water, rising up toward the Refuge farther ahead.

I turned the satlink on long enough to ask the satellite how deep the water ran, but as sophisticated as the machine was, that was something it couldn't perceive. But it was at least three feet deep, deep enough to drown the truck's engine.

I leaped out of the cab and ran down to the edge of the water. The wind was like a living thing, wrapping me in its powerful hands and trying to lift me into the air and fling me aside like another droplet of spray. I had heard of people being blown off mountains by incredibly strong winds, and for the first time I believed that it could happen. The snow sandblasted me, and wrapped as I was in various layers of wool and down, I felt that wind knifing into my skin and knew that it wouldn't take long before I would freeze to death.

For a moment I stood there in an agony of indecision. To enter that water was madness, and yet to stay on this side of it was to abandon Abigail to a death that I now believed was almost certain.

I never had to make that decision; perhaps it was better that way. For I looked up, and saw something moving toward me through the water.

It was Fairchild, and he was carrying Abigail in his arms. They were already halfway across, and I could not believe that he was still upright in the face of that awful storm. The water tore at him, nearly touching her body as he strove to hold it high. I could only imagine the terrible coldness that was eating at him, with the wind only a minor factor now as the coldest water on the eastern seaboard ripped into and past him like a sluice.

I couldn't tell if he saw me or not. His wiry body, whiplash-strong as I have said, plodded forward, step by step. What unbelievable strength that man had; I truly believe that if it weren't for the water itself holding him down, he would have been blown aloft at the center of the airstream, Abigail and all. As it was, he reached the middle of the water and passed it, rising now out of it, faltering for a moment as a particularly violent gust hit, then forging onward. I stepped a few inches into the water and held my hands out to take Abigail. He stepped sideways and walked up onto the snow, still holding her. I couldn't tell if she was alive or dead.

"Why are you here?" he said harshly, standing there, the wind buffeting him, not looking at me, water already freezing up and down the parka that he wore.

I saw that I could increase his paranoia, reinforce his fear that other forces were constantly violating him, or I could give him something to make him feel left alone and in control. In doing the latter, I realized, I was placing myself in the same role that Abigail herself filled, day in and day out.

"For the Refuge," I answered, looking away. "The minute it lets up, I'm going in."

He stood there for a long minute, clothes freezing to his body. I saw that his arms were trembling. Then he nodded, stiffly; he just stood there, as if uncertain what to do.

"Get in the cab and warm up," I said offhandedly. "We'll all go back in together."

Still he swayed there, and then finally his voice came again, the muted power in it beginning to show the strain.

"That truck of yours—it has a satlink?"

"Of course, but . . ."

And abruptly, he began walking forward into the storm.

I waited as long as I dared, long enough for him to make it down to Harold's, then I turned the truck around and drove, as slowly as I could. Even so I almost missed them in the uncertain glare of the headlights, an irregular lump on the road being rapidly covered by snow. I pulled them one by one into the truck, and then, with relief, let the satlink take me through the whiteout to Quentin Harold's driveway.

I touched her face, and she opened her eyes and looked at me. The shocking, deep intelligent grayness hit me, and I felt it all the way down. She saw, and smiled her gentlest, saddest smile.

"The loft blew off," she said, before I had a chance to speak. "I don't think there's a cabin anymore. Most of the dune was gone by the time we started out."

"Never mind," I said, as gently as I knew how. I looked at her in silence, and something must have showed in my eyes, because she looked away.

"Why do you let this kind of thing happen?" I asked her then.

She seemed to reflect, lost in thoughts as incomprehensible to me as a cat's.

"Because I love him," she said at last, looking me again in the eyes, and finally I saw the source of the sadness, the great, kind, empathetic sweetness of her, and I turned away, embarrassed that I was so exposed when I did not hope to be, had never thought or wanted to be.

"And because I am his anchor," her voice said, coming at me. "As long as he loves me, he can't go off the end."

"No, I see that," I said, my face still averted. I wanted no more of this; I never wanted it in the first place.

"I don't think you do," she said. "Love is only the half of it." She stopped for a moment, and then said quietly: "Six years ago he bought me one of those auto/manual cars, the last year you could get them, and he switched it to manual and took me down the controlled highway between D.C. and Baltimore. And he was looking at me, the way he always looked at me. Too long. The car hit the back of a controlled car ahead of us and went off the edge. It hurt me." She reflected a little, and I could feel the pain of the man in her, but of her own bitterness and pain there was nothing, and I was looking for it.

And so he tries to prove his competence, I thought, every way he can. And she knows that if she left him, he would fly apart, like a boiler, under too much pressure, pricked by a bullet. And yet, if she stayed with him, he would test himself, one test more demanding than the other, and the day had to come when he made up one last test, and failed. And if she were still with him then, they would both go down together, *folie à deux*.

"Let it end here," I told her then, knowing that she would grasp what I meant. "Tell him he's proved it; he doesn't need the satellites. He made it here, all by himself, with you in his arms, and blacked out. Tell him that."

"It might work, for a few days," she said to me, her eyes looking directly into mine now, bravery and defiance in them. She was telling me that her decisions were made. She was telling me the way it was.

"The other part is the airchair," she said. "Did you ever think about someone like me without it?"

I let the silence hang, the fire popping and crackling in the air. It hung a long time.

He thought about it, I'll bet. I'll bet his mind approached it constantly, and sheered away, again, and again.

The airchair was necessary. He loved her. It was completely utterly necessary. But it was a machine. It was technology.

He couldn't get away from it.

* * *

Fairchild wasn't that badly off. He thawed out quickly. The storm died out after a while. Seventy-three people had died from Delaware to Nova Scotia. The bugs had led rescuers to snowbound cars and furnaces gone out and woodstove fires, but that was later. During the storm, the wind had blown rescue vehicles into trees and hills and buildings, and the powdery swirling snow got into intakes and choked off engines. Fifteen of the dead had been rescuers themselves.

Wave's Refuge was mostly gone. The house, roofless, still stood, but all the cabins had been swept away. Most of the white pines were down. We found pieces of the cabins a mile and a half inland.

After the storm was over, Fairchild and Abigail called up a private, piloted copter and flew to Bangor, where they boarded a Lear jet, also piloted, and flew away. We never did find out who they were, and that was very hard on our neighbors, who knew everyone else's business, even if they never interfered in it. I think of her, and him, once in a while, and every time I scan the online obituaries I look for short blond hair and gray eyes and a square face, and a brown-haired, light-brown-eyed man, whiplash-strong.

Weston Fairchild. Some might call him a hero. Man against technology, that sort of thing, the stuff of which empires are built and fortunes made. But it seems to me that real heroes are ordinary people who react extraordinarily to some crisis. They don't push their way into places where they then have no choice but to practice heroics. And they surely don't drag someone else with them. Maybe in the cotton-batting comfort of the future, when satellites and MITI computers save mankind from itself everywhere, in everything, people will point to the likes of Weston Fairchild with nostalgia, and trace his spirit back to the movers and shakers of history. They'll forget that many of those movers and shakers were surrounded by corpses. Movers don't always move in the right direction.

Our direction now is surveillance. War, crime, and human suffering are lessening. Most people don't think much about it, but those that do seem happy enough.

As for me, here on the coast of Maine, I will build again. Storms such as that hit Maine now and again; it's part of living here, and the satellites give us ample warning, and insurance is available. The wife and kids and I are content. I intend it so. We are happy here, and I aim to keep it that way. Anything that might threaten it, I will put aside.

Thomas Easton

MOOD WENDIGO

WHEN DID THIS story begin? It's hard for anyone here in town to say. It looped back on itself and tied its bit of time in a knot. No one is really sure just what happened, though we do know we lost a good boy.

Did it start when Lydia Seltzer told her high school biology class about the wendigo? She was talking about the world's mystery beasts, the Abominable Snowman, the Sasquatch, the Loch Ness Monster and its cousins in other lakes around the world. She told them about all the expeditions, the lack of results, the questions—are the searchers simply crackpots? Or do elusive things still exist in the hidden corners of the world? And then she mentioned the wendigo, a thing that had never been more than a story, a superstition, something no one had ever believed in enough to check it out. Its name was Indian, and it was known across the Northeast, from Maine to Ontario. It screamed in the night, and anyone who sought the screamer disappeared without a trace. If they ever returned, they were mad, too blown of mind even to say what had happened to them. There were no descriptions of the wendigo.

Or did it start the day our town acquired a second Lydia? Mad she was, and raving, but she was the same Lydia we had all known for a decade. The same wide mouth, the nose a little larger than she liked, the black hair worn short and curled over her collar. Neither was any beauty, but neither were they ugly, and it seemed surprising that she had never married. Or perhaps it was no surprise after all. She was tough-minded as only a woman can be, and she showed it at an unusually young age. Most women wait till their forties and later to show their steel. But not Lydia. She brooked no nonsense, in class or out, and for as long as we had known her she had been given to severely tailored pant suits, wool for work, denim for evenings and weekends.

When did it start? Who can say? The best I can do is tell you where I came into it. That was some time after the wendigo class. I was at home, sitting at the kitchen table, going over the town budget for the fourth time. Sarah, my wife, was in the living room, watching something inane on TV. We didn't talk much anymore, not about her job at the bank, not

165

about mine. We had no kids.

When the buzzer sounded, I heard her chair creak as she rose to answer the door. There was a murmur of voices, steps in the hall, and "Harry? Miss Seltzer wants to see you." There was a glare with the words. I ignored it, raised my head from the papers and said, "Duty calls, then. Have a seat, Lydia. Coffee, a drink?"

"Do you have any tea?" As Lydia pulled the other chair out from the table, Sarah disappeared. A moment later, the sound of the TV rose, as if to drown out anything that might give my wife's fantasies the lie. But my attention was for Lydia. She seemed more serious than usual, if possible, and there was a folded paper jutting from her bag. I wondered what was on her mind as I filled the kettle. I found out soon enough.

She sat still, watching me as I moved about the room, saying nothing until our tea was before us and I had sat down again. Then she said, "Mayor, I need a leave of absence. A short one."

She stirred her cup, squeezed the bag, and dumped it in the ashtray half full of my pipe ashes. "Of course," I said. "But shouldn't you be asking the superintendent about this?" I was puzzled. It wasn't my chore to handle the teachers, thank goodness. I was the town's unpaid mayor, and there were professionals, paid ones, to handle day to day affairs.

"I will," she replied. She looked at me, her brown eyes unblinking. I remember thinking that for all her mannishness she would be worth shielding from all grief. Perhaps it was the eyes. Maybe it was just Sarah. "But you can help," she said. "You know people, and . . ."

"But what do you need help with?"

She shrugged and took the paper from her bag. She unfolded it and handed it to me. "Look at this," she said. "It's French-Canadian, a rhyme, collected back in the thirties by the WPA people. I found it in the university library, buried in the folklore files."

The paper was covered with a pencilled scrawl, a copy of a poem that must have been set down by someone who wished to capture the flavor of a speech pattern:

>Ze Wendigo,
>Zat crazy beast,
>'E never eats,
>But loves t'go.
>
>In darkest night,
>'E runs and screams
>And stirs ze dreams
>Of second sight.

But when you go
To join ze run,
'E stays unknown,
Ze Wendigo.

I packed and lit my pipe, studying the rhyme, before I spoke. "Interesting," I said. I sent a cloud of smoke toward the ceiling. "But what does it have to do with a leave of absence?"

Her fingers tensed around her tea cup. She had come to me, but she seemed unwilling to reveal her problem. Could it be so rare or odd or shameful? Suppose it was, I told myself, and then I guessed the answer.

"You want to go wendigo hunting," I laughed.

Her lips tightened, and I was immediately sorry for the laughter. That was just the reaction she had feared. Of course. No one wants to be thought a nut, a crackpot, even if their ideas are a bit off the beaten track. "But go on," I said, trying to save the situation. "Maybe I can help. At least, I'm game to try."

She relaxed as if that was all she had wanted. I caught a faint whiff of perfume or cologne. And she began to talk. She told me of the wendigo class, of her own interest in the strange, of her sense of fairness that led her to the library, of her conviction that all the legends must reflect some grain of truth, of her wish to seek that truth. She had come to me for suggestions on where to seek, a guess at the chances of success, perhaps even a partner in the strange quest.

Why me? Well, I do have a reputation for imagination. Last year's ad program for my oil business certainly stirred folks up enough. And then there were the gimmicks I had come up with to get more tourists into the area. And then, too, there had been a few incidents now and again to connect me with the strange. Really, I should have been more surprised if Lydia had not come to me.

But what could I do? I wouldn't know a wendigo if I saw one. Or heard one, rather. She was silent while I relit my pipe and thought. She didn't fidget much, only turning her empty cup back and forth between her hands. Finally, I said, "There's at least one fellow in this town who could help. If you'll come to the town hall tomorrow after school, I'll ask him to meet us there."

She nodded and sighed. Her breath whistled as if she had been holding it. So I would help, after all. Her voice was softer when she spoke. "Do you really think we can . . .'"

"How can we know?" I grimaced, sympathetically, I hoped. "We've no idea what it looks like or where to look. But we can try."

The fellow I wanted to talk to was Howie Wyman. Grizzled, always overalled and booted, he had been doing odd jobs as long as anyone cared to recall. He knew all the stories, too, though he didn't talk much. He seemed to prefer the woods and streams to human company, even his wife, but he was in town at the time, painting a house over on Water Street. I sent a secretary to ask him to come by a little after three.

I was still alone when he showed up, a motley collection of paint spatters, whiskers, and faded cloth completely alien to any civilized conception of a government office. My secretary showed him in, though, as if he were clad in a three-piece suit and fresh from the barber, which tells you something about our town. It's informal. Partly because it's small and partly because its people waste little energy on nonessential appearances. They dress up mostly for church and they try to keep their drinking private.

I said, "Thank you, Bonny," and waved Howie to a seat. He took it, looked for my wastebasket, and got rid of his wad of chewing tobacco. "You wanted me, Mayor."

"Ayuh," I said. "Lydia Seltzer dragged me in on a project of hers. I thought you might be able to tell us something helpful."

"Like what?" He looked doubtful. He knew Lydia was the science teacher, and he knew nothing about science. I doubted he'd ever gotten past the sixth grade. I was starting to tell him about the problem when Lydia walked in, Bonny holding the door until I waved at her. Her wool was pink today, and her face was flushed with eagerness. The combination wasn't attractive, but I didn't imagine it was anything but temporary. I hoped she wouldn't be disappointed.

I introduced Howie to Lydia. "This is the fellow I was talking about. I was just going to tell him the problem."

She took the other chair. "Shall I go on, then?" When I nodded, she produced that paper again and then handed it to Howie. While he read, she said what she wanted, flatly and directly. The nervousness I had seen last night was gone.

When she finished, Howie set the paper on the corner of my desk and said simply, "Pork Hill." I raised my eyebrows, and he went on. "My dad was up there once. Ayuh, huntin' deer in the dark of the moon. He heard that scream. Didn't see nothin', though."

"Where's Pork Hill?"

"North by west, 'bout ten miles."

And that was all he had for us.

We now had a place to look, and the next dark of the moon was just two weeks away, in case that mattered. Lydia could hardly wait. She insisted on borrowing a tent, sleeping bags, a Coleman stove, all the gear anyone could want for a night camping on a lonely hilltop. She got most of it from two members of the school board. She got their sons, too. Keith

Hutchison and Ronny Jackson were two of her best students, and she thought they deserved a field trip, a little hands-on research. They thought so too, especially since it meant a Friday away from school. I didn't argue, since I was sure we could meet no danger from a superstition.

I wish I had been right. Keith was a lanky boy, tall, a forward on the school basketball team. Ronny was shorter, sturdier, a soccer player. Both had family, friends, girl friends, good prospects. Keith, in fact, already had a scholarship for college. They had a lot to lose, but they were eager. Danger was just a myth, and they wouldn't miss this trip for worlds.

They didn't, of course. I didn't believe in any danger myself, so I didn't try to talk them out of it, and Lydia made it sound like a lark. All the way up there, the four of us and the gear crowded into my old station wagon, she waved her camera and ran on about the splash a picture of a real, live wendigo would make.

We loaded the car on Thursday night and left town shortly after noon on Friday. When we met in the town hall lot, I was surprised to see Lydia in dungarees and a red-checked wool shirt. It was so unlike her that, even though the rest of us were dressed similarly, she seemed to stand out. But the clothes were suitable for the trip, and I soon stopped noticing them.

It took us half an hour to reach the foot of Pork Hill, and another two hours to hump the gear to the top. The hill wasn't big, no more than eight hundred feet high, but it was steep and wooded and there was no path. The going was slow until we reached the top, where the trees disappeared. Pork Hill was one of those rocky knobs scattered over the state of Maine, its top scraped clean by glaciers and still inhabited only by lichen, moss, blueberry bushes, and a few stunted birches.

We pitched the tent in a mossy hollow between boulders, and the boys went back down the hill to gather firewood. There were plenty of fallen branches there, and though we had the stove, a fire was a comforting thing to have at night. Even small mountains can get chilly after dark.

By suppertime, the woodpile was large enough to last a week. We had all taken time to explore the hilltop, too, following Lydia as she sought some clue to what a wendigo might be, some trace of something strange. We found nothing but glacial scours and animal droppings and a few weathered shotgun shells, though Lydia was hardly discouraged. As she said when the boys were finally kindling their fire, "It is a traveller, they say. Maybe it never stops here."

I said something which I now wish I hadn't. Though it probably didn't change a thing. "Then you'll have to move quickly to get a picture of it. It won't be waiting for you."

"I suppose I will," she said, fingering the camera on its strap around her neck. She bent, then, to the totebag she had brought and extracted a flash, one of those electronic ones that don't need bulbs. "I'd better be ready."

We ate—hamburgers and potato salad and coffee and bakery pie—and sat around the fire staring, satisfied for the moment by the mystery of its flames. Only Lydia turned her head now and again to the darkness, straining to see what she waited for. But there was nothing but the odor of earth and growing things, the sight of stars like raindrops on a windshield. The air turned chill enough for sweaters, and we listened to the chirps and buzzes of insects, the lazy notes of sleepy birds, the small croaks of tree frogs, and the rare crackling of brush as some animal—deer, coon, rabbit, coyote, even a wild house cat—passed within hearing.

We talked, of what it meant to be a mayor or a teacher or a student, of sports and fishing and hunting, of politics and taxes. We told no ghost stories, though. I suppose that must have been because our mission was too much like such a tale. It would have been tempting fate to describe horrors and frights, and fate never needed tempting.

Eventually, we talked ourselves out and let the fire die. We were readying ourselves for the sleeping bags, washing up, brushing teeth, when it happened. We heard a moan at first, low as if far distant, swelling loud and clear and close. At its peak it sounded like a baby must when it is being dipped in boiling oil.

It was a little after midnight and as black as the inside of a closet. We had been using the light of an electric lantern as well as the glow of the coals. We had been contained in a small and cozy room, but that sound broke down the walls. I shuddered, and Lydia ran, the soap and water spilled on the moss, her camera ready in her hand, Keith hot on her heels. Ronny would have gone too, but I held him still with a hand on his shoulder. "Let go!" he cried. "I want to see it too!"

"Remember the stories," I said as softly as I could over the dying scream. "Someone should mind the camp." He subsided as I'd hoped he would. When the scream was gone and the night was again silent, I added, "Now. Now we can look for them."

We took our flashlights and tried to follow the marks Lydia and Keith had crushed into the moss as they ran. But the tracks soon disappeared in the tangled skein of prints we had made earlier that afternoon. We called and shouted. We covered every inch of that hilltop, again and again, shining our lights down cracks in the rock and under bushes, checking the bottom of every drop we came across, large or small. We searched until our batteries were exhausted, and then we huddled around a rebuilt fire, worrying, starting at every crackle of brush.

With the dawn, we searched and called again, but we had no better luck. Lydia and Keith had vanished without a trace, just as in the legends. I was closer than ever before to believing in the wendigo, and thus in ghosts, banshees, and all the rest of what I had once dismissed as so much claptrap.

Our second search soon ended in futility. We made a hasty breakfast, doused the fire, and broke camp. Then we lugged the gear back to the car. It took longer, since there were fewer of us now. I had plenty of time to berate myself, to think I should never have helped Lydia with her obsession, never have let the boys come along, never have come myself. But who could have expected a myth to be real? Who could have guessed it would cost us half our party? And what was the wendigo? What was it that made a sound that swelled and faded like a freight train's whistle, that screamed like a soul in torment? Like a god on a cosmic treadmill? If only I had known, I might have left the boys in town, but I would still have come with Lydia, hoping to protect her, shield her. I felt as I might for the child I didn't have, and I mourned.

Ronny was less thoughtful. He shivered when he thought of the night, and once he dropped his load with a clatter of pans. He had lost a teacher and a friend. He might have been lost himself. The horror of that scream had almost touched him, and he could barely control his thoughts. He stayed close to me, keeping a wary eye on the woods around us, talking endlessly, trying to imagine what had happened to the others. He failed to disrupt my thoughts only because I was as obsessed myself. There was no conversation. He talked on, while I muttered responsive noises, and we both scurried around our separate skulls, like rats seeking the way out of a trap.

By mid-morning, we were back in town. I stopped the car in front of the town hall. The police station was across the street. We would have to go there first, of course. Missing persons, runaways, lost in the woods, carried off by a mythical beast, had to be reported, search parties organized, motions gone through even if they could do no good. Ronny was still talking, muttering, his skin a cold and clammy white, his eyes glazed. I helped him out of the car and steered him across the road. I remember being glad he hadn't collapsed while we had work to do. It would have been a shame to leave all that gear on top of Pork Hill.

Our town's Chief of Police was a heavy-bellied man whose moon face wore a thin mustache. He was young, about thirty, and as competent as we needed. Most of his energies were spent on rounding up drunks and vandals, occasional burglars, and the odd con man. He could do the work because the town was small and the crime rate low, but he could never hope to improve his lot. He would grow old in the job, the gut would sag, the cheeks jowl and the eyes go piggish. The tattoos on his forearms would fade, and somewhere along the line we would have to get rid of him. I wouldn't miss him; no one would. His sense of social class was far too keen.

When we entered his office, he rose and said, "G'morning, Mayor! I thought you were going wendigo hunting yesterday?"

"We did," I said shortly.

"Ah!" He grinned jovially, as if we shared some secret. "Stealing a march on your great white huntress, hey?"

"Whatever do you mean?" I asked. I was irritated by his tone, impatient with what had to be nothing but nonsense. But his next words set me back.

"Lydia Seltzer. She didn't go with you."

It didn't sound like a question, but what else could it be? "Of course she did. That's why I'm here now. She disappeared last night. She and Keith Hutchison."

The Chief plopped his bulk back into his swivel chair. He looked startled. "But ..." Then he paused, looking at Ronny as if for the first time. "What's the matter with him?"

"Shock and exhaustion," I said. "We were up all night, searching for them. Maybe one of your men would get him over to the hospital and tell his parents where he is."

"Of course, Mayor." He pushed a button on his desk intercom. Then he said, "Maybe you'll tell me what happened when ..." A patrolman entered, was given his instructions, and left with Ronny. The Chief turned back to me. "Now," he said.

I gave him the story. He nodded when I was done. "The shock I can understand," he said. "But why didn't you get here hours ago?"

"I didn't think it was wise to go stumbling through the woods in the dark. Besides, I hoped we might find something in the morning."

"Not that it really makes a difference. A search party wouldn't do any good."

"Why not? They could still be there someplace! Maybe they fell in a hole we didn't see, or got lost in the woods."

"No." He shook his head and rose again. "C'mon. I'll show you."

He led me back to the small cell block. When we entered the narrow corridor, lined with steel bars, I could hear a noise, a jabbering sound, wordless, random. Or almost random. As he steered me toward the noise, I began to pick out shreds that might hold meaning: "fetal train," "stars and stars," "hopper freight," "take yon train," and more, though those were clearest. I wondered what madman he was holding here. And then we faced the last cell in the row. Through the bars, I made out a form strapped onto the narrow bunk, head tossing, face bruised and scratched, denim and wool clothes torn and soiled. It was Lydia.

The Chief spoke. "We picked her up like that yesterday afternoon. She walked into town, went straight to the school, and tried to get into her classroom, raving all the time, just like this. The substitute called the principal, and he called us. I'm waiting for the judge to sign the papers now, and then one of the men'll drive her to Augusta."

AMHI. The Augusta Mental Health Institute. Where they would try to bring her back, perhaps with drugs and electric shocks. But what else could anyone do? I turned away.

Back in the Chief's office, I remembered Lydia's camera. Did he have it? He did, along with everything that had been in her pockets. "Then perhaps," I said, "it might be a good idea to have the film developed. She could have got her pictures after all, and they could help the doctors understand what's wrong with her now."

"Of course," he said, and I left. I wanted sleep, but I should return the gear Lydia had borrowed first and tell Keith's family what had happened. Then, maybe, I could begin to puzzle over how Lydia had disappeared last night and reappeared yesterday. Time travel was impossible, wasn't it?

The Hutchisons and Jacksons were enraged. With me, with Lydia, with the town, with the school. One boy lost, another ill, but the lost one most on their minds. Jack Hutchison swore he would run against me come the next election, sue me for every penny I had, have Lydia fired if she ever regained her wits. But the prospect of no longer being mayor didn't bother me—after all, it didn't pay—and the trip had officially been a school field trip, and the school had insurance to cover lawsuits.

And then that fuss died down. The pictures came out. Lydia had her wendigo, twice. One shot showed a line of shiny boxes stretching down a gleaming tunnel. The other showed Keith walking away from the camera, hand in hand with a figure that wasn't human, through a vast cavern of a room. The shiny boxes covered the floor of that room, and they were surrounded by machines that bore vague resemblances to freight dollies and forklift trucks.

I could guess what the wendigo really was. An interstellar freight train, its tracks looping close to Earth at certain times and places, a freight that could be hopped by anyone who got too close to its passing field. "Fetal?" Maybe "ftl," faster than light. By "take yon" had she meant "tachyon"? I read enough to know what that was, how it might fit, and Keith was alive and well, Earth's envoy to other worlds. Lydia, on the other hand, had been sent back on the next train, going faster than light, backward in time just enough to get her home a day before she left.

By the time Lydia stopped raving and returned to her job, Pork Hill could no longer be visited, either by deer poachers or by would-be interstellar hobos. The army had taken it over, and it was now ringed by wire fence and armed guards while the experts tried to find a way to flag some passing train down.

Fredric Brown

DEATH IS A WHITE RABBIT

THE MAN IN overalls tapped his foot moodily on the running board of my car for a few long moments.

"They screamed, and they died," he said finally.

It wasn't a cheerful topic of conversation; I should have remembered that I had a lady passenger, and desisted in my questioning. But the lady passenger—my cousin—seemed as fully interested as I. In fact, she asked the next question:

"But there *must* have been some cause. Didn't the death certificate reveal anything?"

The man grunted. "It said 'heart disease.' That's what a doc always puts down when he doesn't know." He spat into the dust at the foot of the signpost that read, "You Are Now Leaving St. Agatha" (unnecessary information, as we'd already left the hundred or so scattered buildings of the town half a mile back). He said, "Three healthy men died in a month— all in their sleep. They screamed, and they died."

"But what connection," I asked, "could that have with Professor Allers? Do you mean you think—"

"Mister," he said glumly, "I don't think. You asked me why none of the folks around here would go up to the perfessor's lodge on a bet, and I told you. Maybe there ain't no connection. Take it or leave it."

That, for a Maine Yankee, was a speech; it was the longest statement I'd got out of him thus far. He started to turn away as though he were embarrassed by his own eloquence.

I asked, "Does this road go out to Dick Willis' farm?"

He nodded, grinning at this more pleasant topic. "Yep, if you can call it a farm."

"Suppose he's there now?"

"Sure. He gets in just once a week for supplies. It's five miles beyond Allers, the next place. Very last house at the end of the road."

"If you can call it a road," I called after him. "Anyway, thanks."

I turned to Rita and saw that her eyes were bright with excitement. I wondered whether the cause of the excitement was the fact that she was soon to see her fiance (and my friend), Dick Willis, or because of the dark account we had just heard of the other man—a stranger to us both— whom I intended to see.

In a way, both calls were incidental. I was driving up into deep Maine for the hunting, but I'd promised my boss that I'd pay a business call on Ormond Allers, who had formerly been a good customer of the scientific supply company for which I work. Recently Allers had quit buying from us.

Rita had asked to ride along, for a short surprise call on Dick, who didn't know we were coming. He'd buried himself for the summer on a little Maine farm to write a book on Tahiti.

We'd planned to spend an afternoon with Dick, then drive back to St. Agatha and put Rita on the train. She was to return alone, while I drove on deeper into the game country. But we'd been delayed, and it was almost dark now.

I said, "Look, if we go on to Dick's place now it'll be time to turn around and come back. I'm going to St. Agatha and park you at the hotel—or whatever they use for one. Then I'll get my call on this Allers mug out of the way, and tomorrow I'll take you to Dick's. That way we'll have the whole day—"

"You will not," Rita said firmly. "That whole day with Dick sounds good, and it *is* late to go there now, but I'm going along to see the mysterious 'perfessor.' I want to know, just as much as you do, whether he killed those local people."

"But you know perfectly well," I protested, "that that's silly. Local superstition, coupled with a bit of local awe for an eccentric scientist who used to write books on psychiatry and occultism—"

"Did he really, Sandy? Write about occultism, I mean?"

"Sure. That's why he got kicked out of his chair at the university. He hasn't written any more, and nobody seems to know what he's doing since he holed up here. But, naturally, the people up here would attribute any mysterious things that might happen—"

"You really think it's just local superstition?"

"Of course," I said. "What else?"

She grinned at me impishly. "Then there isn't any reason why I shouldn't go with you to see him, if I want to."

Well, I'd walked right into that one. I hadn't even seen the trap she'd been setting. I grunted an ungracious answer and slid the car in gear again.

As we drove on into the gathering dusk, the road got worse. When it wound into the forest, a few miles further on, it was nothing but a pair of deep ruts leading through a narrow clearing. Meeting another car would have meant backing at least a mile for one of us. But we didn't meet another car. We'd come ten miles and hadn't seen a soul since the man we'd talked to just outside the town.

For a while I thought the road was going to peter out to nothing, but it didn't, quite. I'd turned on my headlights when we entered the deeper dusk of the forest. Suddenly, in their beam—

"Stop!" Rita cried breathlessly. "Sandy, it's beautiful. But—"

I saw what she meant by the qualifying "but." Ahead of us crouched a mountain lion. Uncaged and free, it can be a beautiful animal—at a safe distance. They don't attack human beings without provocation—few animals do, for that matter—but if you're unarmed you'd rather have a rear view of a mountain lion than a front view.

For a moment, I thought the snarling furry fury ahead of us was blinded by our headlights, and would jump aside the moment I turned them off. I stepped on the brake and pushed the light switch, and we rolled to a stop ten feet from it. With the car stopped, we could clearly hear its snarl; there was just enough light for us to make out the outline of it and catch the gleam of its eyes.

"It isn't going to move," said Rita. "Drive around—no, you can't. Toot the horn, Sandy. Scare it away. Don't run over it."

I wouldn't have, of course. If my rifle had not been knocked down and packed at the bottom of the rear trunk, I'd have asked nothing better than a shot at this range. I think I'd have put a hole through my own windshield, if necessary, to do it. But a hunter, even an amateur like myself, doesn't care to do his hunting with a V-8.

I tooted the horn. The lion moved a little then, from the center of the roadway to one of the deep ruts in which I had to keep my wheels in order to clear the trees on either side. When it moved, I saw that it was hobbling on three legs.

"Sandy, it's crippled," Rita said. "One back leg— Can't you scare it away, with a club or something?"

"I can not," I told her. "A mountain lion on three legs can still move faster than I can on two. And in these woods and without a gun—no thanks. I'll edge the car up closer. Maybe—"

I put the car in low, and gunned it forward a couple of yards. The cat didn't budge. I could just see it now, over my left fender.

"Back up until you're out of sight of it," Rita suggested. "Maybe it's too scared to move. When you're out of sight, it'll get off the road."

I didn't have any better idea myself, so I put it in reverse and started back.

Before I'd moved a foot back, Rita gave a little scream, and I darned near let out a yip myself. For the lion had jumped at our radiator, and was snarling right in our faces. For a nervous fraction of a second, I forgot that

good strong windshield glass was between us. Then the lion wasn't there
any more; there was a heavy thud on the top of the car above our heads.

"Sandy! Is the top—"

"Sure," I told her. "All-steel body." I shoved the gear-shift back into low
and let in the clutch. "Well, that's that. He'll jump off or jump onto a tree
when we get going."

"But at that speed, won't he hurt himself, Sandy?"

I snorted. "At ten miles an hour? And anyway, what do you want me to
do, get out and lift him off, or wait here till morning?"

We'd picked up speed now, as much as we could along that road. Rita
said, "I wish—" and then stopped. We couldn't hear any sound from
overhead; probably the lion was still there.

I wished we'd never met that lion, and not, mainly, because of what it
might do to the top of my car and the scratches in the paint on my
radiator.

That lion wasn't acting right. It wasn't behaving the way a mountain
lion is supposed to. I couldn't put my finger on my reason for worrying
about it, but I felt it, just the same.

We hit a straight stretch then that was just a bit better than the road
we'd been covering. I stepped her up to possibly twelve or fifteen miles—
and then it happened.

There was a thud and a scratch of claws on my radiator. We had a momentary glimpse of fur. Then the car lurched, even as I reached for the brake, and there was another bump as the back wheel went over, too, before the car stopped.

Rita gave a little gasp, but didn't say anything. I raised up off the seat to look out the back window, and I could see the lion lying there. It looked dead. It certainly should be dead, but I'm a soft-hearted cuss.

I opened the door on my side and said, "Stay in here. I'll be sure." I closed the door and walked around to the rear trunk. I got out my rifle, put it together and loaded it. Then I walked back for a look at the lion.

It was dead, all right, and not particularly pleasant to see. I don't know just why, but I bent down and turned my flashlight on its hind legs. There was a bullet hole through the left one, just below the middle joint.

I walked back to the car. I left the rifle loaded, though I had the safety on, and I put it in the back seat where I could reach it without getting out of the car.

"Sandy, wasn't that queer? Almost like—like it deliberately *made* you kill it. First it wouldn't get out of your way, and then—"

"Nuts," I said. "Animals don't commit suicide. It was scared and got confused, that's all. It'd been wounded."

She said, "Oh," and sounded satisfied.

"Listen," I said, "it's pretty dark, and it's getting kind of late for a call. Hadn't we better go back to town? I'll look up Allers in the morning?"

"Well—but you can't turn around here anyway. According to the instructions we got, it can't be more than a few miles on. Go on till we get there. If his light's out, we'll know he's turned in."

That sounded sensible, and I drove on. I told myself I was being very silly to keep on thinking about that lion. But I hadn't liked the way he acted. . . .

Then we were out in the open—a sudden transition to sandy dune country, and ahead of us was a light. As we drove closer, it resolved itself into a lantern that bobbed down to the edge of the road to meet us. It was held by a stocky man in a plaid mackinaw; in his other hand he carried a single-barreled shotgun. Two dogs—huge mastiffs—walked beside him.

The road turned, and my headlights briefly illuminated the darkened house, a hundred feet back, from which he had started his walk to the road. He must have heard our engine when we were still back out of sight, and started then.

I stopped the car, but, instead of getting out, I rolled a window part way down. I said, "Is this where Professor Allers lives? Or are you Professor Allers?"

The mastiffs were sniffing at the car. The man said, "Back!" to them before he answered my question. They returned to heel, growling. "It is," he said, "But I ain't."

"Is the professor here? I want to see him on a business matter. Of course, if he's turned in for the night, I'll come back tomorrow. I—"

"He's asleep, all right, mister. But it won't do you any good to come back t'morrow. He don't see no one."

I said, "But it's purely business. If you'll tell him I represent the Burkwald Company, I'm sure he'll see me."

"I'll tell him, t'morrow. You'll waste your time driving out. He don't see no one. Back, Donner!" The latter remark was directed at the larger of the dogs, which had again started for the car.

"I'll be back tomorrow," I told him. I rolled up the window again, and started the engine. He stood there without speaking, but apparently not intending to return to the house until I'd driven away.

It hadn't been an enthusiastic reception, but probably Allers, when he learned whom I represented, would see me all right. Not that it mattered a lot; if he really refused to see me, then that was that, as far as I was concerned. The matter wasn't of sufficient importance to try to force an interview. A few hundred dollars worth of business a year isn't a major issue to a company the size of Burkwald Scientific.

There was room to turn here. I twisted the wheel as I let the clutch in, but Rita said, "Wait, Sandy," and put her hand on my arm.

"Listen," she said, "we're only five miles from Dick's place. Perhaps we ought to let him know we're here. If he doesn't know, suppose he should go into the woods on a hunting or fishing trip tomorrow, leaving before we got there?"

It was a possibility. Dick Willis wasn't much of a hunter or fisherman, but his letters had mentioned occasional all-day trips through the woods. It might be just our luck that he'd be gone on one when we drove out in the morning.

Besides, it was only nine o'clock or so, and Dick might want to come into town with us and visit a couple of hours before we took rooms for the night. Even if he'd turned in early, I knew he wouldn't mind being awakened on an occasion like this.

I said, "Good idea, Rita," and drove straight on, instead of turning. If the road became no worse, it wouldn't take up more than twenty minutes to make that extra five miles.

A new moon rode above the horizon and, except for the stretches that tunnelled through the forest, it was bright enough for us to see without headlights.

We saw the place a few hundred yards ahead of us as we came around a low hill. It was a huge, ramshackle frame building, looking quite lost there all by itself in that desolate country. There was a light, at a gabled window on the third floor, and a man's head and shoulders silhouetted against the light.

"That's Dick!" said Rita, a bit tremulously. "Won't he be surprised when he finds out who his callers are!"

"Doubt if he gets many callers way out here," I said. "Even strangers ought to be a novelty. Golly, with a house that size he sure has room enough to write! A different chapter in each room."

We were closer now, and from Rita's side of the car I didn't think she could see that lighted window any longer. I could—and I saw something that puzzled me. The man in the window was Dick, all right; I recognized him, although I knew he couldn't recognize me in the car. But there was heavy chicken netting nailed across that window; two thicknesses of it.

Dick had a rifle in his hand. It was pointed our way, right at the car, so it hadn't been noticeable in silhouette. He wasn't sighting along the barrel; he was simply holding it ready.

We swung into the yard. I cut the ignition and brought the car to a stop. I said, "I'll be damned. Oh, pardon—"

She said, "Never mind. So will I, Sandy. What on earth?"

I said, "It's a moose."

Yes, there was a moose in the yard—a dead moose. But it was the manner of its death that was strange. Dick's automobile—or what was left of it—stood there in the drive, facing us.

The moose—a huge one—lay dead, with broken antlers and a broken neck, directly in front of the battered radiator of Dick's car. Apparently it had charged full tilt, at express train speed, directly into the front of the stationary car. The impact had stove in the radiator completely, had even shattered the windshield; and the wheels looked as though the front axle had been bent. Possibly that part was my imagination; it seemed difficult to believe that even the full charge of a moose could have done so much. But the car was as definitely ruined as though it had run into a telephone pole at, say, twenty miles an hour.

"It must have been loco!" I muttered.

I wasn't watching Rita, and before I could have stopped her anyway, she was out of the car. She called up to the lighted window.

"Dick! It's Sandy and I!"

I got out after her, taking my .30-30 with me.

I couldn't see the expression on Dick's face because the light was behind him. But his voice was hoarse. He called down, "Rita! Sandy! Get back in that car quickly. Go back to town! You're in danger standing there ... in terrible danger!"

He still held that gun ready, but not pointed directly at us. He held it, with the muzzle against the mesh of the wire, as though to guard us from whatever mysterious danger he thought might threaten us.

If I hadn't known Dick as well as I did, I'd have taken him less seriously. After all, I was armed, and what danger could threaten us in the open in a Maine farmyard?

But I said to Rita, "Get back in the car!" I spoke sharply, and so authoritatively that she actually took a step to obey. Then she looked up at Dick again and called, "Dick, what is wrong? What's the danger?"

"Rita, *please!* Believe me! I can't explain; it would take a long time, and I don't know what danger you may be in right now. No, don't come in the house—that would be worse. Just believe me, and drive back, quick!

"Sandy! Force her into that car. Don't just stand there! Go back to town, please."

I took Rita's arm tightly. "Can't you see that whatever's wrong, you're making him frantic with worry for you just by standing there? Get in the car and shut the door, then we'll find out what's up. Be a good girl, for his sake!"

Reluctantly, she obeyed. "Just till you get him to tell us. I *won't* go back if he's in danger, unless he comes with us!"

When I'd closed the car, I looked up again. "Look, Dick," I called. "I've got my .30-30 and it's ready to shoot if anybody attacks me. Now what's this all about? We're *not* moving until we know what's what."

"It's too hard to explain, Sandy. Listen—oh, let's say that somebody's trying to kill me because of something I happen to know, see? And as long as you and Rita stay here, you're in danger too. You'd better take her back to town."

"If she'll go, I'll have her drive back herself. But I've got a gun too. I'll come in there and help you against—whatever it is. Or, still better, why not let us drive you in?"

"Because, Sandy, you'd never make it if I were with you. Look at this car—ready for the scrap heap now. Yet, I was just starting the motor when that happened. And that's just what would happen to yours, if I was in it. It may anyway; I don't know whether he'd let you through or not, now you've been here. That's why you can't send Rita back alone, see?"

I did see, and I didn't. I said, "Who is this mysterious 'he'? Ormond Allers? I thought there was something darned funny about—" Then I kept quiet, remembering the things I'd heard back in St. Agatha.

"I'll take a chance, Dick. Allers is responsible for those three mysterious deaths and either you found out, or found proof that he was, and—"

"For God's sake, Sandy, shut up! *No,* that's not it! Oh—hell, that's torn it. You might as well come in now, both of you. You'd never get back alive. Listen, I'll come down and let you in. Till I get there, keep watching out."

"What shall I watch for?"

"Heaven only knows, Sandy. But *shoot anything that moves!*"

His head and shoulders disappeared from the window, and I heard doors opening, footsteps running down stairs. Then the door at the side of the house opened and Dick stood there, a flashlight in one hand and a rifle in the other.

He said, "Come on, quick."

Rita, of course, had been listening to everything we'd said. She was out of the car already, and running toward him. He caught her in his arm and pressed her body to his, but he didn't kiss her.

He slammed the door and bolted it, then led the way to the second floor and along a hallway toward where a steep little flight of steps, almost like a ladder, led to a trap door in the hall ceiling.

The trap door was open and light from a kerosene lamp shone down through it; I knew that this was the third-story room with the window where he'd kept his vigil.

"Keep watching behind, Sandy," he warned me. "You're the rear guard."

I mounted the stairs backwards, rifle at ready—to shoot at I knew not what. Then we bolted the trap door.

I strode across to the window and looked out. Behind me, I heard Dick exclaim, "Rita! Good Lord, kid, what a welcome you found here. I'm sorry—"

And Rita's voice, a bit smothered. "Oh, Dick—I'm *glad* we came. Now tell us."

He took a deep breath and said, "Okay."

"Listen," I said, "just one thing before you tell us what it's all about. Isn't it darned dangerous for us to be standing here at a window—even with wire in front of us? With that light behind us, we're perfect targets."

Dick shook his head. "He won't shoot. Bullets leave marks; there are inquests and investigations. We're slated to be killed some way that will look accidental, or natural. See?"

"Not exactly."

"All right," said Dick. "When I first came up here a couple of months ago, Allers seemed friendly enough—to me, anyway, if not to the natives. I was over there several times, and he was here once or twice. He talked about his experiments. He talked well, too, but what he was trying to do sounded incredible. I didn't tell him so, but I thought he was just a little— just a little off his rocker."

"In which of his fields—psychology or occultism was he chiefly interested in?"

"I'd say this covered both," said Dick. "He told me he was making unusual experiments in animal hypnosis, with some rather startling results. In fact, he claimed that he was able to go further than hypnosis, as we ordinarily understand it—that, with his own body in a state of auto hypnosis, he was able to obtain complete control of an animal mentality."

I whistled softly. "Do you mean—that moose? The lion?"

"What lion?" Dick demanded quickly, and I explained.

He nodded. "It tried to break into the house here, about two hours ago. I shot, and lamed it. The lion was then useless to Allers and he wanted out."

"Rita was standing so close to me that her shoulder touched my arm, and I felt her shudder. "Wanted out?" she asked.

"Just that," Dick told us quietly. "That was one thing he discovered about this 'control,' as I guess you'd call it; the animal had to die in order for him to—to relinquish control, to—it sounds absurd to say it—to return to his own body. Or to enter another animal."

There in that room lighted by a kerosene lamp, looking out over a wild moonlit landscape, it didn't sound as mad as it might have elsewhere.

"Did you ever see any of his experiments, Dick?"

"No, I didn't. I listened when he talked about them, but I didn't quite believe him. Oh, I didn't show my skepticism, but it sounded too fantastic. That a man, asleep or hypnotized or drugged—yes, he took some sort of a drug, and was secretive about what it was—could project his own personality into an animal—"

"Were the animals he took over necessarily right in the room with him when the experiment started?"

"Oh, yes, at first. Then he said, he found he was able to go farther. He could concentrate on a certain type of animal, and find himself in—in control of one somewhere nearby. And then, to get 'back' he'd have to kill the animal—make it commit suicide, in a way. He, himself, didn't feel any pain, so he said it was always easy to get it killed somehow."

"And now you believe he is—in some animal form which he has under control—trying to kill you, Dick?" There was sheer horror in Rita's voice.

He nodded somberly. "And the worst thing—the thing that makes it hard to fight—is that killing any of those animals accomplishes nothing. It only frees him for another attempt."

"But the men who died? What about them, Dick?"

He took a deep breath before he answered. "He talked about his experiments, up to a month ago. Then he became secretive; I didn't guess why. Matter of fact, I hadn't really believed him and was so busy working on my book that I didn't think about it until yesterday. Then I ran out of tobacco, and walked over to his place to borrow some.

"He wasn't there. He and that fellow who works for him had gone away somewhere. Even the dogs were gone. Well—to make it short, I took the liberty of borrowing a few ounces of tobacco.

"I looked in the drawer where he kept it and I found the notebook in which he'd been recording his experiments. I had no business doing it, of course, but I did. And that's how I learned about those men."

"You mean he—he murdered them, Dick?"

"I mean just that. Oh, not deliberate murder in the ordinary sense. He didn't try to kill them. He regarded the experiments as failures; yes, he had tried to carry his experiments over from animals to men, and he'd failed. The human psyche, he wrote, is more delicate than that of the lower animals. There wasn't—you might call it room—room for him to take control in that way. In each case he chose someone sleeping—yes, that's true of animals, too; he has to catch them asleep—but the shock killed them."

I remembered how the Yankee I'd talked to back at St. Agatha had put it: "They screamed, and they died."

Somehow, there and then, I wasn't feeling skeptical. Back home in New York, I'd have howled with derision at an idea like that. But now I merely asked, "What did you do?"

"It was evidence of murder, Sandy. It was my duty to turn it over to the authorities. I took out three pages that contained the incriminating entries."

"Why not the whole book?" Rita wanted to know.

A big bird of some sort was circling high overhead. Dick gripped his gun more tightly as he answered.

"You see I was afoot; I had to come back here to get my car. And I thought if Allers got back before I was safely past his place on the way to town, he'd miss the book right away. He wouldn't miss the pages unless he happened to open the book. But apparently that's what happened. I hot-footed it back here and got in my car ready to start, and—"

"The moose?"

Without taking his eyes off the circling bird, he said, "Yes. Then like a fool I started out afoot. There's another dead lion out in that field."

"But surely, Dick, with two rifles, and the car, we—"

"Oh, he'll stop the car all right. A moose or a deer is the most dangerous, and it's easier for him to get them at night. But even so—see how this window was smashed before I put up the wire?"

I nodded. "I've been meaning to ask how—"

"A gull. This isn't far from the coast here. Flew right through the glass. Broke its neck, of course, but—"

I shuddered. The thought of an owl or gull power-diving into the windshield of the V-8 was not pleasant.

I said, "Sit down, Dick, take a rest. I'll watch here. But what if we don't go out at all? What if we merely stand seige here?"

He turned away from the window and I saw again the fatigue lines in his face and his strained and bloodshot eyes.

"Sooner or later," he said, "one of us will sleep. And then ... Remember those men? He can't touch us personally while we're awake." He looked at Rita again. "Lord, kid, I wish you hadn't walked into this."

She said, "You'd better rest, Dick. I'll—I'll talk to you to keep you awake."

I listened to Dick and Rita talking behind me, and occasionally chipped in a remark or two of my own. And the odd thing is that we talked about New York, about our college days, about people we knew, about everything and anything except what was happening to us tonight.

Once I heard Rita say, "Dick!" sharply. I turned my head and saw that she was shaking him by the shoulders. He'd almost dropped off to sleep.

He opened his eyes and there was a scared look in them that I hadn't seen there before. He said, "Thanks, Rita. I—I'd better not sit down any more."

He got up and began to pace slowly back and forth across the room— three steps each way like a caged animal. Rita walked with him for a while, then she sat down and simply watched him.

I said, "Take the window for a while, Dick. I'm going down to forage for some coffee. I guess I can boil some water over that lamp."

He said, "Fine, but be careful, going down. Maybe I'd better go down with you. There may be—" He broke off. We looked at one another and I knew we were thinking the same thing.

It had been too quiet, too peaceful, for an hour now. Could it be that something was being prepared for me? That something was already lying in wait?

I asked, "Are all the windows tight down below, Dick? Could something—?"

"How about snakes?" Rita asked. "Can he—"

Dick answered her question first. "I don't think so. There was a mention of his trying in his notes. A reptilian mind is something so different; I believe he failed. About the windows, Sandy—I'm afraid they're not so good. A couple of the cellar windows were broken, and another was loose on its hinges."

I'd crossed to the bolted trap door which, with the window, was one of the only two openings of our stronghold. There was, I noticed, a large knothole, almost two inches in diameter, in the center of the door.

"I'll see if I can hear anything," I told them, and put my finger to my lips for silence, then bent down and put my ear to the knothole.

At first there was nothing—only dead silence. Then I began to hear what seemed to be a faint scraping sound.

I cupped my hands around the knothole to shut off all light from my side of it, and put my eye down.

At first, I saw nothing but darkness. Then—something small and white. I couldn't see what it was. But it was at the foot of the ladder-like steps that led up to the trap door. It moved—I was sure that it moved!

I stood up quietly and reached for my gun. "There's something down there," I whispered. "Maybe I can shoot it from here. Rita, turn off that lamp for a moment. But be ready to light it again."

I put the muzzle of my rifle through the knothole, and then there was sudden darkness. But when my eyes became accustomed to the dimness, I saw the sights in the faint moonlight.

I could see the deeper black of the knothole in the trap door. I moved my head, and my rifle with it, until I thought I could see something white, or gray, through that hole. Then I pulled the trigger.

The crash of the rifle was deafening in that little room. I said to Rita, "Okay, the lamp!" and I heard the scratch of her match. Something clicked in my mind then, and I knew what that faint sound from below had been. It had been the scratch of a match across wood!

The light grew brighter and steadied as the flame touched the wick of the lamp and I heard the click as the chimney went back into place. I threw the bolt of the trap door, and Dick stood ready.

I shot the beam of my flashlight down the steep stairway, and for a moment I almost laughed at myself. A white rabbit lay motionless at the foot of those stairs. Then I heard Dick suck in his breath.

We'd been right in thinking that something horrible had been getting ready for us, but we hadn't thought of fire . . . .

A little pile of waste paper and shavings had been gathered there by the bottom step. It hadn't been there when we came up; I was practically certain of that. And right by the head of the motionless white rabbit lay several ordinary kitchen matches. When I ran down the steps and picked them up, I noticed that they were moist in the middle, as though they'd been held in the mouth of a small animal.

Dick was right at my heels coming down those steps.

"Fire!" he said. "My God, I never thought of that! And this old house would go like tinder, Sandy. We'll have to patrol the whole house if he's thought of that. Lord, I thought we were safe up there on the top floor!"

There was sheer horror in his eyes, and I knew he was thinking not of himself but of Rita.

I looked down at that quite-normal-looking white rabbit, and the matches that I'd picked up, and a cold chill ran down my spine. Then I saw the rabbit move a bit; a hind paw jerked convulsively.

"Dick," I said, "it's still alive! Say—"

He bent down to look at it closely. "You creased it," he said. "There's a streak of fur off just back of the ear. I'll finish it all right." He stood up and aimed his rifle, and I heard the snick as he threw off the safety.

I shouted "Don't!" and managed to knock the barrel of his gun aside just as it roared.

"Dick," I yelled. "Don't you see what it means? As long as that rabbit stays alive, we're *safe!*"

I reached down and picked it up with both hands and started up the steps, telling Dick to bring my gun. The rabbit suddenly came back to consciousness then, with a convulsive attempt to leap out of my hands that nearly threw me off balance and backwards down the steps.

I said, "Oh, no you don't!" and held it tighter. I made the top of the steps with it, and saw Rita's eyes wide with horror as she backed away from me. Dick followed, and slammed the trap door.

The rabbit writhed in my hands, twisted its neck in an insane frenzy to bite my hands. Its eyes were red lights of malignancy. It was stronger than one would believe possible, so strong that it took all the strength I had to hold it.

I said, "Throw something over its head, Dick. It's going to—" But I spoke too late.

It leaped directly for the window first, struck the wire and fell back. It rolled and I grabbed for it, but it was on its feet again in a flash and had taken its next leap in another direction. "The lamp!"

But Rita had been quicker than I. She had seen that the white rabbit was going to leap directly into the kerosene lamp, and she grabbed the lamp and held it high over her head. We seemed to have him cornered then. He bared his teeth and his eyes . . . But even now I don't want to think about them.

He got away, through Dick's hands and between his legs. He bounded across the room and raced head-on into the wall. His head hit it with a thud. Dick sighed and said, "Well, that's done it—"

But I ran across to the rabbit, and still it wasn't dead.

I took off my coat and wrapped it quickly about the animal, as tightly as a straitjacket. Only its nose stuck out.

I said, "Well, if it lives . . ." And it was living, even through the coat I could feel the faint beat of its heart. I said, "Listen, now we can take my car and go out of here. We're safe so long as we keep the rabbit alive. Aren't we?"

Dick nodded. He leaned back against the wall and I believe he would have collapsed if Rita hadn't supported him. But he said, "Come on, let's—"

"No!" The protest was Rita's, and it was as vehement as it was unexpected. "Dick needs sleep; he can't travel this way. And you say you're sure we're safe as long as it lives. Look, Dick's out on his feet right now. Let him catch a few hours sleep—"

"But what if the damned thing dies?" Dick asked weakly. "It's had two good hard wallops, and—"

"And what if we leave here and it dies?" Rita demanded. "We'd be caught out there, and isn't that worse even than taking our chances later—with Dick rested and ready?"

It made sense all right, once we granted the original premise that the professor had told Dick the truth about his experiments and their limitations.

I said, "Okay. Must be near dawn now anyway. We've been here—"

Rita looked at her wrist watch. "It's not midnight yet," she said. "We've been here an hour and a half."

I whistled. An hour and a half—and Dick had been through two days of this, alone, without sleep, and without help! No wonder he looked the way he did.

I said, "Rita's right, Dick. I'll watch this—this thing in my coat, and if it dies we'll wake you quick."

It was the strangest night I ever spent. Rita sat on the floor, leaning back against the wall, and Dick went to sleep with his head in her lap. After a while she too dozed.

At about one o'clock, the rabbit began to act up again. But this time, confined as he was in that tightly wrapped coat I was able to manage him. There was something fearful about those convulsive struggles inside that coat; something diabolic in their very silence.

That rabbit was trying to die. Time and again I had to struggle with him to keep his nostrils clear of the coat so he would not smother, and at the same time avoid being bitten.

Two hours of it was all I could stand. At three o'clock there was a faint trace of dawn in the sky outside. I roused Rita and Dick.

The three of us, I still carrying the white rabbit, went out into the still grayness and got into my car. Dick drove, Rita sitting beside him in front. We took both rifles.

We talked but briefly, and our campaign was simple. We were going to take Ormond Allers—asleep or awake—into town with us. And the complete notebook as well as the especially incriminating pages Dick had torn from it.

The first rim of the sun was pushing up over the horizon when we stopped the car in front of Allers' lodge. We didn't know whether or not Allers' man would make trouble when he saw there were two of us, but we made Rita lie down out of sight on the floor of the car.

The two dogs were inside; they'd heard the car coming and were giving tongue so loudly we could hear them clear down at the road. Dick tooted the horn.

After a moment he opened the door. The dogs came out first, bounding down to the car, growling ferociously. Then the man in the mackinaw—

he must have been sleeping fully dressed—came out after them, the shotgun under his arm. He too started down toward the car.

"We've got to see Professor Allers right away," I called to him. "Important."

"Important, hell! He isn't seeing anybody. His own orders. Move on, before I—"

I touched Dick's shoulder and simultaneously the muzzles of our rifles came into sight, aimed at him.

"Drop that shotgun," I ordered. He hesitated only a moment before he threw it down. It was, as I'd noticed the night before, a single shot and with two of us having the drop on him he couldn't have got both of us.

"Now tie up those dogs if you don't want them shot," I told him. When they were tied to a tree clear of the path that led back to the lodge, we got out of the car.

With the white rabbit under one arm and my rifle under the other, I started up the path. Dick picked up the shotgun and handed it to Rita.

"Go in ahead of us," Dick ordered. "Take us to Allers' room."

That was when it happened.

There was a wild convulsive movement under my arm. I lost my grip and the coat dropped to the ground with a thud. I dropped my rifle and grabbed at it with both hands, but I was too late.

The white rabbit rolled once and was clear of the coat. He was off like a streak. He ran straight for the two mastiffs, leaped straight at the larger of them.

The mastiff's jaws snapped once.

In the instant of silence that followed, we all heard clearly the noise from the house—a single high-pitched scream. We ran in. Dick was the first to reach the room from which the scream had come.

I stopped Rita in the main living room of the lodge, and in a minute Dick reappeared. "Allers," he said, "is dead. I should have thought of that possibility—"

"What? What killed him?"

"Being out too long. I remember now reading that in his notes. For him to be 'away' for more than half an hour at a time was dangerous. He'd decided an hour was maximum; once he'd held control that long and had had difficulty getting back control of his own body. What happened to him was something similar to what happened to the three men he killed—only it worked the other way."

He took a deep breath and then crossed over to a desk at one side of the room, and took a notebook from a drawer. He took some folded pieces of paper from his own pocket, then walked across to where a fire smouldered in the huge fireplace.

I said, "Dick, don't! Listen, those notes—"

"I'm going to burn them, Sandy," he said. "This—it's something a bit too near diabolic for comfort. Knowledge like that in the wrong hands. . . .!"

Rita took my arm and said, "He's right, Sandy. And it isn't needed for evidence, now that Allers is dead. . . ."

Dick took a rest from his writing and three days later, with Rita on the train back for New York, he and I were driving through bright Maine sunshine, headed for the woods farther north.

Things are different in sunshine.

"Dick, old egg," I said, "I've been thinking it over. Maybe we're a couple of superstitious old women. Those deaths could have been natural; they *were* diagnosed as heart failure. Or maybe Allers' notes were a blind for what he was really doing—something he wrote down because he knew it wouldn't be believed. Possibly he was dabbling in some strange drug or poison, and tried it out on a few of the local boys. That would account for the similarity in the manners of their deaths and his, and—"

"How about the animals?"

"That's even easier. There's a drug called arrytol—one of the sulfanilimide derivatives. Injected into an animal's bloodstream, it would cause exaggerated ferocity, and an impulse toward self-destruction. Possibly he'd been experimenting with—"

I caught a side glimpse of Dick's face, and he was grinning.

"Sandy," he said, "do you ever plan to get married and settle down, with a nice little home of your own in the suburbs?"

"Huh?" I said, a bit startled at the sudden transition. "Maybe. Matter of fact I met a girl a few months ago who. . . . Buy why?"

"Let me know when," he said. "I want to send you a present."

"Sure, but—"

"A cute white rabbit, Sandy. To keep for a pet."

I knew he was kidding me, of course, but just the thought of it made me shudder.

I drove on, and shut up.

Fritz Leiber

YESTERDAY HOUSE

THE NARROW COVE was quiet as the face of an expectant child, yet so near the ruffled Atlantic that the last push of wind carried the *Annie O.* its full length. The man in gray flannels and sweatshirt let the sail come crumpling down and hurried past its white folds at a gait made comically awkward by his cramped muscles. Slowly the rocky ledge came nearer. Slowly the blue *V* inscribed on the cove's surface by the sloop's prow died. Sloop and ledge kissed so gently that he hardly had to reach out his hand.

He scrambled ashore, dipping a sneaker in the icy water, and threw the line around a boulder. Unkinking himself, he looked back through the cove's high and rocky mouth at the gray-green scattering of islands and the faint dark line that was the coast of Maine. He almost laughed in satisfaction at having disregarded vague warnings and done the thing every man yearns to do once in his lifetime—gone to the farthest island out.

He must have looked longer than he realized, because by the time he dropped his gaze the cove was again as glassy as if the *Annie O.* had always been there. And the splotches made by his sneaker on the rock had faded in the hot sun. There was something very unusual about the quietness of this place. As if time, elsewhere hurrying frantically, paused here to rest. As if all changes were erased on this one bit of earth.

The man's lean, melancholy face crinkled into a grin at the banal fancy. He turned his back on his new friend, the little green sloop, without one thought for his nets and specimen bottles, and set out to explore. The ground rose steeply at first and the oaks were close, but after a little way things went downhill and the leaves thinned and he came out on more rocks—and realized that he hadn't quite gone to the farthest one out.

Joined to this island by a rocky spine, which at the present low tide would have been dry but for the spray, was another green, high island that the first had masked from him all the while he had been sailing. He felt a thrill of discovery, just as he'd wondered back in the woods whether his might not be the first human feet to kick through the underbrush. After all, there were thousands of these islands.

Then he was dropping down the rocks, his lanky limbs now moving smoothly enough.

To the landward side of the spine, the water was fairly still. It even began with another deep cove, in which he glimpsed the spiny spheres of sea urchins. But from seaward the waves chopped in, sprinkling his trousers to the knees and making him wince pleasurably at the thought of what vast wings of spray and towers of solid water must crash up from here in a storm.

He crossed the rocks at a trot, ran up a short grassy slope, raced through a fringe of trees—and came straight up against an eight-foot fence of heavy mesh topped with barbed wire and backed at a short distance with high, heavy shrubbery.

Without pausing for surprise—in fact, in his holiday mood, using surprise as a goad—he jumped for the branch of an oak whose trunk touched the fence, scorning the easier lower branch on the other side of the tree.

Then he drew himself up, worked his way to some higher branches that crossed the fence, and dropped down inside.

Suddenly cautious, he gently parted the shrubbery and, before the first surprise could really sink in, had another.

A closely mown lawn dotted with more shrubbery ran up to a snug white Cape Cod cottage. The single strand of a radio aerial stretched the length of the roof. Parked on a neat gravel driveway that crossed just in front of the cottage was a short, square-lined touring car that he recognized from remembered pictures as an ancient Essex. The whole scene had about it the same odd quietness as the cove.

Then, with the air of a clockwork toy coming to life, the white door opened and an elderly woman came out, dressed in a long, lace-edged dress and wide, lacy hat. She climbed into the driver's seat of the Essex, sitting there very stiff and tall. The motor began to chug bravely, gravel skittered, and the car rolled off between the trees.

The door of the house opened again and a slim girl emerged. She wore a white silk dress that fell straight from a square neckline to hip-height waistline, making the skirt seem very short. Her dark hair was bound with a white bandeau so that it curved close to her cheeks. A dark necklace dangled against the white of the dress. A newspaper was tucked under her arm.

She crossed the driveway and tossed the paper down on a rattan table between three rattan chairs and stood watching a squirrel zigzag across the lawn.

The man stepped through the wall of shrubbery, called, "Hello!" and walked toward her.

She whirled around and stared at him as still as if her heart had stopped beating. Then she darted behind the table and waited for him there.

Granting the surprise of his appearance, her alarm seemed not so much excessive as eerie. As if, the man thought, he were not an ordinary stranger, but a visitor from another planet.

Approaching closer, he saw that she was trembling and that her breath was coming in rapid, irregular gasps. Yet the slim, sweet, patrician face that stared into his had an underlying expression of expectancy that reminded him of the cove. She couldn't have been more than eighteen.

He stopped short of the table. Before he could speak, she stammered out, "Are you he?"

"What do you mean?" he asked, smiling puzzledly.

"The one who sends me the little boxes."

"I was out sailing and I happened to land in the far cove. I didn't dream that anyone lived on this island, or even came here."

"No one ever does come here," she replied. Her manner had changed, becoming at once more wary and less agitated, though still eerily curious.

"It startled me tremendously to find this place," he blundered on. "Especially the road and the car. Why, this island can't be more than a quarter of a mile wide."

"The road goes down to the wharf," she explained, "and up to the top of the island, where my aunts have a treehouse."

He tore his mind away from the picture of a woman dressed like Queen Mary clambering up a tree. "Was that your aunt I saw driving off?"

"One of them. The other's taken the motorboat in for supplies." She looked at him doubtfully. "I'm not sure they'll like it if they find someone here."

"There are just the three of you?" he cut in quickly, looking down the empty road that vanished among the oaks.

She nodded.

"I suppose you go in to the mainland with your aunts quite often?"

She shook her head.

"It must get pretty dull for you."

"Not very," she said, smiling. "My aunts bring me the papers and other things. Even movies. We've got a projector. My favorite stars are Antonio Morino and Alice Terry. I like her better even than Clara Bow."

He looked at her hard for a moment. "I suppose you read a lot?"

She nodded. "Fitzgerald's my favorite author." She started around the table, hesitated, suddenly grew shy. "Would you like some lemonade?"

He'd noticed the dewed silver pitcher, but only now realized his thirst. Yet when she handed him a glass, he held it untasted and said awkwardly, "I haven't introduced myself. I'm Jack Barr."

She stared at his outstretched right hand, slowly extended her own toward it, shook it up and down exactly once, then quickly dropped it.

He chuckled and gulped some lemonade. "I'm a biology student. Been working at Wood's Hole the first part of the summer. But now I'm here to do research in marine ecology—that's sort of sea-life patterns—of the inshore islands. Under the direction of Professor Kesserich. You know about him, of course?"

She shook her head.

"Probably the greatest living biologist," he was proud to inform her. "Human physiology as well. Tremendous geneticist. In a class with Carlson and Jacques Loeb. Martin Kesserich—he lives over there at town. I'm staying with him. You ought to have heard of him." He grinned. "Matter of fact, I'd never have met you if it hadn't been for Mrs. Kesserich."

The girl looked puzzled.

Jack explained, "The old boy's been off to Europe on some conferences, won't be back for a couple days more. But I was to get started anyhow. When I went out this morning Mrs. Kesserich—she's a drab sort of person—said to me, "Don't try to sail to the farther islands." So, of course, I had to. By the way, you still haven't told me your name."

"Mary Alice Pope," she said, speaking slowly and with an odd wonder, as if she were saying it for the first time.

"You're pretty shy, aren't you?"

"How would I know?"

The question stopped Jack. He couldn't think of anything to say to this strangely attractive girl dressed almost like a flapper.

"Will you sit down?" she asked him gravely.

The rattan chair sighed under his weight. He made another effort to talk. "I'll bet you'll be glad when summer's over."

"Why?"

"So you'll be able to go back to the mainland."

"But I never go to the mainland."

"You mean you stay out here all winter?" he asked incredulously, his mind filled with a vision of snow and frozen spray and great gray waves.

"Oh, yes. We get all of our supplies on hand before winter. My aunts are very capable. They don't always wear long lace dresses. And now I help them."

"But that's impossible!" he said with sudden sympathetic anger. "You can't be shut off this way from people your own age!"

"You're the first one I've met." She hesitated. "I never saw a boy or a man before, except in movies."

"You're joking!"

"No, it's true."

"But why are they doing it to you?" he demanded, leaning forward. "Why are they inflicting this loneliness on you, Mary?"

She seemed to have gained poise from his loss of it. "I don't know why. I'm to find out soon. But actually I'm not lonely. May I tell you a secret?"

She touched his hand, this time with only the faintest trembling. "Every night the loneliness gathers in around me—you're right about that. But then every morning new life comes to me in a little box."

"What's that?" he said sharply.

"Sometimes there's a poem in the box, sometimes a book, or pictures, or flowers, or a ring, but always a note. Next to the notes I like the poems best. My favorite is the one by Matthew Arnold that ends . . ."

> Ah, love, let us be true
> To one another! for the world, which seems
> To lie before us like a land of dreams,
> So various, so beautiful, so new,
> Hath really neither joy, nor love, nor light,
> Nor certitude—

"Wait a minute," he interrupted. "Who sends you these boxes?"

"I don't know."

"But how are the notes signed?"

"They're wonderful notes," she said. "So wise, so gay, so tender, you'd imagine them being written by John Barrymore or Lindbergh."

"Yes, but how are they signed?"

She hesitated. "Never anything but 'Your Lover.'"

"And so when you first saw me, you thought—" he began, then stopped because she was blushing.

"How long have you been getting them?"

"Ever since I can remember. I have two closets of the boxes. The new ones are either by my bed when I wake or at my place at breakfast."

"But how does this—person get these boxes to you out here? Does he give them to your aunts and do they put them there?"

"I'm not sure."

"But how can they get them in winter?"

"I don't know."

"Look here," he said, pouring himself more lemonade, "how long is it since you've been to the mainland?"

"Almost eighteen years. My aunts tell me I was born there in the middle of the war."

"What war?" he asked startledly, spilling some lemonade.

"The World War, of course. What's the matter?"

Jack Barr was staring down at the spilled lemonade and feeling a kind of terror he'd never experienced in his waking life. Nothing around him had changed. He could still feel the same hot sun on his shoulders, the same icy glass in his hand, scent the same lemon-acid odor in his nostrils. He could still hear the faint *chop-chop* of the waves.

And yet everything had changed, gone dark and dizzy as a landscape glimpsed just before a faint. All the little false notes had come to a sudden focus. For the lemonade had spilled on the headline of the newspaper the girl had tossed down, and the headline read:

HITLER IN NEW DEFIANCE

Under the big black banner of that head swam smaller ones:

FOES OF MACHADO RIOT IN HAVANA
BIG NRA PARADE PLANNED
BALBO SPEAKS IN NEW YORK

Suddenly he felt a surge of relief. He had noticed that the paper was yellow and brittle-edged.

"Why are you so interested in old newspapers?" he asked.

"I wouldn't call day-before-yesterday's paper old," the girl objected, pointing at the dateline: July 20, 1933.

"You're trying to joke," Jack told her.

"No, I'm not."

"But it's 1953."

"Now it's you who are joking."

"But the paper's yellow."

"The paper's always yellow."

He laughed uneasily. "Well, if you actually think it's 1933, perhaps you're to be envied," he said, with a sardonic humor he didn't quite feel. "Then you can't know anything about the Second World War, or television, or the V-2s, or bikini bathing suits, or the atomic bomb, or—"

"Stop!" She had sprung up and retreated around her chair, white-faced. "I don't like what you're saying."

"But—"

"No, please! Jokes that may be quite harmless on the mainland sound different here."

"I'm really not joking," he said after a moment.

She grew quite frantic at that. "I can show you all last week's papers! I can show you magazines and other things. I can prove it!"

She started toward the house. He followed. He felt his heart begin to pound.

At the white door she paused, looking worriedly down the road. Jack thought he could hear the faint *chug* of a motorboat. She pushed open the door and he followed her inside. The small-windowed room was dark after the sunlight. Jack got an impression of solid old furniture, a fireplace with brass andirons.

"Flash!" croaked a gritty voice."After their disastrous break day before yesterday, stocks are recovering. Leading issues . . ."

Jack realized that he had started and had involuntarily put his arm around the girl's shoulders. At the same time he noticed that the voice was coming from the curved brown trumpet of an old-fashioned radio loudspeaker.

The girl didn't pull away from him. He turned toward her. Although her gray eyes were on him, her attention had gone elsewhere.

"I can hear the car. They're coming back. They won't like it that you're here."

"All right, they won't like it."

Her agitation grew. "No, you must go."

"I'll come back tomorrow," he heard himself saying.

"Flash! It looks as if the World Economic Conference may soon adjourn, mouthing jeers at old Uncle Sam who is generally referred to as Uncle Shylock."

Jack felt a numbness on his neck. The room seemed to be darkening, the girl growing stranger still.

"You must go before they see you."

"Flash! Wiley Post has just completed his solo circuit of the globe, after a record-breaking flight of seven days, eighteen hours and forty-five minutes. Asked how he felt after the energy-draining feat, Post quipped . . ."

He was halfway across the lawn before he realized the terror into which the grating radio voice had thrown him.

He leaped for the branch overhanging the fence, vaulted up with the risky help of a foot on the barbed top. A surprised squirrel, lacking time to make its escape up the trunk, sprang to the ground ahead of him. With terrible suddenness, two steel-jawed semicircles clanked together just over the squirrel's head. Jack landed with one foot to either side of the sprung trap, while the squirrel darted off with a squeak.

Jack plunged down the slope to the rocky spine and ran across it, spray from the rising waves spattering him to the waist. Panting now, he stumbled up into the oaks and undergrowth of the first island, fought his way through it, finally reached the silent cove. He loosed the line of the *Annie O.*, dragged it as near to the cove's mouth as he could, plunged knee-deep in freezing water to give it a final shove, scrambled aboard, snatched up the boathook and punched at the rocks.

As soon as the *Annie O.* was nosing out of the cove into the cross waves, he yanked up the sail. The freshening wind filled it and sent the sloop heeling over, with inches of white water over the lee rail, and plunging ahead.

For a long while, Jack was satisfied to think of nothing but the wind and the waves and the sail and speed and danger, to have all his attention taken up balancing one against the other, so that he wouldn't have to ask himself what year it was and whether time was an illusion, and wonder about flappers and hidden traps.

When he finally looked back at the island, he was amazed to see how tiny it had grown, as distant as the mainland.

Then he saw a gray motorboat astern. He watched it as it slowly overtook him. It was built like a lifeboat, with a sturdy low cabin in the bow and wheel amidship. Whoever was at the wheel had long gray hair that whipped in the wind. The longer he looked, the surer he was that it was a woman wearing a lace dress. Something that stuck up inches over the cabin flashed darkly beside her. Only when she lifted it to the roof of the cabin did it occur to him that it might be a rifle.

But just then the motorboat swung around in a turn that sent waves drenching over it, and headed back toward the island. He watched it for a minute in wonder, then his attention was jolted by an angry hail.

Three fishing smacks, also headed toward town, were about to cross his bow. He came around into the wind and waited with shaking sail, watching a man in a lumpy sweater shake a fist at him. Then he turned and gratefully followed the dark, wide, fanlike sterns and age-yellowed sails.

II

The exterior of Martin Kesserich's home—a weathered white cube with narrow, sharp-paned windows, topped by a cupola—was nothing like its lavish interior.

In much the same way, Mrs. Kesserich clashed with the darkly gleaming furniture, Persian rugs and bronze vases around her. Her shapeless black form, poised awkwardly on the edge of a huge sofa, made Jack think of a cow that had strayed into the drawing room. He wondered again how a man like Kesserich had come to marry such a creature.

Yet when she lifted up her eyes from the shadows, he had the uneasy feeling that she knew a great deal about him. The eyes were still those of a domestic animal, but of a wise one that has been watching the house a long, long while from the barnyard.

He asked abruptly, "Do you know anything of a girl around here named Mary Alice Pope?"

The silence lasted so long that he began to think she'd gone into some bovine trance. Then, without a word, she got up and went over to a tall cabinet. Feeling on a ledge behind it for a key, she opened a panel, opened a cardboard box inside it, took something from the box and handed him a photograph. He held it up to the failing light and sucked his breath in with surprise.

It was a picture of the girl he'd met that afternoon. Same flat-bosomed dress—flowered rather than white—no bandeau, same beads. Same proud, demure expression, perhaps a bit happier.

"That is Mary Alice Pope," Mrs. Kesserich said in a strangely flat voice. "She was Martin's fiancée. She was killed in a railway accident in 1933."

The small sound of the cabinet door closing brought Jack back to reality. He realized that he no longer had the photograph. Against the gloom by the cabinet, Mrs. Kesserich's white face looked at him with what seemed a malicious eagerness.

"Sit down," she said, "and I'll tell you about it."

Without a thought as to why she hadn't asked him a single question—he was much too dazed for that—he obeyed. Mrs. Kesserich resumed her position on the edge of the sofa.

"You must understand, Mr. Barr, that Mary Alice Pope was the one love of Martin's life. He is a man of very deep and strong feelings, yet as you probably know, anything but kindly or demonstrative. Even when he first came here from Hungary with his older sisters Hani and Hilda, there was a cloak of loneliness about him—or rather about the three of them.

"Hani and Hilda were athletic outdoor women, yet fiercely proud—I don't imagine they ever spoke to anyone in America except as to a servant—and with a seething distaste for all men except Martin. They showered all their devotion on him. So of course, though Martin didn't realize it, they were consumed with jealousy when he fell in love with Mary Alice Pope. They'd thought that since he'd reached forty without marrying, he was safe.

"Mary Alice came from a purebred, or as a biologist would say, inbred British stock. She was very young, but very sweet, and up to a point very wise. She sensed Hani and Hilda's feelings right away and did everything she could to win them over. For instance, though she was afraid of horses, she took up horseback riding, because that was Hani and Hilda's favorite pastime. Naturally, Martin knew nothing of her fear, and naturally his sisters knew about it from the first. But—and here is where Mary's wisdom fell short—her brave gesture did not pacify them; it only increased their hatred.

"Except for his research, Martin was blind to everything but his love. It was a beautiful and yet frightening passion, an insane cherishing as narrow and intense as his sisters' hatred."

With a start, Jack remembered that it was Mrs. Kesserich telling him all this.

She went on. "Martin's love directed his every move. He was building a home for himself and Mary, and in his mind he was building a wonderful future for them as well—not vaguely, if you know Martin, but year by year, month by month. This winter, he'd plan, they would visit Buenos Aires, next summer they would sail down the inland passage and he would teach Mary Hungarian for their trip to Budapest the year after, where he would occupy a chair at the university for a few months ... and so on. Finally the time for their marriage drew near. Martin had been away. His research was keeping him very busy—"

Jack broke in with, "Wasn't that about the time he did his definitive work on growth and fertilization?"

Mrs. Kesserich nodded with solemn appreciation in the gathering darkness. "But now he was coming home, his work done. It was early evening, very chilly, but Hani and Hilda felt they had to ride down to the station to meet their brother. And although she dreaded it, Mary rode with them, for she knew how delighted he would be at her cantering to the puffing train and his running up to lift her down from the saddle to welcome him home.

"Of course there was Martin's luggage to be considered, so the station wagon had to be sent down for that." She looked defiantly at Jack. "I drove the station wagon. I was Martin's laboratory assistant."

She paused. "It was almost dark, but there was still a white cold line of sky to the west. Hani and Hilda, with Mary between them, were waiting on their horses at the top of the hill that led down to the station. The train had whistled and its headlight was graying the gravel of the crossing.

"Suddenly Mary's horse squealed and plunged down the hill. Hani and Hilda followed—to try to catch her, they said—but they didn't manage that, only kept her horse from veering off. Mary never screamed, but as her horse reared on the tracks, I saw her face in the headlight's glare.

"Martin must have guessed, or at least feared what had happened, for he was out of the train and running along the track before it stopped. In fact, he was the first to kneel down beside Mary—I mean, what had been Mary—and was holding her all bloody and shattered in his arms."

A door slammed. There were steps in the hall. Mrs. Kesserich stiffened and was silent. Jack turned.

The blur of a face hung in the doorway to the hall—a seemingly young, sensitive, suavely handsome face with aristocratic jaw. Then there was a click and the lights flared up and Jack saw the close-cropped gray hair and the lines around the eyes and nostrils, while the sensitive mouth grew sardonic. Yet the handsomeness stayed, and somehow the youth too, or at least a tremendous inner vibrancy.

"Hello, Barr," Martin Kesserich said, ignoring his wife.

The great biologist had come home.

III

"Oh, yes, and Jamieson had a feeble paper on what he called individualization in marine worms. Barr, have you ever thought much about the larger aspects of the problem of individuality?"

Jack jumped slightly. He had let his thoughts wander very far.

"Not especially, sir," he mumbled.

The house was still. A few minutes after the professor's arrival Mrs. Kesserich had gone off with an anxious glance at Jack. He knew why and wished he could reassure her that he would not mention their conversation to the professor.

Kesserich had spent perhaps a half hour briefing him on the more important papers delivered at the conferences. Then, almost as if it were a teacher's trick to show up a pupil's inattention, he had suddenly posed this question about individuality.

"You know what I mean, of course," Kesserich pressed. "The factors that make you you, and me me."

"Heredity and environment," Jack parroted like a freshman.

Kesserich nodded. "Suppose—this is just speculation—that we could control heredity and environment. Then we could recreate the same individual at will."

Jack felt a shiver go through him. "To get exactly the same pattern of hereditary traits. That'd be far beyond us."

"What about identical twins?" Kesserich pointed out. "And then there's parthenogenesis to be considered. One might produce a duplicate of the mother without the intervention of the male." Although his voice had grown more idly speculative, Kesserich seemed to Jack to be smiling secretly. "There are many examples in the lower animal forms, to say nothing of the technique by which Loeb caused a sea urchin to reproduce with no more stimulus than a salt solution."

Jack felt the hair rising on his neck. "Even then you wouldn't get exactly the same pattern of hereditary traits."

"Not if the parent were of very pure stock? Not if there were some special technique for selecting ova that would reproduce all the mother's traits?"

"But environment would change things," Jack objected. "The duplicate would be bound to develop differently."

"Is environment so important? Newman tells about a pair of identical twins separated from birth, unaware of each other's existence. They met by accident when they were twenty-one. Each was a telephone repairman. Each had a wife the same age. Each had a baby son. And each had a fox terrier called 'Trixie.' That's without trying to make environments similar. But suppose you did try. Suppose you saw to it that each of them had exactly the same experiences at the same times . . . ."

For a moment it seemed to Jack that the room was dimming and wavering, becoming a dark pool in which the only motionless thing was Kesserich's sphinxlike face.

"Well, we've escaped quite far enough from Jamieson's marine worms," the biologist said, all brisk again. He said it as if Jack were the one who had led the conversation down wild and unprofitable channels. "Let's get on to your project. I want to talk it over now, because I won't have any time for it tomorrow."

Jack looked at him blankly.

"Tomorrow I must attend to a very important matter," the biologist explained.

IV

Morning sunlight brightened the colors of the wax flowers under glass on the high bureau that always seemed to emit the faint odor of old hair combings. Jack pulled back the diamond-patterned quilt and blinked the sleep from his eyes. He expected his mind to be busy wondering about Kesserich and his wife—things said and half said last night—but found instead that his thoughts swung instantly to Mary Alice Pope, as if to a farthest island in a world of people.

Downstairs, the house was empty. After a long look at the cabinet—he felt behind it, but the key was gone—he hurried down to the waterfront. He stopped only for a bowl of chowder and, as an afterthought, to buy half a dozen newspapers.

The sea was bright, the brisk wind just right for the *Annie O.* There was eagerness in the way it smacked the sail and in the creak of the mast. And when he reached the cove, it was no longer still, but nervous with faint ripples, as if time had finally begun to stir.

After the same struggle with the underbrush, he came out on the rocky spine and passed the cove of the sea urchins. The spiny creatures struck an uncomfortable chord in his memory.

This time he climbed the second island cautiously, scraping the innocent-seeming ground ahead of him intently with a boathook he'd brought along for the purpose. He was only a few yards from the fence when he saw Mary Alice Pope standing behind it.

He hadn't realized that his heart would begin to pound or that, at the same time, a shiver of almost supernatural dread would go through him.

The girl eyed him with an uneasy hostility and immediately began to speak in a hushed, hurried voice. "You must go away at once and never come back. You're a wicked man, but I don't want you to be hurt. I've been watching for you all morning."

He tossed the newspapers over the fence. "You don't have to read them now," he told her. "Just look at the datelines and a few of the headlines."

When she finally lifted her eyes to his again, she was trembling. She tried unsuccessfully to speak.

"Listen to me," he said. "You've been the victim of a scheme to make you believe you were born around 1916 instead of 1933, and that it's 1933 now instead of 1953. I'm not sure why it's been done, though I think I know who you really are."

"But," the girl faltered, "my aunts tell me it's 1933."

"They would."

"And there are the papers . . . the magazines . . . the radio."

"The papers are old ones. The radio's faked—some sort of recording. I could show you if I could get at it."

"*These* papers might be faked," she said, pointing to where she'd let them drop on the ground.

"They're new," he said. "Only old papers get yellow."

"But why would they do it to me? *Why?*"

"Come with me to the mainland, Mary. That'll set you straight quicker than anything."

"I couldn't," she said, drawing back. "He's coming tonight."

"He?"

"The man who sends me the boxes . . . and my life."

Jack shivered. When he spoke, his voice was rough and quick. "A life that's completely a lie, that's cut you off from the world. Come with me, Mary."

She looked at him wonderingly. For perhaps ten seconds the silence held and the spell of her eerie sweetness deepened.

"I love you, Mary," Jack said softly.

She took a step back.

"Really, Mary, I do."

She shook her head. "I don't know what's true. Go away."

"Mary," he pleaded, "read the papers I've given you. Think things through. I'll wait for you here."

"You can't. My aunts would find you."

"Then I'll go away and come back. About sunset. Will you give me an answer?"

She looked at him. Suddenly she whirled around. He, too, heard the *chuff* of the Essex. "They'll find us," she said. "And if they find you, I don't know what they'll do. Quick, run!" And she darted off herself, only to turn back to scramble for the papers.

"But will you give me an answer?" he pressed.

She looked frantically up from the papers. "I don't know. You mustn't risk coming back."

"I will, no matter what you say."

"I can't promise. Please go."

"Just one question," he begged. "What are your aunts' names?"

"Hani and Hilda," she told him, and then she was gone. The hedge shook where she'd darted through.

Jack hesitated, then started for the cove. He thought for a moment of staying on the island, but decided against it. He could probably conceal himself successfully, but whoever found his boat would have him at a disadvantage. Besides, there were things he must try to find out on the mainland.

As he entered the oaks, his spine tightened for a moment, as if someone were watching him. He hurried to the rippling cove, wasted no time getting the *Annie O.* under way. With the wind still in the west, he knew it would be a hard sail. He'd need half a dozen tacks to reach the mainland.

When he was about a quarter of a mile out from the cove, there was a sharp *smack* beside him. He jerked around, heard a distant *crack* and saw a foot-long splinter of fresh wood dangling from the edge of the sloop's cockpit, about a foot from his head.

He felt his skin tighten. He was the bull's-eye of a great watery target. All the air between him and the island was tainted with menace. Water splashed a yard from the side. There was another distant *crack*. He lay on his back in the cockpit, steering by the sail, taking advantage of what little cover there was.

There were several more *cracks*. After the second, there was a hole in the sail.

Finally Jack looked back. The island was more than a mile astern. He anxiously scanned the sea ahead for craft. There was none. Then he settled down to nurse more speed from the sloop and wait for the motorboat.

But it didn't come out to follow him.

V

Same as yesterday, Mrs. Kesserich was sitting on the edge of the couch in the living room, yet from the first Jack was aware of a great change. Something had filled the domestic animal with grief and fury.

"Where's Dr. Kesserich?" he asked.

"Not here!"

"Mrs. Kesserich," he said, dropping down beside her, "you were telling me something yesterday when we were interrupted."

She looked at him. "You *have* found the girl!" she almost shouted.

"Yes," Jack was surprised into answering.

A look of slyness came into Mrs. Kesserich's bovine face. "Then I'll tell you everything. I can now."

"When Martin found Mary dying, he didn't go to pieces. You know how controlled he can be when he chooses. He lifted Mary's body as if the crowd and the railway men weren't there, and carried it to the station wagon. Hani and Hilda were sitting on their horses nearby. He gave them one look. It was as if he had said, "Murderers!"

"He told me to drive home as fast as I dared, but when I got there, he stayed sitting by Mary in the back. I knew he must have given up what hope he had for her life, or else she was dead already. I looked at him. In the domelight, his face had the most deadly and proud expression I've ever seen on a man. I worshipped him, you know, though he had never shown me one ounce of feeling. So I was completely unprepared for the naked appeal in his voice.

"Yet all he said at first was, 'Will you do something for me?' I told him, 'Surely,' and as we carried Mary in, he told me the rest. He wanted me to be the mother of Mary's child.

Jack stared at her blankly.

Mrs. Kesserich nodded. "He wanted to remove an ovum from Mary's body and nurture it in mine, so that Mary, in a way, could live on."

"But that's impossible!" Jack objected "The technique is being tried on cattle, I know, so that a prize heifer can have several calves a year, all nurtured in 'scrub heifers,' as they're called. But no one's ever dreamed of trying it on human beings!"

Mrs. Kesserich looked at him contemptuously. "Martin had mastered the technique twenty years ago. He was willing to take the chance. And so was I—partly because he fired my scientific imagination and reverence, but mostly because he said he would marry me. He barred the doors. We worked swiftly. As far as anyone was concerned, Martin, in a wild fit of grief, had locked himself up for several hours to mourn over the body of his fiancée.

"Within a month we were married, and I finally gave birth to the child."

Jack shook his head. "You gave birth to your own child."

She smiled bitterly. "No, it was Mary's. Martin did not keep his whole bargain with me—I was nothing more than his 'scrub wife' in every way.

"You *think* you gave birth to Mary's child."

Mrs. Kesserich turned on Jack in anger. "I've been wounded by him, day in and day out, for years, but I've never failed to recognize his genius. Besides, you've seen the girl, haven't you?"

Jack had to nod. What confounded him most was that, granting the near-impossible physiological feat Mrs. Kesserich had described, the girl should look so much like the mother. Mother and daughters don't look that much alike; only identical twins did. With a thrill of fear, he remembered Kesserich's casual words: "... parthenogenesis ... pure stock

. . . special tchniques . . ."

"Very well," he forced himself to say, "granting that the child was Mary's and Martin's—"

"No! Mary's alone!"

Jack suppressed a shudder. He continued quickly. "What became of the child?"

Mrs. Kesserich lowered her head. "The day it was born, it was taken away from me. After that, I never saw Hilda and Hani, either."

"You mean," Jack asked, "that Martin sent them away to bring up the child?"

Mrs. Kesserich turned away. "Yes."

Jack asked incredulously, "He trusted the child with the two people he suspected of having caused the mother's death?"

"Once when I was his assistant," Mrs. Kesserich said softly, "I carelessly broke some laboratory glassware. He kept me up all night building a new setup, though I'm rather poor at working with glass and usually get burned. Bringing up the child was his sisters' punishment."

"And they went to that house on the farthest island? I suppose it was the house he'd been building for Mary and himself."

"Yes."

"And they were to bring up the child as his daughter?"

Mrs. Kesserich started up, but when she spoke it was as if she had to force out each word. "As his wife—as soon as she was grown."

"How can you know that?" Jack asked shakily.

The rising wind rattled the windowpane.

"Because today—eighteen years after— Martin broke all of his promise to me. He told me he was leaving me."

VI

White waves shooting up like dancing ghosts in the moon-sketched, spray-swept dark were Jack's first beacon of the island and brought a sense of physical danger, breaking the trancelike yet frantic mood he had felt ever since he had spoken with Mrs. Kesserich.

Coming around farther into the wind, he scudded past the end of the island into the choppy sea on the landward side. A little later he let down the reefed sail in the cove of the sea urchins, where the water was barely moving, although the air was shaken by the pounding of the surf on the spine between the two islands.

After making fast, he paused a moment for a scrap of cloud to pass the moon. The thought of the spiny creatures in the black fathoms under the *Annie O.* sent an odd quiver of terror through him.

The moon came out and he started across the glistening rocks of the spine. But he had forgotten the rising tide. Midway, a wave clamped around his ankles, tried to carry him off, almost made him drop the heavy object he was carrying. Sprawling and drenched, he clung to the rough rock until the surge was past.

Making it finally up to the fence, he snipped a wide gate with the wire-cutters.

The windows of the house were alight. Hardly aware of his shivering, he crossed the lawn, slipping from one clump of shrubbery to another, until he reached one just across the drive from the doorway. At that moment he heard the approaching *chuff* of the Essex, the door of the cottage opened, and Mary Alice Pope stepped out, closely followed by Hani or Hilda.

Jack shrank close to the shrubbery. Mary looked pale and blank-faced, as if she had retreated within herself. He was acutely conscious of the inadequacy of his screen as the ghostly headlights of the Essex began to probe through the leaves.

But then he sensed that something more was about to happen than just the car arriving. It was a change in the expression of the face behind Mary that gave him the cue—a widening and sideways flickering of the cold eyes, the puckered lips thinning into a cruel smile.

The Essex shifted into second and, without any warning, accelerated. Simultaneously, the woman behind Mary gave her a violent shove. But at almost the same instant, Jack ran. He caught Mary as she sprawled toward the gravel, and lunged ahead without checking. The Essex bore down upon them, a square-snouted, roaring monster. It swerved

viciously, missed them by inches, threw up gravel in a skid, and rocked to a stop, stalled.

The first, incredulous voice tht broke the pulsing silence, Jack recognized as Martin Kesserich's. It came from the car, which was slewed around so that it almost faced Jack and Mary.

"Hani, you tried to kill her! You and Hilda tried to kill her again!"

The woman slumped over the wheel slowly lifted her head. In the indistinct light, she looked like the twin of the woman behind Jack and Mary.

"Did you really think we wouldn't?" she asked in a voice that spat with passion. "Did you actually believe that Hilda and I would serve this eighteen years' penance just to watch you go off with her?" She began to laugh wildly. "You never understood your sisters at all!"

Suddenly she broke off and stiffly stepped down from the car. Lifting her skirts a little, she strode past Jack and Mary.

Martin Kesserich followed her. In passing, he said, "Thanks, Barr." It occurred to Jack that Kesserich made no more question of his appearance on the island than of his presence in the laboratory. Like Mrs. Kesserich, the great biologist took him for granted.

Kesserich stopped a few feet short of Hani and Hilda. Without shrinking from him, the sisters drew closer together. They looked like two gaunt hawks.

"But you waited eighteen years," he said. "You could have killed her at any time, yet you chose to throw away so much of your lives just to have this moment."

"How do you know we didn't like waiting eighteen years?" Hani answered him. "Why shouldn't we want to make as strong an impression on you as anyone? And as for throwing our lives away, that was your doing. Oh, Martin, you'll never know anything about how your sisters feel!"

He raised his hands baffledly. "Even assuming that you hate me"—at the word "hate" both Hani and Hilda laughed softly—"and that you were prepared to strike both at my love and my work, still, that you should have waited . . ."

Hani and Hilda said nothing.

Kesserich shrugged. "Very well," he said in a voice that had lost all its tension. "You've wasted a third of a lifetime looking forward to an irrational revenge. And you've failed. That should be sufficient punishment."

Very slowly, he turned around and for the first time looked at Mary. His face was clearly revealed by the twin beams from the stalled car.

Jack grew cold. He fought against accepting the feelings of wonder, of poignant triumph, of love, of renewed youth he saw entering the face in the headlights. But most of all he fought against the sense that Martin Kesserich was successfully drawing them all back into the past, to 1933 and another accident. There was a distant hoot and Jack shook. For a moment he had thought it a railway whistle and not a ship's horn.

The biologist said tenderly, "Come, Mary."

Jack's trembling arm tightened a trifle on Mary's waist. He could feel *her* trembling.

"Come, Mary," Kesserich repeated.

Still she didn't reply.

Jack wet his lips. "Mary isn't going with you, Professor," he said.

"Quiet, Barr," Kesserich ordered absently. "Mary, it is necessary that you and I leave the island at once. Please come."

"But Mary isn't coming," Jack repeated.

Kesserich looked at him for the first time. "I'm grateful to you for the unusual sense of loyalty—or whatever motive it may have been—that led you to follow me out here tonight. And of course I'm profoundly grateful to you for saving Mary's life. But I must ask you not to interfere further in a matter which you can't possibly understand."

He turned to Mary. "I know how shocked and frightened you must feel. Living two lives and then having to face two deaths—it must be more terrible than anyone can realize. I expected this meeting to take place under very different circumstances. I wanted to explain everything to you very naturally and gently, like the messages I've sent you every day of your second life. Unfortunately, that can't be.

"You and I must leave the island right now."

Mary stared at him, then turned wonderingly toward Jack, who felt his heart begin to pound warmly.

"You still don't understand what I'm trying to tell you, Professor," he said, boldly now. "Mary is not going with you. You've deceived her all her life. You've taken a fantastic amount of pains to bring her up under the delusion that she is Mary Alice Pope, who died in—"

"She *is* Mary Alice Pope," Kesserich thundered at him. He advanced toward them swiftly. "Mary, darling, you're confused, but you must realize who you are and who I am and the relationship between us."

"Keep away," Jack warned, swinging Mary half behind him. "Mary doesn't love you. She can't marry you, at any rate. How could she, when you're her father?"

"Barr!"

"Keep off!" Jack shot out the flat of his hand and Kesserich went staggering backward. "I've talked with your wife—your wife on the mainland. She told me the whole thing."

Kesserich seemed about to rush forward again, then controlled himself. "You've got everything wrong. You hardly deserve to be told, but under the circumstances I have no choice. Mary is not my daughter. To be precise, she has no father at all. Do you remember the work that Jacques Loeb did with sea urchins?"

Jack frowned angrily. "You mean what we were talking about last night?"

"Exactly. Loeb was able to cause the egg of a sea urchin to develop normally without union with a male germ cell. I have done the same thing with a human being. This girl is Mary Alice Pope. She has exactly the same heredity. She has had exactly the same life, so far as it could be reconstructed. She's heard and read the same things at exactly the same times. There have been old newspapers, the books, even the old recorded radio programs. Hani and Hilda have had their daily instructions, to the letter. She's retraced the same time trail."

"Rot!" Jack interrupted. "I don't for a moment believe what you say about her birth. She's Mary's daughter—or the daughter of your wife on the mainland. And as for retracing the same time trail, that's senile self-delusion. Mary Alice Pope had a normal life. This girl has been brought up in cruel imprisonment by two insane, vindictive old women. In your own frustrated desire, you've pretended to yourself that you've recreated the girl you lost. You haven't. You couldn't. Nobody could—the great Martin Kesserich or anyone else!"

Kesserich, his features working, shifted his point of attack. "Who are you, Mary?"

"Don't answer him," Jack said. "He's trying to confuse you."

"Who are you?" Kesserich insisted.

"Mary Alice Pope," she said rapidly in a breathy whisper before Jack could speak again.

"And when were you born?" Kesserich pressed on.

"You've been tricked all your life about that," Jack warned.

But already the girl was saying, "In nineteen hundred and sixteen."

"And who am I then?" Kesserich demanded eagerly. "Who am I?"

The girl swayed. She brushed her head with her hand.

"It's so strange," she said, with a dreamy, almost laughing throb in her voice that turned Jack's heart cold. "I'm sure I've never seen you before in my life, and yet it's as if I'd known you forever. As if you were closer to me than—"

"Stop it!" Jack shouted at Kesserich. "Mary loves me. She loves me because I've shown her the lie her life has been, and because she's coming away with me now. Aren't you, Mary?"

He swung her around so that her blank face was inches from his own. "It's me you love, isn't it, Mary?"

She blinked doubtfully.

At that moment Kesserich charged at them, went sprawling as Jack's fist shot out. Jack swept up Mary and ran with her across the lawn. Behind him he heard an agonized cry—Kesserich's—and cruel, mounting laughter from Hani and Hilda.

Once through the ragged doorway in the fence, he made his way more slowly, gasping. Out of the shelter of the trees, the wind tore at them and the ocean roared. Moonlight glistened, now on the spine of black wet rocks, now on the foaming surf.

Jack realized that the girl in his arms was speaking rapidly, disjointedly, but he couldn't quite make out the sense of the words and then they were lost in the crash of the surf. She struggled, but he told himself that it was only because she was afraid of the menacing waters.

He pushed recklessly into the breaking surf, raced gasping across the middle of the spine as the rocks uncovered, sprang to the higher ones as the next wave crashed behind, showering them with spray. His chest burning with exertion, he carried the girl the few remaining yards to where the *Annie O.* was tossing. A sudden gust of wind almost did what the waves had failed to do, but he kept his footing and lowered the girl into the boat, then jumped in after.

She stared at him wildly. "What's that?"

He, too, had caught the faint shout. Looking back along the spine just as the moon came clear again, he saw white spray rise and fall—and the figure of Kesserich stumbling through it.

"Mary, wait for me!"

The figure was halfway across when it lurched, started forward again, then was jerked back as if something had caught its ankle. Out of the darkness, the next wave sent a line of white at it neck-high.

Jack hesitated, but another great gust of wind tore at the half-raised sail, and it was all he could do to keep the sloop from capsizing and head her into the wind again.

Mary was tugging at his shoulder. "You must help him," she was saying. "He's caught in the rocks."

He heard a voice crying, screaming crazily above the surf:

> Ah, love, let us be true
> To one another! for the world—

The sloop rocked. Jack had it finally headed into the wind. He looked around for Mary.

She had jumped out and was hurrying back, scrambling across the rocks toward the dark, struggling figure that even as he watched was once more engulfed in the surf.

Letting go the lines, Jack sprang toward the stern of the sloop.

But just then another giant blow came, struck the sail like a great fist of air, and sent the boom slashing at the back of his head.

His last recollection was being toppled out onto the rocks and wondering how he could cling to them while unconscious.

VII

The little cove was once again as quiet as time's heart. Once again the *Annie O.* was a sloop embedded in a mirror. Once again the rocks were warm underfoot.

Jack Barr lifted his fiercely aching head and looked at the distant line of the mainland, as tiny and yet as clear as something viewed through the wrong end of a telescope. He was very tired. Searching the island, in his present shaky condition, had taken all the strength out of him.

He looked at the peacefully rippling sea outside the cove and thought of what a churning pot it had been during the storm. He thought wonderingly of his rescue—a man wedged unconscious between two rock teeth, kept somehow from being washed away by the merest chance.

He thought of Mrs. Kesserich sitting alone in her house, scanning the newspapers that had nothing to tell.

He thought of the empty island behind him and the vanished motorboat.

He wondered if the sea had pulled down Martin Kesserich and Mary Alice Pope. He wondered if only Hani and Hilda had sailed away.

He winced, remembering what he had done to Martin and Mary by his blundering infatuation. In his way, he told himself, he had been as bad as the two old women.

He thought of death, and of time, and of love that defies them.

He stepped limpingly into the *Annie O.* to set sail—and realized that philosophy is only for the unhappy.

Mary was asleep in the stern.

Charlotte Armstrong

THREE-DAY MAGIC

DO YOU BELIEVE in magic? Old-fashioned magic? That which can twang the threads of cause and effect, take a swipe right across the warp and woof of them, and alter the pattern?

If you ask George this question, he will get a look on his face, a certain look, as if he were remembering a time, an hour, maybe only a certain feeling that once he had. He'll answer, yes, he believes in magic. But he won't explain.

You'll concede he has the right to mean whatever he means by that. You'll like George.

The Casino at the Ocean House, up in Deeport, Maine, was a long room with windows to the sea. Its tables and soft lights, the dance music, gave the hotel's guests something to do in the evening. It was a huge success. Even the village oldsters were proud of it. "Beth'z down to the Casino, last night," they'd say. "George'z got a new trumpet. Fellow from Bath. Ayah. Pretty good, she says."

George Hale and his band played in the Casino every summer, but George, himself, belonged to Deeport, as had his Pa and his Grandpa and many other Hales before him. Tourists exclaimed over the old Hale house, up on the slope, when they saw it glimmering behind the lilacs, under the elms. But George always thought it was most beautiful in the winter when the flounces and ruffles of green fell away and it stood forth, bared and exquisite, etched by delicate shadow, white on white.

Here, also, lived his mother and two of her sisters, all three of them widows, all three doting on George, but each pretending, with a native instinct towards severity, that this was not so. Nor did Nellie Hale, Aunt Margaret or Aunt Liz ever admit that the way he earned a living was "work" at all. George had too much fun. George knew he had fun and he knew the Casino was a success. But he did not suspect what a huge success *he* was.

He was perfect for the Casino. For George felt he was in the middle of a party, any night; therefore, when he took up his saxophone as if he *had* to join, something better than the seabreeze blew across the floor. George's music may have been a little bit corny. He liked all kinds, George did, but whatever he, himself, touched, came out with a jig quality, a right foot, left foot, whirl-me-around-again t-ra-a-boom-de-ay effect. But he was right for the Casino. He kept the customers remembering that here they were, up on the coast of Maine, breathing deeper than they breathed in town, and in touch for two weeks, more or less, with some simple source of joy.

The Casino paid George well, in fact, enough to last him a frugal winter. But it never occurred to George to push onward. Winters, he went right on enjoying himself. Then the band, and at local fees, would play for the Elks, or the High School prom. In fact, for some miles around, wherever people gathered together for fun and society, George was usually right there, beating out the festive rhythm of their mood. Deeport was proud of him, for in the winter, like the streets and the shore, he was theirs alone.

George was nearly 29, and unmarried. The neighbors speculated about this, sometimes. But his mother and the Aunts, if they speculated, said nothing. Aunt Liz darned his socks exquisitely. Aunt Margaret ironed his shirts to perfection. And his mother, without seeming to do so, based the menus on his preferences.

Naturally George had his secrets. For one thing, he played some pretty highbrow records when he was alone. For another, he believed in true love. He wasn't so naive as to think it happened to everybody, but he did hope it was going to happen to him. There were certain volumes of English poetry, never caught off the shelves in the old Hale house, which grew, nevertheless, dog-eared and loose at the bindings. Oh, George had his secrets.

One evening in August, George was leading the boys through a waltz, when a red-haired girl in a white dress floated out of the dimness in somebody's arm. Something about the line of her back, the tilt of her head as she took the turns (George played a fast bright waltz, nothing dreamy) pleased him very much for no reason he could trap by taking thought. When later, she danced by with John Phelps 3rd, an old-timer among the summer people, George gave the baton to his second fiddle, climbed down, and sought Phelps out.

She was sitting at a table with an elderly bald-headed man, who had a long sour face and cold gray eyes over which horny lids fell insolently. She was Miss Douglas. He was Mr. Bennett Blair. George held her off, the prettiest way to waltz, and somehow, on the crowded floor there was plenty of room. They flew along, dipping like birds. Her long white skirt fanned and flared. Her bright hair swung. Her brown eyes smiled at George and he smiled gently down.

She had no "line." Neither did George, of course. They exchanged a little information. They told each other where they lived. She lived in New York with Mr. Blair who was no kin but her guardian. She liked Maine very much. George said he'd been to New York twice and he liked it very much. It was a wonderful city. She said it was wonderful up here, she thought. And they waltzed.

When it was over, there was a small warm spot, somewhere under George's dress shirt, a little interior glow, perhaps in the heart.

The next morning George was hanging around the drugstore when she came in. It wasn't much of a coincidence, because all the summer people went to the drugstore at least twice every day. She came in alone. She wore a blue dress that was solid in the middle. He'd known she wouldn't come down to the drugstore with her ribs bare. He felt very close to her, having known this in advance as he had.

Her name was Kathleen. After she accepted his invitation to a coke so graciously, it seemed all right to ask her.

She said she was called Kathy. He said there wasn't any nickname for George, except Georgie, but he'd outgrown that of course, by the time he was six. Then he was telling her about his mother and the Aunts. Pretty soon, George and Kathy were walking up High Street towards the old Hale house, and inside, against their coming, Aunt Liz was wiping the pink hobnail pickle dish, Aunt Margaret was straightening the antimacassars in the sitting room, and Nellie Hale was adding just a little more milk to the chowder.

Kathy stopped at the gate and said the exact right thing. She said, "It must be just beautiful in the winter time!" George's hand on the gate shook a little as he opened it. There was a meaning to the time. It would be remembered, this moment in which Kathy Douglas stepped through his front gate.

Nellie Hale and the Aunts, for all one could tell, were absolutely hardened to George's well-known habit of bringing strange and beautiful red-haired girls home for dinner. They thought nothing of it at all. But in a little while they began to unbend from this stiff proud nonchalance. For Kathy talked about old things and she understood them, too. Old things that had belonged here a long long time. She asked about Captain Enos Gray, whose cherry table they sat around. And about Captain Mark, who'd brought the china home. She listened, bemused, while the ships went out again and some went down . . . the tales were spun . . . the worn rosary of family legend was told out, bead by bead.

It was after three o'clock before George took her back to the Ocean House. They laughed a lot, skipping along the afternoon streets, her hand in his arm.

They were a little giddy, both of them.

Phelps 3rd was on the veranda, looking concerned. Mr. Blair, in a formidable beach outfit, was waiting in the lobby. He shooed Kathy upstairs. He looked at George from under his horny lids and grunted and walked away.

George came, blinking, out on the veranda again and now, too late, Phelps 3rd told him.

Kathy Douglas had as her inheritance about $5,000,000 of her own. Bennett Blair had about $10,000,000 of his own and was a power in the land. Also, upright and cold, he was a guardian who really guarded. Nobody would get Kathy except the creme de la creme in blood, character, business ability and financial standing.

She was a flower, a lovely lovely flower, but not a wild flower, nor one that had grown under amateur culture in a suburban garden. No, delicately and expensively nurtured, precious and unobtainable was Kathy. She was not, admitted Phelps 3rd, for such as he, who was heir to only half a million from Phelps 1st, toothpaste.

She was not . . . oh, heavens, never! . . . for such as George!

For a dashed moment or two, it seemed to George that he must give her up. But then his vision cleared. By definition it was no solution to give her up. So he dismissed the notion from his mind.

The aroma of millions clung to Mr. Blair and around Kathy, too. It wafted along the harsh Maine sand to the beach, where Kathy and her Fraulein spent most of the day. Naturally, George took to the beach. Afternoons, he would greet Mr. Blair, back from his morning golf to stretch his knobby white knees to the sun. But George couldn't for the life of him dig up any mutual interests. Mr. Blair looked wearily down from an eminence of age and experience and nothing George had to offer seemed worth his response. Yet George knew he was not ignored. He felt, in the afternoons, the weight of that cold glance. He felt himself being labeled and filed in some compartment of that shrewd old brain. Mr. Blair was a guardian who really guarded. Phelps 3rd had known what he was talking about, all right.

But, somehow, seeing Kathy every day, the problem postponed itself and hung suspended in a golden time. For Kathy wasn't discouraging at all.

A golden week went by and then, one morning, Kathy came running to tell him, "George, we're leaving. We have to go!" Clouds fell over the day. "Mr. Blair had planned another week, but something has come up."

"Gosh," said George from the bottom of his heart. "I'm sorry to hear that." And yet, somewhere inside his head a little lick of triumph told him that nothing had come up at all.

George folded himself up and sat down where he was and Kathy knelt beside him. "When, Kathy?" he asked bleakly.

"This afternoon." She was frankly full of woe.

George bit his lip thoughtfully. "Back to New York?"

"Yes."

George looked at the ocean and something closed in his mind. Something said 'goodbye' to it. "Me, too," he said. "Right after Labor Day, when the Casino closes, I'm coming down."

"Oh, George! You'll come to see me?" She was all vivid and glad. Her hand moved on the sand towards his.

"I can't say anything, Kathy. I can't ask you anything, yet."

"Ask me what?" Her eyes were shining.

But George, in the bottom of his soul, agreed with Mr. Blair. Nothing was too good for Kathy. Of course, she was infinitely precious and she must have the very best, the very best of everything. So he put his lips on her hand, just once, and let it go. "I'm going to be able to ask Mr. Blair," he said grimly, "the very same day."

Yet, here on the beach in the sunshine, with Kathy near and the dark blue sea and the whole world sparkling around them, the future cleared before him. He'd go down to New York and settle himself and make about a million dollars in some sound respectable way and then he'd ask her. It seemed not only clear and simple, but certain that all this must come to pass.

For Kathy wasn't discouraging at all.

George's decision was the result of a marching logic. Now, in the blood and character departments, George was fine. What he lacked was in the success department. So he must abandon this easy-going life. He must acquire the proof, that is to say, the money. Nothing he could do in Deeport would lead to the kind of money Mr. Blair probably had in mind. So . . .

The boys in the band were disconsolate. The manager of the hotel set up such a pained and frantic howl that George fled his office, with bitter reproaches of ingratitude, pleas for mercy, predictions of the Casino's ruin, ringing in his ears. George thought this was shock. He was sorry.

He arranged to leave the bulk of his earnings in the bank for his mother and the Aunts where it would, as it always had, take them nicely through the winter. "So you see," George explained to them hopefully, "it's not going to make any difference to you."

The three ladies tightened their mouths and agreed. Aunt Margaret, although plump, was the one who tended to fear the worst, but, of course, she didn't weep. Aunt Liz, tiny and angular, chose to look on the bright side, and smiled mysteriously to herself as if she'd been tipped off by a private angel. Nellie Hale, a blend of both temperaments, simply tightened her mouth. "George is grown," she said, and that was all she would say.

So, darned and mended, cleaned and pressed, and fed to the utter limit, George, with $200 in his pocket and his saxophone in his hand, took the train one September evening, without the faintest conception of the gap his departure tore in the whole fabric of the town's life. All hints of this he took for kindliness and so he was spared. He suffered only the wrench of his own homesickness.

New York received George and his saxophone with her customary indifference. Yet he was lucky in the first hour, for he walked by Mrs. McGurk's four-story brownstone on West 69th Street just as her hand in the front window hung up the vacancy sign.

George, trained all his life to pretend that only cleanliness mattered, saw that the square ugly room on the fourth floor was clean and so said he'd take it. Mrs. McGurk sniffed. Take it, indeed! She said she'd take him. Rent by the month, in advance. That was her rule. George paid and looked about him. The room had no charm but George, although he had always lived in the most charming surroundings, knew not the word or its definition. The place felt queer. He imagined, however, that it was only strange.

Mrs. McGurk was a widow, 40-odd, toughened by her career. The poor woman had a nose that took, from head-on, the outline of a thin pear, and was hung, besides, a trifle crookedly on her face. Her character, though scrupulously honest, was veiled by no soft graces. Like the room, she was clean but she had no charm.

What other roomers might hole up, two to a floor, below him in this tall narrow house, George did not know. He tried to say "Good day" to a man who seemed about to emerge from the other door on his landing, but he got no answer. All he saw was a brown beard, a narrow eye, and the door, reversing itself, closing softly to wait 'til he had gone by.

George shrugged. He had other matters on his mind. First, he had to get a job. This was not very difficult since he was a member of the union in good standing. Pretty soon George had hired himself and saxophone out to Carmichael's Cats, a small dance band, playing in a small night club. It wasn't such a wonderful job, but George felt that, in this great city, first one got a toehold and then one took the time to look around.

His first night off, he called on Kathy. She lived only just across the Park in Bennett Blair's gray stone house that looked to George exactly like a bank building. He was received in a huge parlor, stuffed full of ponderous pieces, dark carving, stifled with damask in malevolent reds and dusty greens, lit by lamps whose heavy shades were muddy brown.

Kathy was glad to see him. Bennett Blair was not.

George walked home through the Park and on its margins the tall buildings glittered, high and incredible in the dark. "Tisn't going to be so darned easy!" George thought to himself. And he tightened his mouth.

George, from his toehold, had no time to look around because the toehold gave way. Carmichael's Cats were sorry but they couldn't use him. He wasn't right.

George had to stir himself and get another job with Barney and his Bachelors. They played, as had the Cats, a jagged and stylized kind of music, full of switches and turns. Barney liked to ambush himself, to leap on a sweet passage with an odd blue interruption, to fall from a fast blare to a low whimper with shock tactics. These tricks were no ingredient of George's bag. It wasn't that he didn't like the effect. He admired it. But he couldn't do it. Barney could jerk and shake up the whole band, but not George. George would try, but first thing he knew, there he'd be, tootling along in his own jig time, following one note with the probable next at the probable interval. Being obvious! Barney was disgusted!

So George left the Bachelors, unhappily, and approached Harry and his Hornets.

Each new month, Mrs. McGurk waited for dawn to crack, but no longer. Pay in advance was her rule and her system had no flaws. Rarely, indeed, did the sun go down upon a deficit, or a roomer escape to carry his debt unto the second day.

On the fourth floor, George, occupationally a late riser, was just getting up when she sang out, "First of the month, Mr. Hale." Her initial assault was always blithe and confident.

"Why, sure," drawled George. "Come in a minute." He fumbled under his handkerchiefs in the top drawer. "Hey," cried George in honest surprise, "I don't seem to have much money!"

The landlady's nostrils quivered, scenting battle.

"Gosh," said George reasonably. "I can't give you all of this!" In the midst of turmoil, changing jobs, George had not noticed how low his capital funds were getting. He stared at calamity. He had been here a month and a half, now, and he had not only made no progress toward his million dollars, he dared not pay the November rent!

Mrs. McGurk was nagging monotonously. "Month in advance. Told you my rule. Took the room, didn't you?"

Up in Deeport, of course, money lay in the bank. But it was not his.

"Rent's due," shrilled Mrs. McGurk. "You've got it!"

George pulled himself together. "How about taking half of it?"

She looked at the bills he offered and on her lop-sided face there was no recognition. "Half of it now," urged George. "I've just got a new job. All I want to do is see the man and get an advance." George was not going to let next week's meals out of his fingers. He couldn't. This crisis had sneaked up on him but his instinct was to meet it with caution and compromise. There was a sense, here, in which Greek met Greek.

Mrs. McGurk snorted. "Why don't you pay me and *then* go get this advance?"

"Because I'd rather do it the other way around," said George.

"Nope," said Mrs. McGurk.

"Yup."

"Nope."

"Do you think I'm trying to cheat you?" George was really curious.

"I got my rules, young man, and nobody's talked me out of them for twenty years."

George sat down on the bed and ran his hand through his hair. "I wish a little bird would tell me where the money's gone," he said ruefully.

"Either pay up or get out!" Mrs. McGurk wanted no persiflage. "I'll take two weeks notice money. You want it like that? Eh?"

George said, "The first of the month lasts 'til midnight. Take half. If I bring you the rest before midnight, it's my rent on time. If I don't, then this is notice money." Her face, if possible, hardened. "That's fair," said George.

"That's not the way I do business."

"But it's fair," he protested.

"You got it, right there, and I want it!"

"You're not going to get it," said George quietly. He put the bills on the bed.

Mrs. McGurk was wild. George swung around. "Of course, there's another way that's just as fair. Give me back a half, tonight, if things go wrong. Want *me* to trust *you?*" George smiled. "O.K."

Head down, she glowered at him. Her hand snatched at the money on the bed and stuffed it furiously into her old brown handbag. Mrs. McGurk was fit to be tied. During the years of shortages, what with rent ceilings and rising costs, she had not grown rich and avarice was not her trouble.

But she had acquired a taste for power, and she was not going to be jockeyed out of position. "You gimmee the rest before midnight," she cried, "or I'll rent the room out from under you tomorrow." She flung herself out the door and pounded across the hall. "Mr. Josef! Mr. Josef!"

George closed his door gently. He had to think, what to do. As a matter of fact, Harry, the bandleader, hadn't been absolutely definite about taking George on. And no use looking for Harry this early. George sat down on the bed and removed all artificial props from under his spirits. Promptly they sank, way down. This ugly room was more unfriendly, uglier than ever.

But the mood was one George had been taught to cast off. He thought he'd go across the Park and see Kathy for a minute.

Kathy came in a little girl's hop down the great stairs, seeming, as always, glad to see him. But she said, "Oh, George, Mr. Blair is home. He wants to have a talk with you and I promised . . ." George felt a chill of foreboding. "Maybe," she added hopefully, "he's too busy."

But Mr. Blair was not too busy. George was taken from Kathy's side and ushered through the high rooms to the library where Mr. Blair, entrenched behind his desk, frostily received him.

Mr. Blair was old and cold and his past lay around him here in this sanctum, relics of past enthusiasms, the accumulations of his mind. The total effect was overwhelming. There was so much, and everywhere each single item in the mass reeked of its expense. The smell of money rose like dust. George nearly choked.

Mr. Blair massaged the vague arthritic pains in his knuckles. "Mr. Hale," he said crisply, "am I correct in guessing that your reason for transplanting yourself to this city is your interest in my ward?"

"Correct," croaked George.

A faint sigh came out of Mr. Blair. It seemed to set the dust dancing. "I envy you your youth," he said in his rusty voice. George thought of the knobby old knees that had never tanned, in all that Maine week, though he had held them so faithfully to the sun, and felt, oddly in this place, a brief pang of pity. "But," the tough old lids lowered, "I must ask you to consider my point of view."

"I recognize your point of view, sir. I wouldn't think of asking for Kathy . . . yet."

Mr. Blair pushed out his lower lip. George had jumped the interview several steps ahead. "You expect to be in a position to ask for her, ever?"

"Yes, sir. I do."

Mr. Blair went into a fast rhythm. "What is your work?" He barked.

"I . . . uh . . ."

"You play a saxophone." Mr. Blair knew the answers, too. "How much do you earn?"

"Uh . . . "

"Not very much. What prospects for the future?"

"Well . . ."

"Few," said Blair. "As a matter of fact, you are just floundering. And even if you had a job, at this moment, what prestige, what standing in the community are you aiming for?"

"But . . . "

"When can you hope to ask for Kathleen?"

George wilted. "I don't know," he admitted.

Mr. Blair took another tack. "Now, if," he purred, "you point out to me that Kathleen already has enough mere money, I would agree with you. But I'll ask you this. Have you had any business training? Have you the slightest idea how to watch over and guard her estate?"

"I intend to learn," said George desperately.

Mr. Blair let his lids fall in pure disdain. "Let me speak plainly. If you were to defy my expressed opinion, I am empowered to divert her estate into charitable channels . . . "

"No, sir," said George promptly. "That won't happen."

Bennett Blair's lids lifted and he stared a moment. "I don't accuse you of fortune hunting," he said stiffly. "I merely say, that since it will take you many years to achieve the standing I consider necessary, will you ask her now, to fix her affections on you? Can't you see that's unfair?"

George leaned back. "It certainly is," he answered steadily. "I shouldn't even risk her liking me, now. Somebody better for *her* than I am might be shut out. That's what you mean sir, isn't it?" Mr. Blair's fish mouth remained a little open. "It does me a lot of good to see her," said George wistfully. "But I'll have to get along without that."

"Quite right," snapped Mr. Blair. "You realize what it means?"

"Yes," said George sadly.

"I cannot," said Mr. Blair crossly, "be so swayed by my admiration for your handsome attitude that I will forget to insist upon a strict accord between your principles and your actions."

"Did you think I was just talking?" asked George forlornly. He got up. "Is there some back way out?"

Mr. Blair caught his tongue between his teeth and around this physical arrangement crept a reluctant grimace verging on a smile. "Oh, no, no, no," he waved a hand. "You may speak to Kathleen, of course. You might tell her," he added ruthlessly, "how we agree."

Kathy was waiting in the parlor. George took her hands. "Goodbye," he said.

She scrambled out of the chair in alarm.

"Mr. Blair's been explaining some things and he's right, Kathy. I'd better not see you any more. Until maybe . . . someday."

Kathy's hair gleamed as if it brightened with her temper. "I won't be seeing you at all? Because Mr. Blair says you mustn't?"

"But he's right, Kathy. Maybe you don't realize. . ."

"You haven't asked me what I realize."

"I know *you* never think about money or success or things like that," groaned George. "But they have a meaning, just the same. I . . . I have a lot to do." He stepped away from her. "In the meantime, don't wait."

"What?"

"Don't . . . don't wait . . ." said George, ready to bawl.

Kathy flung out her hands in a gesture that might have been despair. "There's only one thing to do," babbled George.

Kathy cocked her head. "Are you sure you know what it is, George?"

George's eyes were storing up the sight of her.

"I haven't any intention of waiting for you!" said Kathy boldly.

George was beyond heeding. "Then . . . Kathy, goodbye," he groaned. She looked so lovely, so tempting, so perfect, George felt he couldn't bear it another minute. He blurted out, "I hope I'll be seeing you . . . but if I never do, it was wonderful to have seen you at all. Goodbye. Goodbye."

He turned and fled.

Kathy began to breathe very quickly, in angry little gasps. She ran after him. She cried out, to the door that had already closed behind him, "Aren't you going to ask me what I mean?" The last word went up in a outraged wail. But Kathy took her hand from the door and drew away.

It was a black morning. George walked along, staggering under a succession of blows. He was about as far down as he could get. But, gradually, the bottom began to feel solid under his feet.

He wouldn't be seeing Kathy, so he must use every moment to claw and fight his way back to her. Definitely, he must kick away the toehold of his musical background. That meant no Hornets. That meant no advance! That meant raising the rest of his rent some other way.

Well, he'd sell his saxophone. So much was settled. George's spirits began to bounce. He would close his mind to what Kathy had said. Whether she waited or not, nothing could keep him from hoping, from *trying*.

By sheer luck, he caught the landlady off guard and ran up the long stairs. On the last flight he overtook the bearded figure of his fourth-floormate. "Pardon," said George. The man flattened himself against the wall, palms in, head turned, eyes furtive. He stood as if he felt himself to be invisible against the protective coloration of the wallpaper.

George paid him no mind. He knew what he had to do. When his hand went cozily around the handle of his instrument case, he beat down the sentimental pang. He reconnoitered. Mrs. McGurk's voice was raised, back in her kitchen regions, so he fled past the last newel post and escaped.

He tramped along the street, west, his mind busy solidifying plans. Sell the sax, pay the rent, read the ads, go to employment agencies, poke and pry, wedge himself in, somewhere. His imagination glanced off miracles of one kind or another, bouncing, steadying.

There probably weren't going to be any miracles, George reminded himself. He mustn't expect any magic.

He didn't believe in magic, at this time.

Something told him to stop walking. He saw that he stood before a pawnshop, looking into a very dirty window at a jumble of stuff that gleamed in the dust, whether jewelry or junk, he couldn't tell. But deeper within he could discern the dim shapes of larger objects, among them the unmistakable curve of a violin. Musical instruments? Well, he could ask.

George opened the door and went in. A bell made a flat clank over his head. Out of the shadowy back regions, the proprietor approached, a very small man, humped and telescoped with age, his face netted with a million wrinkles. He had a dark eye, this little man, dark, liquid and gleaming.

"Yess?" he said.

George lifted his case. "How much for this?" he asked, speaking distinctly in case these ancient ears were deaf.

The proprietor fluttered back of the counter. He moved silently and somehow weightlessly. "Sixteen dollarsss," he said in a dry wisp of sound.

"Not enough," said George's Yankee blood promptly.

The old man moved his shoulders in light indifference. But the dark eyes swam to look up, as if to suggest a hesitation. So George stood still, although his urgency, the glow of his resolution, the steam George had up, tumbled and churned around him.

The old man said, "I've got things I give you to boot."

"What things?" said George. "Look, I don't want to swap, you know. I want . . ."

"Yesss . . . but come . . ." The whole little man was nodding, now.

George followed him along a dark lane that led to the darkest interior corner. The proprietor paused in a clearing in the jungle of objects, picked up something and set it on a low table. "If you wish," said the proprietor, "sixteen dollarsss and thisss . . ." "Thisss" was an old carpet bag.

"What's in it?"

"See . . ."

George pulled at the double handle. "Nuh-uh. what would I want with . . . ? Hey, what's that?" He reached in. There was an old sword wedged diagonally in the bag. George had a fancy for old things and a small-boyish love for swords. He fondled the hilt of this one. The scabbard was some worn crimson stuff.

George waked himself out of a dream. The old man's bright eyes were avid and sly. "No, no," said George.

"Maybe isss antique . . ."

"Looks antique, all right," George fished into the bag and found a small curved box. The lid opened by sliding. There was nothing in it but a flower. A rose. Artificial, he supposed. He dropped the box and rummaged again. There were soft cloth masses. There was a piece of flat metal, framed with a wrought design, burnished in the center. Old, very old. There was a small dark leather pouch. "What's this?"

"Open," said the proprietor softly.

George pulled the thong fastenings. Inside, he found a single piece of metal. Flat, lopsided, with some worn engraving on it, perhaps it was gold. "Hey," said George, "did you know this was in here?" The old man made his butterfly shrug. "Is it a coin? Is it gold?"

"Maybe . . ."

"This might be worth something," George said honestly. "Old coins, y'know."

"May be . . ." said the proprietor indifferently. "You take?"

"Wait a minute," said George, "how do you know this isn't gold? How do you know it isn't worth a lot of money?"

"I am tired," said the old man.

George looked dubious. He chewed on his lip. The whole thing was queer. Queer shivery feeling to this place. "I certainly don't want this bagful of junk. Give me $25 and the coin. How about that?"

"I give twenty and all thisss. So no more, not less." The sibilants sighed in the dusty air.

"You seem to want to get rid of it," murmured George. His imagination was jumping. Maybe this coin was worth a lot. Maybe the sword would sell for something to a man who knew about swords.

"I am going," said the proprietor softly, "to California."

Ah! George relaxed. He had a sense of satisfaction, and clearing of confusion. Of course! Anyone who was going to California flung off the winter garments of old caution. *He* wouldn't want to bother, this old fellow whose bones were promised to the sun!

But George was young and full of beans, and George could spare the energy that lurks at the bottom of most strokes of luck. George said, "It's a deal."

The old man's hands came up as if he would rub them together, but cautiously, he did not. He simply nodded, all over, as before, and fluttered towards his till.

When George lugged his new property out into the street, he felt perhaps he'd been had. One thing led him to hope he'd done well. The queer stark look with which the old man's eyes clung to the carpet bag, there at the last . . . as if there were something . . . something unusual . . . about this carpet bag.

As a matter of fact, it was old-fashioned, ungainly, misshapen, distended ridiculously at one bottom corner because the sword inside was really too long, and it made George feel foolishly conspicuous. The only thing to do was dump it in his room.

Even as he gained the second floor, he heard a hen-like flutter in the lower hall. He went up fast, anyway, shut himself in and began to empty the carpet bag out on his bed. Might as well see what he had here.

Across the hall, Mr. Josef held his ear against the inside panel of his own door. His eyes rolled, relishing this pose. His fat hand, on which the nails were chewed away, caressed the inner knob with delicious stealth.

Down below, Mrs. McGurk muttered to herself and began to climb.

Outside the city roared.

George looked at what he had here. There was the pouch. He tossed it aside. The box that held a rose, the sword... George balanced it a moment in his hand and it felt alive. He had a terrible suspicion that he could never sell it.

There was that flat metal oval. Then there was a strange object, in metal that resembled a teapot and yet was not a teapot. Baffled, George put it down. He fished out a queer old flask. It seemed to be made of pinkish stone, with a stony stopper, the whole bound in an intricate metal lattice. Something swished inside. George could not get the stopper out to sniff at whatever was in there. He put it down and delved deeper.

Now he came to the fabric. First, he drew out an odd garment, made of a black, rather porous cloth that was opaque and yet so soft it seemed to melt under his fingertips. The thing was designed to be worn. The top of it was cut, obviously, to fit around one's shoulders. George blinked and put it by.

He certainly did not understand what kind of person packed this bag, nor of what kind of household these things could be the relics. There must be some rhyme or reason to this conglomeration. True, all these things were old. But what other quality they had in common he couldn't ... at this time ... imagine.

Rolled tightly at the bottom of the bag there now remained a small thin, old, and shabby Oriental rug. As George extracted it, something else dropped. The last object of all in the bag was a ring.

Very old. Not gold, however. Perhaps it was blackened silver. On a plain band, a wrought setting in the same dark metal held an uncut lumpish stone of bluish-gray color. This stone was curiously filmed over. George put his thumb on it. It wasn't dusty. Nothing rubbed off. It was certainly a queer-looking ring. He held it in his palm, thinking suddenly of Kathy.

Mrs. McGurk rapped sharply, opened the door, and stepped in. She loosened the set of her mouth long enough to let out a "Well?"

George dropped the ring and felt for the coin in his pocket. "It's not midnight yet," he said mildly. It occurred to him that he had better hunt up an old coin man as soon as possible.

"Lying, weren't you?" she sneered. "You got no new job, and no man to see!"

George didn't answer. He just met her steady glare with a steadier look of patience and regret. Mrs. McGurk's eyes fell away. They spied the bed. "I'd thank you to keep that junk off my bedspread," she snapped.

"Sorry," said George gently. "I've got to go out again, now."

Mrs. McGurk said venomously. "Don't hurry. I've decided not to accept your full month's rent. I'm giving *you* notice, Mr. Hale."

"All right," said George patiently. "Excuse me?" He went out, past her, leaving her there.

He felt stiff and sad. There was no need for such unpleasantness. It served no purpose except to sadden and embitter the innocent day.

Mr. Josef stood in the hall. When George appeared, he turned his back and pretended to be entering his room. George started downstairs. He looked back. Mr. Josef was in a ridiculous position. He seemed to be staring into the blank wood, a foot and a half from his face. He was not, of course. His eyes, sideways, were watching George.

"Who," wondered George, "does he think he is, anyway?"

Mrs. McGurk, having been rude, ugly and unjust, was of course furious. She stalked about George's room, looking for something to pin her fury on. George, however, kept his things clean and orderly as effortlessly as he breathed. There was nothing for his landlady to pounce on, except the bed and its array of strange objects.

Mrs. McGurk approached it then, with nostrils dilated. But, dusty and old as many of these things appeared, nothing, no dust of any kind, had been transferred to the bedspread. Mrs. McGurk's fury began to give way to sheer curiosity.

The cloak she made nothing of. It couldn't belong usefully to a personable young man like George. The metal things she shook her head over. Junk. She wouldn't, she huffed to herself, give them houseroom.

What quiet there was, existing under the constant flow of sound from the city, was being broken hideously by a cat, down below. He was a displaced feline who lived by his wits in the deep yards in the heart of the block. He was sitting on a fence, wailing his heart out. Mrs. McGurk winced at the piercing pain of his cries.

She picked up the pinkish stone flask and shook it, but she couldn't get the stopper out, either. She opened the pouch and drew her mouth down at the sight of the flattened lump of gold that lay within it. She could not know that George, even now, was taking a similar coin out of his pocket to show it to a man behind a counter, two blocks south. Nor could she know that George had not the slightest idea of the existence of this second coin. No thief, she merely drew the thongs tight and cast the pouch down, impatiently.

The cat wailed as if the world's end were at hand. Mrs. McGurk moved to the window and joined the neighbors in a lively exchange of shouted despair. The cat had no mind for the troubles of humans. It wailed on.

Shaking her head, Mrs. McGurk drew it into the room again. She picked up the ring. A curious piece of work. She slipped it on her finger, where it fit with a pleasant weight to it and looked, for all its queerness, rather well on her work-bitten hand.

The cat thought of something particularly outrageous and screamed in an ecstasy of self-pity. "I wish to goodness," said Mrs. McGurk out loud, "that cat would stop its yowling!"

On her hand, the dull bluish lump of stone in the ring began to catch light. For a brief moment, it gleamed. The dusty look of it seemed to burn away.

The cat stopped it. Abruptly. His current yowl, in fact, was cut off in the middle and never finished. Silence poured down like water and extinguished the noise.

Mrs. McGurk blinked. The precipitous quiet was just a trifle uncanny. She listened with a curious eagerness for the cat to resume, but it did not. She took off the ring and dropped it back on the bed, vaguely sorry, in an inexplicable way, that she had ever touched it.

For just a moment, the things lying on the bed up here in George's room were more than queer. Their antiquity was worse than puzzling.

"Fifty?" said the old man, casually. His thumb came up in a caressing pinch. His junior clerk wasn't breathing.

George made a low mirthful sound. "You've certainly been helpful," he said cheerfully. "May I see your classified directory?"

"One hundred dollars," said the man.

"Two hundred," said George gaily.

"It's a deal," snapped the man and now George staggered. In a tense silence, the junior took the coin, the money was fetched and George signed something.

"I'm satisfied, you know," said George. "But I wish you'd tell me . . . "

"Rare!" babbled the man. "Rare? Not even listed. And indisputably genuine. The inscriptions, the feel of the gold . . . " He rubbed his fingers, "greasy with time . . . " He slapped the counter jubilantly. "Now tell me. Where *did* you get it?"

"Found it, like I told you," said George cheerfully. "I'm certainly glad you liked it. Tell you what, if I ever run across another one, I'll let you know. So long."

George went off jauntily. The boss's mouth curled. "He'll bring us another one! Ha!"

"Ha ha!" echoed the clerk.

Mrs. McGurk had shaken off her funny feeling. She went on examining this queer collection, and at last she picked up the little carved box with the sliding lid and looked sourly at the rose inside. Artificial, she presumed. Yet . . . no . . . Or, if it were, it was a marvel! Her woman's eye could see as much. She touched it and the petals were sweet and cool. Mrs. McGurk raised the box to her crooked nose. To her senses came the

unmistakable fresh rich fragrance of the living rose.

Just then, George opened his door.

Rose to nose, Mrs. McGurk looked full at him.

Until this day, Mrs. McGurk's impression of George had been mild. Her trained gaze had gone over him and not finding the mark of the complainer, or the destroyer of rented property, or the innocent stare of the deadbeat, she had looked no more.

This morning, however, he had offered her good faith and fair play and she had been obliged to turn them down. Under her tough protective crust still existed an uneasy heart that knew and recognized her losses. George had what she had no more... the capacity for trusting. Something about him was sweet to the core, and it hurt! So, of course, she had been stubbornly angry.

But now, as the perfume of the rose penetrated her senses, something very strange happened to Mrs. McGurk. This crust of hers seemed suddenly and for no cause to dissolve. Her bosom swelled as if some withered seed, lying dormant in her heart, had been touched by magic moisture so that it sprang into life and began to grow. Looking full at George, the light in her eye grew suddenly tender. How was it she had not noticed before the gentleness of his eyes, the sweetness of his smile? This was such a boy as one could be fond of, as if he were one's own, almost. Mrs. McGurk had the sensation of melting. She swayed a little. She put the rose, in its box, down on the bed and she smiled.

Even in its best day, Mrs. McGurk's smile had been rather terrifying, involving her long teeth bared to the upper gums and somehow the illusion that the bulbous end of her nose had taken a sudden twitch farther off center. "I'm sorry, Mr. Hale," said she contritely. And her inner being swooned and swam in the luxury of this humility. "I was rude and unjust to you and I'm terribly sorry."

George realized at last what she thought she was doing with her face. However, to him a kindly feeling was the most natural thing in the world and he accepted it immediately. "That's all right, Mrs. McGurk. I was probably irritating. I've got the money, now," he added gently. "Do I owe you anything?"

"My dear boy!" cried Mrs. McGurk, "of course not! You paid me for two full weeks ahead! And you must stay! This room is yours. I want you to feel at home!"

It was the first time the sweet sense of home had come to her mind for years and years. Mrs. McGurk's eyes filled. She wanted to do more for George. She felt a compelling urge to make him happy. "Please let me show you my second floor front," she snuffled. "Such a lovely room it is, Mr. Hale. It would just suit you! Only one flight up and a private bath."

"That's mighty nice of you," said George, somewhat bewildered. "But you know I can't afford . . ."

"Same price!" cried she. "And handy to the phone!"

"Well, I . . . uh . . . if you say so," said George weakly. "It's very nice of you. But I want to pay my full month ahead. Please. I know it's your rule."

"One has to have rules, Mr. Hale. The people I meet . . . "

"Sure, I know. I don't bla—"

"But I should have *seen*," said his landlady, "that *you* are *different!*"

George realized, with some dismay, that Mrs. McGurk was trying to be charming. There she stood, in her shapeless print dress, with her hair piled up in the usual slapdash coiffure, the same woman . . . and yet . . . The head was cocked, now, in a kind of old-fashioned coquetry, the curled lip bared the long teeth; the glance came sideways from under arched brows, with the left eye not quite in focus. It was a formidable sight!

George swallowed. But, being George, he gave her full marks for effort. He thanked her.

"Oh, you will stay?" cried she. "I'll go right down. And freshen up the room a bit. Don't bother about your things. I'll move them. It's no trouble. I feel," said Mrs. McGurk, "so happy to have someone like you in the house, I can't tell you . . . !" The brows ached with sweetness. She went out with a bob and a flirt of her skirt.

George sank down on the bed. He rubbed the back of his head. The money was in his hand. He stared down at it. It occurred to him that this was one of the strangest days of his life.

But here was $200, here in his hand. He began to wonder if there was more, disguised in the heap of stuff beside him. He shoved the money into a pocket and reached for that flat oval . . . But his thoughts drifted off to Kathy. Now that he had $200, was he any nearer? When would he see her again, her sweet pretty face, the red gold of her hair, the enchanting lights in her tawny eyes?

Kathy was standing in the middle of a dainty bedroom . . . on a thick white rug . . . near a soft green chair . . .

George inhaled a great gasp.

He *was* seeing her!

He had been looking absently into the burnished metal and now it was acting like a mirror but what it reflected was not here! He could see Kathy!

He lifted the thing in both trembling hands. The vision did not go. It trembled a little, but the tiny Kathy began to fumble at the fastenings of her dress!

George's hair rippled on the back of his neck. He'd heard there were people who could see things in a crystal ball. Now, he, George Hale, of Deeport, Maine, was seeing things! Why, the strength of his love was so great . . . !

Kathy began to wiggle out of her dress. She stood in her slip, bare shouldered, adorable. Another figure crossed the little reflected scene. Fraulein!

Now, George knew darned well he wasn't in love with Fraulein!

He breathed. He had to. The image in the Magic Mirror shook with his body but did not fade.

Magic?

Kathy pushed the straps of her slip down and took hold of it at the hem. She was going to take it off. No doubt of it. Right now, across the Park, Kathy was undressing!

But George, in spite of his state of absolute astonishment, was yet a gentleman, and, above all, he adored her. So he tore his gaze away from the enchanted bit of metal, turned it over, dull side up, and slid it away from him, under the pillow.

He put his reeling head in his hands.

In a little while, he lifted his face. It was rather white. Not everyday does a man run into old-fashioned magic! Slowly, he drew the pouch to

him, opened it, and observed with only a dull thud of verified suspicion the presence therein of another golden coin. He took this out and put it in his pocket, drew the thongs together for a moment, and looked inside again. Sure enough. There lay the third coin. George left it there. This was the Magic Purse that never stayed empty!

Here? On 69th St.?

But what else? Suddenly he was in a frenzy to know what else. That carpet. Well, of course! He had no doubt it was the one that could fly! He got up and began to paw over his strange loot. He took up the soft black cloak, put it over his shoulders, and vanished.

That is, of course, George remained standing right where he was, but when he looked down along his body, he couldn't see it! This was the Cloak of Darkness! The very one!

He shuddered out of the thing. Cold chills were racing in his spine. He hung the Cloak in his closet, aimlessly, without thought.

Ah, the thing like a teapot! He recognized it now! He'd seen it drawn, in a hundred illustrations. It was the Lamp, the only Lamp that could qualify for this collection! Aladdin's! Must be! Must be! But George wasn't going to rub it. Not now. He didn't want to meet the Slave of the Lamp! Not this afternoon!

George inched it aside. He was excited and he was scared. He daren't stop and think. That ring? Ah, but all the old tales were full of rings, with one magic property or another. He slipped it on his finger, where it seemed to fit comfortably. Nothing happened.

His eye lit on the pink stone flask and he picked it up. He was convinced, now, that this, too, was magically endowed. Somehow, he had here the strangest of all collections.

(The little old proprietor must have known! How old? How old was that man? A thousand? Five thousand? He'd said he was tired! George trembled. Never mind. Don't think of it!)

Oh yes, everything here, logic insisted, must be magical.

The pink flask was heavy in his right hand. He rubbed his head. "I wish," he murmured, "a little bird would tell me what's in here."

"Water from the Fountain of Youth." This sentence came into the air. It was like a line of music, high and full of flats. George turned his head in sharp alarm. Had he heard it? Or thought it? No sound now, certainly. Only beyond the window sill, the flutter of wings . . . Some sparrow . . .

Water from the Fountain of Youth! George loosened his fingers. He wanted none of that! Suddenly, he wanted none of any of it. He stripped off the Wishing Ring and threw it down. He understood that one might wish to get rid of these things.

It wasn't . . . well, it wasn't right! He wanted to crawl back within the safety of the possible, the steadiness and order of the natural world, the sane and simple world of splitting atoms, of nebulae, of radar and penicillin.

It is not so easy to believe in magic.

George paced up and down, conquering his fright, assimilating his wonder.

There remained the Rose and the Sword. He mistrusted the Rose. He had a shadowy recollection of the Rose and the tale of the Rose. He picked up the Sword and drew it from the scabbard.

It leaped in his hand. What a piece it was! George swung his wrist over and sliced off the top of the bedpost. The hard brass separated, clean and sharp. The upper six inches fell off on the floor.

It was impossible not to take another swipe at something. George brought his arm around. The Sword leaped and flashed down through the back, the seat, the springs of his tough, hard-cushioned leather chair. Clattering, it fell apart in two perfectly neat sections. Wood, fabric, metal, anything! Lord, lordy, what a sword! The Sword of Swiftness, or maybe Excalibur itself! He whirled the blade around his head. Whistling sweetly, it descended and cleaved the washbasin as if it were butter. A chunk of the hard porcelain came clean away and dropped with a bang on the floor. Lucky he'd missed the plumbing, for heaven's sakes! George realized he'd better restrain himself. This thing was dangerous! Much, much too dangerous to play with.

He flicked the Sword at the window sill, cutting a swift notch with the bare tip. He took a neat triangle delicately out of the mirror. He fought temptation. Sweating, he made himself take up the crimson scabbard and insert therein the wicked and utterly fascinating blade.

(Outside in the hall, Mr. Josef stood quivering. His beard was agitated. His eye yearned for George's keyhole.)

But George sheathed the Sword and put it away from him. He puffed out his breath. What to do now? Anybody else might have run for a good stiff drink, but to George came the thought that he'd had no lunch! No wonder he felt queer. Besides, he'd think better on a full stomach.

Oh, he hadn't forgotten what he was really after. It would take more than a bag of magic to make George forget what he'd wrapped his whole life around. Now, somehow, he was going to be able to ask for Kathy! All he had to do was calm himself, and think it out!

He shoved all the stuff back into the carpet bag, or thought he did. He hadn't counted the nine objects. He was too excited to check. He forgot the Mirror, still under his pillow, and the Cloak, in his closet.

The rest he packed and then he shoved the bag under the bed with the instinct to hide it. He felt of his money. He was whistling a Georgish version of *Tonight We Love* as he slammed out of his door, and went downstairs with swift heels beating out the jig time of his tune.

No sooner did George depart, in the very backwash of the sound of his going, Mr. Josef oozed across the hall. His ears shadowed George out the door far below, checked the finality of its slam. Then, softly, he put his own key into George's lock. It yielded. Mr. Josef poured himself around the edge of the door and inside.

He stared at the empty room as if he would hypnotize this space to remain empty. The closet door was half open. Mr. Josef went slinking along the wall towards it, his right hand in his pocket. Finally, he took a leap and a whirl and brought himself up sharp with the closet door wide open and he confronting and threatening George's blue serge and other garments.

Mr. Josef watched the blue serge closely for a moment. Then he took his hand out of his pocket, arranged the muscles around his eyes, and began to rake the place methodically with a narrowed glance. When he spied the chair, lying so absurdly in two pieces, his eyes rounded. In fact, they popped.

But he moved cooly to examine it. He saw the washstand and blinked incredulously at the thick raw edge where George had sliced it, at the hunk of the outer curve that lay like a piece of melon on the floor. As he crept over and touched it gingerly, there came from deep in the house the thump of feet on the stairs.

It was, in fact, Mrs. McGurk, coming up.

Mr. Josef rolled himself a glance of dark warning, via the mirror. He took long crouching steps across to the door. He skated down the hall.

When Mrs. McGurk, humming *My Wild Irish Rose* in a gay wobbly soprano, had gone into George's room, Mr. Josef slipped like shadow in soft pell-mell down the stairs to the telephone.

"X?"

"Y."

"Z!" breathed Mr. Josef. "Listen, I have stumbled on something terrific! I must have help at once! Something bigger even than A. You know what I mean?"

"Frankly, no," said Y, wearily.

"A, I say!"

"A for apple?"

"No, no, no. Nuclear Fission," hissed Mr. Josef. "Send Gogo. At once! I tell you, they have a secret weapon!"

"Yeah?"

"I saw results with my own eyes, you fool! This is of desperate importance! *Mother must know!*"

"Hm? Oh, yeah," mumbled Y. "Mother Country, that is."

"Stupid!" Mr. Josef spat into the phone. "Send Gogo. At all costs, I will secure for us this secret!"

"O.K.," said Y. "Keep your shirt on. O.K. O.K."

"I will expect him here in five minutes," said Mr. Josef silkily. He hung up, silkily.

Y looked across the plain office toward the other desk. "Josef. That clown. He's got a spy complex."

"He *is* a spy," said the other man, placidly. "We all are, I suppose." He wrote down a neat numeral.

"I'd better send somebody around, if only to keep an eye on him. It's embarrassing. Why doesn't the FBI pick him up?" frothed Y. "We've betrayed him, six times over."

The other man shook his head, went on totalling some figures, compiling information received.

Y got on the phone again, angrily.

Mrs. McGurk stopped humming for a moment, when she saw the broken chair, the washbasin, the bedpost. But the warm flood of happy activity on which (under the spell of the Rose) she was floating bore her right by such details. If George had done the damage, he, being George, would of course make it right. They would talk it over, once he was snug downstairs.

She found his empty suitcase under the bed, beside an old carpet bag, already packed up. Mrs. McGurk opened George's dresser drawers and began to fill the suitcase. At last, staggering a little, she lugged both pieces to the top of the stairs and started down.

The second floor front was a room of pleasing proportions. Mrs. McGurk felt proud of it. Into the clean paper-lined drawers of her best dresser she put George's clothing, fussing daintily with the arrangement. She was an absolutely happy woman. She was creating, with love. She was Making a Home.

She closed the drawers. The top of the dresser was bare. Ah, but his own things ... all the little touches ... She dove into the carpet bag. This flask, now, was a pretty thing. But the metal lattice work seemed dull. Mrs. McGurk fetched a rag and some scouring paste. Snatches of old tunes came humming out of her as she worked. Her fingers felt tireless. She was so light of heart that she wondered, intermittently, if she were not coming down with something.

At last the flask shown as bright as she could make it and she set it on the dresser and cocked her head. It looked well, but certain artistic instincts were stirring in Mrs. McGurk today. It needed balancing. She dug into the carpet bag and came out with the lamp.

Naturally, at the first swipe of her cleaning rag across its surface, the

Genie materialized. It seemed for a moment that steam was pouring out of the spout-like protuberance on the lamp, but the cloud fell away rapidly to reveal a rather pleasant-looking man, whose skin was on the dark side, and who wore, of course, an Oriental costume of Aladdin's day. He was standing in the air about a foot above the floor.

Mrs. McGurk leapt. She screamed! The lamp rolled off her lap. Before the Genie had time to make his set speech about being the Slave of the Lamp and so forth (which perhaps he delayed in the process of translating it from the Arabic) Mrs. McGurk cried, "Eek! Go away!"

The Slave of the Lamp, of course, obeyed her.

Mrs. McGurk stood trembling in an empty room. Then she fled that place. Ricocheting from wall to wall, blindly, she raced for the sanctuary of her kitchen.

George munched his lunch, considering ways and means. The thing was, he concluded, to show the old man that Kathy would be safe and sound as George's wife, even without her inheritance. That George, all by himself, with his own resources, could take care of her.

At last, George rose and paid for his meal and sloped his course towards Mrs. McGurk's stepping jauntily, trying to beat down a persistant little twinge of uneasiness. He told himself that with the Lamp, with the bottomless Purse, all *must* be magically smooth. There was a legless man, begging in the street. George put two fingers on the old gold coin in his pocket, tossed it into the cup and went swiftly on. It made him feel a trifle better to do this.

He had forgotten about his new quarters. He proceeded up the stairs, as usual, put his key in the lock of the door, and waltzed blithely in. Something hard jabbed him in the ribs. A thousand motion pictures, from childhood on, had conditioned him to know, at once, exactly what it was. His arms began to go up.

The voice behind him said, "My dear Mr. Hale, won't you ... sit down?"

George saw the mocking eye of Mr. Josef, gleaming with pleasure. A second man came from behind the door, a large creature with a flat impassive face. George recognized the type. A henchman!

"Close the door," hissed Mr. Josef. The henchman kicked it shut.

George let the tail of his eye explore the room. The bedspread had been flung up over the pillow. He could see the curls of dust on the bare floor under the bed. The carpet bag was not where he had left it.

"Now, if you please," said Josef sternly, "the secret, and quickly!"

"What secret?"

"Come now, Mr. Hale. Surely we needn't pursue the childish course of torture?"

"I don't know what you're talking about," said George. "My money's in my pocket." He pointed with his elbow.

Mr. Josef put his head to one side. "Gogo, he is going to be stubborn."

"What did *that?*" said Gogo suddenly in a reasonable tone of curious inquiry.

"Did what? Oh . . ." George saw that he meant the cut-up washbasin. "Why . . . uh . . ." He swallowed hard. "Accident," he croaked. It did not seem possible to answer this question. George realized he was in quite a spot. The fourth floor was well removed from a policeman. The house had been so quiet, no help could be in it. And there were two of them.

"What kind of accident?" Gogo asked skeptically.

Josef shoved himself between them. The gun looked wicked and unsafe in his gloved hand. "Mr. Hale, naturally you are loyal to your government. But we will, you know, by one means or another, possess this new ray."

"Huh?" said George.

Mr. Josef chuckled. "So it *is* a ray!" he purred triumphantly.

"Ray!" said George in perfect astonishment.

"You would never," teased Mr. Josef, "make your fortune on the stage."

George simply goggled.

"Can we bribe you, Mr. Hale?" inquired Josef suddenly.

"Bribe me to do what?"

"Oh, give us specifications. We wish to know the source of this ray's power, how it is controlled, all about it. Come now."

"There is no such thing!"

Mr. Josef smiled.

"I don't know what you mean!" cried George.

Mr. Josef's eyebrows rose, pityingly.

George knew, now, he had to get away. There wasn't anything he could say. They had in their heads an explanation for the damage in his room that was just about as preposterous as the real one. They weren't going to listen to his old-fashioned stuff. And torture wasn't going to get anybody anywhere, especially George. He said, in an artful whimper, "Don't hurt me." He stumbled back a little farther. "I can't tell you anything."

"A hero," said Mr. Josef regretfully. "Ah, well, we have our little ways. No one regrets these necessities more than I do," cried Mr. Josef, frothing a bit at the mouth, "but we must know what you know, and know it now! And if we pay eventually with our lives for what we do . . . be it so!" The gun quivered with his fervor.

George made up his mind and leaped backward into the closet. He wound himself into the Cloak and leaped out again as the gun in Mr. Josef's startled hand went off. The bullet got George's blue serge in the heart, but George, in his gray, invisible and whole, slid along the wall away from danger.

"A secret passage!" screeched Mr. Josef, tearing his beard. He staggered towards the closet, eyes bulging. George lifted an invisible foot and kicked Gogo hard on the seat. The shock on the toe of his shoe felt wonderful. He only wished it had been Mr. Josef.

His visitors did not notice the door apparently open by itself, for Gogo was growling in his throat, looking on all sides for what had hit him. And Mr. Josef, with his eyes so narrowed that he could hardly see at all, was frantically clawing the inside closet wall.

George, still in the Cloak, flitted down to the second floor. The carpet bag was there, all right. He had deduced as much. Furthermore, it had been opened. George spotted the Flask. Then he saw the Lamp, on the floor. When he also saw the cleaning rag, where Mrs. McGurk had let it fall, George deduced the rest.

He sighed. He supposed the poor lady had been frightened out of her wits. He hated to sneak out on her now, especially since she had been so kind. But he could not stay in the same house with Mr. Josef's obsession. And his new plans involved leaving here, anyhow.

So George scribbled a note. "Inclosed please find a full month's rent . . . also what I hope will pay for the damages . . . Many thanks for your

kindness ... All best wishes ..."

Then he listened to the house. There was a muted, though furious, buzzing still going on upstairs. He guessed he was safe here for a few more minutes.

George slid out of the Cloak and packed it. He took up the Lamp. Gently and somewhat fearfully, he brought his palm to its side and rubbed.

When the Genie appeared, George, having been braced for this, found himself unalarmed. This Genie looked like a nice fellow. Nothing ferocious about him. Little bit up in the air, of course. George smiled cordially.

"I am the Slave of the Lamp," said the Genie slowly. "What are your commands?" He used the broad A, George noticed.

"Uh, how about getting me a reservation at the Waldorf for the night?" asked George a bit nervously. "Single room, with bath. Name of Hale."

The Genie bowed his turbanned head. "I hear and obey," he murmured.

"Wait a minute," said George, more easily. "As long as you're here, listen. You could build me a house, I suppose? A real nice house, furnished, and with pretty grounds? Fix it, with servants and all, so I could invite some people, say, to lunch?"

The Genie bowed.

"Lessee," said George. "About how long would it take you? Could I count on that by the middle of November?" The Genie looked simply scornful. "By next week then?" The Genie's expression remained haughty. "Tomorrow?" cried George joyfully.

The Genie drew air whistling in through his teeth. "I hear and obey," he said, as before.

"Wait a minute. Don't be in a hurry," George wished this fellow would relax and chat. "Fix it up. . . say . . . uh . . . in one of the nice parts of Westchester County. I want it to look rich, you know. Maybe there should be a swimming pool. But everything the best quality. Nothing flashy. How will I know my address?" demanded George, who liked things clear.

"I will return, Master."

"Call me...uh...Mr. Hale," said George, shuddering. "And, by the way, the servants should be regular. Not ...uh...slaves, y'know. O.K.? Then, tomorrow morning, I'll be seeing you."

The Genie appeared to shimmer in the air. George didn't say any more. The Genie quietly vanished. George took up the Lamp and packed it. He felt exhilarated, with something of the sensation of one who defies the laws of gravity on a tightrope and walks on the wings of mere balance. Things were moving fast, all right.

He got out of the house without any trouble. The spies must have still been rooting around in the upstairs closet, and poor Mrs. McGurk was nowhere to be seen. George hefted the carpet bag and set off down the street. Whatever way he was going, he knew he was headed for Kathy.

He went by way of the Waldorf. George's natural caution . . . just common sense, after all . . . told him he'd better check on this Genie's powers, before assuming too much. But everything was fine. The great hostelry swallowed him in without a ripple in its digestion. George looked around the room they gave him, which was extremely handsome, and he decided the Genie must be the McCoy.

The time had come, here, now, and on the same day. He could call up Kathy. His throat all but closed up when he heard her voice. He managed to say, "It's George."

"Oh, George!" Kathy wasn't anything but glad. "Where are you?"

"At the Waldorf."

"What?"

"Kathy, I . . . did you miss me?" He knew it was ridiculous, but he couldn't help it.

"Oh, George," she said. "I've missed you terribly!" Then they both knew that they meant the long vista of empty days ahead of them, not the mere afternoon behind.

"Kathy, darling," cried George, in spite of himself. "Will you marry me?"

"I certainly will!" said Kathy. "Oh, George, I'm so glad you called!"

"I love you, I love you, I love you," he said.

"I'm so glad . . . so glad you c-called. . . ."

George felt like crying, too.

"Are we going to run away?" she asked. "Shall we go to Maine? Oh George, let's! Mr. Blair can't do anything that matters."

"Kathy, I'm going to ask him for you and he's going to be glad about the whole thing . . ."

"But . . ."

"Listen, I want you and Mr. Blair to come to lunch tomorrow at my house . . ."

"Your house? Do you mean in Maine?"

"No, no . . . my new house."

"But . . ."

"Tomorrow, Kathy. I'll call him up myself. You'll come to lunch and you'll see. Because I can take care of you, Kathy. And I can prove it. You're going to be surprised."

"George, are you coming over?"

He said, "Kathy, I'd better not, because I promised. Sweetheart, until I can *ask* him . . . and I can, tomorrow . . . Don't you see?"

"George, are we engaged to be married?"

"I meant to wait," he groaned.

"But you didn't and I said, 'yes.' So we are!"

"We sure are!"

"Well, then," said Kathy. "I don't see what difference anything else makes. Honestly, I don't. But do it your own way. I'll *give* you 'till tomorrow."

"Kathy, don't be mad! Kathy, would you like an emerald?"

"I've got an emerald," she wailed.

George said, "I can't stand it! Will you meet me in the tearoom on Madison, right now?"

"No," said Kathy, female that she was. "You promised. Besides, I'm all dressed for the evening. Tomorrow, dear . . . dear George . . ."

"Until tomorrow," said George. "Oh, dearest Kathy . . ."

He loved her, he loved her, he loved her!

Most of Mrs. McGurk's roomers were in their rooms on Sunday morning. Ordinarily, therefore, this was Her Day, to which Mrs. McGurk looked forward as quite the liveliest day in the week. But this Sunday, she was not in the mood.

The evening before, having finally conquered her fright, she had gone up to the second floor and found George's note. It seemed to her to be the sweetest letter she'd ever had, and it broke her heart. Mrs. McGurk did not see how she could Go On.

Mysteriously, he had left his clothing behind in the drawers. She puzzled all night long over this. She hoped it meant he would return, if ony for a few minutes . . . Oh, she could not rent his room! No, indeed! It would remain as it was, yearning for him, and maybe . . . someday . . . she took to comforting herself with dreams.

Came the dawn, she realized that there was no sense maintaining two shrines to George's memory, on two different floors. So, rather early Sunday morning, Mrs. McGurk climbed up to his old room. She let herself in. Yes, she thought sadly, here was the real shrine, after all. For had it not been George, himself, who had broken that washbasin? Mrs. McGurk saw other traces of his being, and she flung herself on his bed for a good cry. Dimly, she perceived the luxury of this, how even her tears were a bath and a refreshing. Still, she wept with all her heart, until her nose, burrowing against the pillow, met something hard.

She explored with her hand and drew out the Mirror.

Mrs. McGurk sat up and wiped her eyes. This, whatever it was, had been His. Her hands caressed it. Oh, if he had only told her where he had gone! She could let him know. She could get in touch with him. But he had disappeared into the outer world and she had no clue. Oh, would she ever again see his dear face or his darling smile?

Mrs. McGurk was ready to fling herself howling into the pillow once more, when she noticed a moving image on the burnished metal surface she held in her hands. This was odd! Stony with shock, Mrs. McGurk watched the magic scene. She had been thinking of George, so, of course, it was George she saw.

George was walking on grass, looking up at the facade of a magnificent house. He moved beside beds of gorgeous flowers, chrysanthemums in white and bronze masses. He strolled on the edge of a great pool that lay like a jewel in the leaf-strewn lawn.

But it was George! George, with his hands in the pockets of a new tweed suit ... Mrs. McGurk clutched the Mirror. She was over 40. In her day, Bluebeard had murdered all his wives but one without benefit of Dick Tracy. Ah, Mrs. McGurk had known the old tales, the classics! Furthermore, just yesterday, she had seen a Genie! Now, two and two whirled together in her head. She didn't understand, but she recognized, and her heart began to beat in wild elation.

Even as she stared, George was strolling down a long curving drive. Where was he? Where? Ah, if he kept on as he was going, she might find out! Since it was the Magic Mirror and her thought controlled it, the image shifted, running ahead of George. Yes, there it was, on a stone pillar there at the end of the drive. She began to mutter, over and over again, "2244 Meadow Lane ... 2244 Meadow Lane...." Now George strolled into the scene and stopped, with that look on his face, that dear baffled look he was wearing, to touch his own name on the handsome mailbox.

Mrs. McGurk sighed in a flood of peace and joy. George was at a place of his own and she had the address. She pressed the Mirror to her heart. It should never leave her!

Away down below, somebody was leaning on her doorbell. Mrs. McGurk, light as a girl, flew downward. She thrust the Mirror inside the bosom of her dress, where it was extremely uncomfortable, flung open her front door, and lavished one of her toothiest smiles on a perfect stranger who was teetering, in an obvious rage, on the stoop.

"George Hale live here?" yelped this man.

"He isn't here right now," trilled she.

"You can tell him from me, he's a dirty crook!" cried the caller. "Look at that!" In his trembling palm lay two old gold coins, exactly alike. "You can tell him from me," stormed the rare coin dealer, for it was he, "that he needn't send any more beggars around to my competitors with any more of this junk! He can't kid around with the Law of Supply and Demand! Maybe he tricked me once! But you tell him, if any more of these show up, I'll get the Government after him for hoarding gold! And I mean it! Good day!"

"Good day," said Mrs. McGurk. She closed the door. Her surprise gave way to a belated but loyal anger. She was about to open and shout defiance at the enemy's back when she realized that she was not alone. Somebody was breathing on her neck.

It was Mr. Josef, who had crept close behind her in his furtive way. He fingered his beard. His eyes were sly.

"Morning," said his landlady shortly.

"Oh, Mrs. McGurk," said the spy, "could you supply me with Mr. Hale's forwarding address?" She looked at him sourly. "I am rather anxious to get in touch with him," drawled Mr. Josef. "Something to his advantage . . ."

The end of Mrs. McGurk's nose twitched thoughtfully. "You don't happen to have a street map, do you?"

"Many. Many." He rubbed his hands together. "Of what district?"

"Well . . . uh . . . I don't know. You see, I . . . happen to have the street number, but not the . . . uh . . . community," blushed Mrs. McGurk.

"Quite a pretty little problem!" cried Mr. Josef, in great delight. "Come, we shall solve it. This," said he happily, "is just the sort of thing I am rather good at. Ah, fear not! We shall ferret him out, you and I!"

George had, somehow, envisioned a larger or perhaps fresher copy of the old Hale house, when he had given his orders. He had certainly expected something simpler in line and decor than this! But the Genie, naturally, George supposed, would have more Oriental ideas of what luxury was. Anyhow, George conceded, it was sure some house! It would certainly impress Mr. Blair. Since that was the point, George felt he should be satisfied.

It was still quite early Sunday morning. He had come up by Genie. That is, as soon as he'd shaved and had breakfast, he'd rubbed the Lamp. The Genie had materialized somewhat tardily. He'd seemed rather out of breath, too, and there had been definite beads of sweat on his coffee-colored brow. George had asked him, in all sympathy, if anything was the matter, but the fellow had only rolled his eyes in a stiff unfriendly way. George didn't wish to offend by insisting. He'd let himself be whisked up here.

In fact, George didn't know exactly where he was.

He'd gone through the whole place, picked out a suit he liked, up in the master chamber, and put it on. He'd given orders to the butler about luncheon. Now he was restless. He was anxious to get Bennett Blair out here and impress him and get it over with.

He'd drive himself back into town, he decided, incidentally finding out where he was and how to get back again. He'd call for Kathy and her guardian in the . . . lessee . . . the Cadillac.

As he drove out the gate, a state cop stopped him. "You live here?"

"Guess so," said George cheerfully. "Hale's my name."

"O.K.," said the cop mildly. He spat at the pavement.

"Say," said George, "what's the best way to get to New York from here?"

The cop told him and George rolled smoothly off, waving his thanks. In a mile or two, he wondered whether or not he had a license plate. If so, was it on the records, somewhere in the vast recesses of the Bureau of Motor Vehicles? George shook off the thought. It made his head ache. He began to experiment with the throttle. He felt, all of a sudden, that he'd better hurry.

The cop, left behind, stayed where he was for a while, rubbing his chin on his palm, gazing thoughtfully at the house.

The funny thing was, he'd been by here, yesterday, and there'd been no house.

His head was aching a little, too.

Mr. Blair sat like an old toad, motionless, in the tonneau. The sweet air blew on him in vain. When they turned in at the gates, however, he roused. They bowled up to the front entrance. A man servant came to hand them from the car. The butler stood respectfully in the great doorway.

Within, sunshine sifted through splendid drapery to glow on the polished floor. This entrance hall, alone, would knock the old man's eye out, thought George to himself. The great stairs winding up, the rich dark paneling, the white cockatoo in his silver cage, adding that one exotic note . . .

"Kathy said, "Ooooooh!"

Mr. Blair said nothing. George led them into the drawing room. It was baronial. On the vast floor lay a rug of such exquisite color and pattern, such size, such texture, that Mr. Blair was forced to cover a covetous gasp with a fake clearing of his throat. George bit on his own smile. Blandly, he ordered cocktails in the library. Then, with the tail of his eye on the old man's face, George ushered them through the green and silver music room (with its silver piano) to the colossal coziness of the library. A soft fire bloomed in the grate. Cocktails came at once in a gold and crystal shaker.

The somber beauty of the room was absolutely still. Kathy, since her first gasp, had made no sound. Mr. Blair was stricken dumb. But he was not paralyzed. He walked to and fro. He went over to the bookshelves and drew out a volume or two. Then he began to pat his hand along the shelf and mutter in his throat. He went close to a painting, peering at the corner of it. He turned on George.

"You inherited this place!"

"Well, in a way," said George. "Anyhow, it belongs to me, sir."

"Furnished, as it *is*?"

"Oh, yes. Sure."

"Did you know," demanded Mr. Blair, going so far as to point, vulgarly, with a forefinger, "that whole shelf there, is ALL first editions?"

"Is that so?" said George pleasantly.

"That rug in the other room . . . Where did it come from?"

"It was just here," said George.

"You realize this is a Matisse?" snapped Mr Blair, indicating the painting.

"I'll be darned," said George feebly. "I guess I hadn't noticed."

What there was of hair on Mr. Blair's head seemed to stir as if it would rise on end. He fell into a chair and seized his drink, thirstily.

Kathy went over to look out of the window. George stood behind her. "It's pretty . . . uh . . . big . . ." he murmured. Kathy nodded. "Too big," said George quietly.

Kathy leaned back just enough to seem to say, "Thou art my shield . . . in thee I trust. . ."

"Don't worry," he whispered. "We don't have to live here." She turned her cheek against his lips.

Meanwhile, Mr. Blair had picked up a small china bowl from the table. Now he looked at the under side of it and began to curse softly.

"Looking for an ashtray, sir?" George gave a host-like leap. "I guess that will do, won't it, sir?"

Mr. Blair cast George a wild glance and leaned back and blew his breath in puffs toward the ceiling.

Luncheon was served in the 40-foot dining room where they gathered like two kings and a queen in great carved chairs. At once, Mr. Blair began to examine the lace in the tablecloth.

"Kinda pretty, isn't it?" George beamed innocently. "My Aunt Liz used to crochet a lot."

"Your Aunt Liz," exploded Mr. Blair, "never crocheted this!"

"Well, no, of course she didn't."

"Came with the place, eh?"

"Oh, yes. . ."

"Don't know much about lace, do you?"

"Well—uh—no."

"No," said Mr. Blair.

Kathy was looking blankly at the china, the crystal. Her puzzled eyes kept coming back to George's face, to say "It's all right, of course. Because it's you."

George squirmed a little. He felt, himself, that the food was, well, astonishing. He had tried to tell the butler what he would like served for this meal, but he must have been vague, or left a lot of leeway somehow, because he didn't recognize one single dish. Although it tasted fine. Mr.

Blair seemed to think so.

Also, the butler kept filling wine glasses with different kinds of wine and each time, Mr. Blair would sip and then close his eyes as one in pain. George didn't drink much wine. It all tasted alike to him, anyhow, he explained cheerfully. Kathy sat, hardly eating anything but a little of the cucumber mousse, and George couldn't really eat, either.

Just so Mr. Blair had a good lunch. Because, after lunch would be the time to ask him.

In the drawing room, George's manservant brought cigars and coffee.

George cleared his throat. "Mr. Blair, I wanted you to come today because . . ."

"Yes," Mr. Blair's attention came away from the furnishings with a snap.

"Because I want to marry Kathy," said George. "I wanted to show you that I can take care of her. So now I . . . uh . . . ask your permission to . . . uh . . ." George forgot the sentences he had made up ahead of time. "I love her so darned much!" he cried, "And she . . ."

Kathy's hand was in his. It had flown there. "Me, too," said Kathy. Their hands, holding each other tight, lifted between them, entreating him.

Suddenly Mr. Blair looked very old and very patient. He said gently, "I take it all this magnificence is supposed to impress me."

"It does," said George, sharply, for him.

"Oh, it does. It does, George," conceded Mr. Blair. He leaned back and said, coldly, "I would like very much to meet what friend of yours so kindly loaned you this place for the day."

George said, "Nobody loaned it to me, sir. It's mine."

"You will produce certain proofs?"

"Proofs?"

"A deed to the property, perhaps. The inevitable records of ownership. My dear chap, this is rather astonishing, you know. For Kathleen's sake, I must see the proof and you cannot afford to be offended that I ask for them."

"Well, of course not," stammered George. "Gosh, I . . ."

"However," said Mr. Blair, "granting the existence of such proof, if you then think you have proved your capacities in such a way as to satisfy me, I am sorry you are so deceived. What you have done," said Mr. Blair, opening his eyes wide with an effect of pouncing, "is exactly the opposite! You've proved yourself a perfect ignoramus!"

"Huh?"

"You have no more idea what is in this house than a Hottentot!" rasped Mr. Blair. "You offer me a bowl of priceless porcelain for an ashtray! You never heard of Matisse! Don't tell me! How you imagine that I will permit . . ."

"Just a minute," said Kathy, very quietly. "George and I are engaged to be married."

"I'm sorry to hear that, Kathleen," said her guardian levelly and coldly.

"Wait," cried George. "Maybe I don't know very much, but I can learn, and anyhow, it doesn't matter!"

"It matters," snarled Mr. Blair. "Kathleen's fortune will never pass into the hands of . . ."

"I don't *need* Kathy's fortune!"

"I don't *care!*" said Kathy.

"Sit down, Kathleen," barked Mr. Blair. "There is a good deal that must be explained. I want to know, and so should you, my dear, exactly how a saxophone player without a penny to his name, yesterday, claims to be in possession of a place like this, today. If, as I all along suspected, he's only borrowed it, then he is a cheat. And you'd better know it. So sit down."

With an expression of perfect disdain on her face, an expression that signified her perfect faith in George, Kathy sat down.

"Now," snapped Mr. Blair. "Do one of two things, George, if you please. Produce your papers and explain how you got them. Or name the real owner." Suddenly Mr. Blair's toe rubbed across the soft silk of the rug, as if it had been waiting to do so for minutes. "In a way," he said, with genial brutality, "I hope you can prove yourself the owner, because, if you do, George, I intend personally to swindle you out of several things you don't *yet* know you've got here."

George looked about him, wildly. It was as if his fairy godmother had turned and bit him.

But then the butler, at George's elbow, said, "I beg pardon, sir."

"Hm?"

"People are approaching the house, sir. In fact, there are persons at the door. I don't quite know what you wish in the matter . . ."

They all became aware of crowd noises. George strode to the window. Men were milling around, out there.

"Excuse me," said George. He walked down the long drawing room to the hall and he opened the front door. The first face he saw was that of the cop he had spoken to, that morning. "Say, what is all this?" asked George, in his friendly fashion.

Everybody began to talk at once. The group converged on the door. It advanced and invaded. George was soon surrounded. Competing voices rose louder and louder.

"Who inspected your wiring here?" "Permit?" "Fire law says . . ." "Why didn't the Building Department get an application?" "I'm from the union . . ." "Who put in the plumbing here?" "Zone . . ." "You can't put up a pre-fab unless . . ." "My client . . ." "Second mortgage . . ." "Title." "Tax."

Somebody was snapping the lights off and on. It seemed that others were darting off in all directions, into the depths of the house. "Hey!" said George.

"Electricians local won't ..." "Painters and Paperhangers got a beef if you ..." "Where's your meter?"

Some were returning and screaming, now.

"My God, he's into the gas lines!" "Who inspected ..." "What about the sewers? He can't ..." "Wait 'till the water company ... !" "Slap a summons on him ..." "Wrong type construction ..." "Have to tear it out ..." "Permit ..."

George, in the center of the mass, struggled.

A little dark man screeched, "Telephone!" He fought his way towards the instrument. "Can't be a telephone," he whimpered. Now the state cop was braying down the noise. He achieved an uncertain quiet. He said, in it, "O.K. Mr. Hale. Your turn." The whole house vibrated.

The little man could be heard moaning low into the phone. "You're wrong. Operator! There *is* no such number!"

George clutched his hair. "Listen, I . . . I don't know what to say." A wordless growl rose from the pack. "I didn't mean to break the regulations."

The state cop said, sourly, "I figgered, when I saw this place, which wasn't here, yesterday . . . I figgered you mighta forgot a few dee-tails."

"This ain't no pre-fab!" said one. "Moved it in?" "Say, listen, you can't move a house ..." "Permit?" "Wait till the office opens ..." "Jeese," said one, furiously, "who does this guy think he is!" "Yeah," they cried, "who do you think y'are?"

Kathy, cowering in the sofa, murmured, "Oh, please, Mr. Blair!" Her guardian, who had sat stonily through the beginning of it, now rose.

"Not here YESTERDAY!" said the gas man, suddenly, with distended eyeballs. They grew quiet. All grew quiet. Mr. Blair stood still.

"Not here!" screamed the white cockatoo, from his silver cage. "Not here!" Something like a shudder passed through the crowd. They moved closer to each other. They seemed to press in on George, now, silently. Their breathing alone was very loud.

"Yesterday! Yesterday!" squawked the pink-eyed bird.

George threw out his arms, thrusting them back. "Now, listen, whatever I have to do to make this right, I'll do. So go away. Write me letters, will you?"

"Will you?" said the cockatoo.

Sound began to swell again from their throats. It was working up.

"My name is Blair," said that gentleman. "Bennett Blair." The perfume of his wealth, the strong odor of much money, was wafted on the heated air. "I think my young friend," said Mr. Blair with the faintest accent on the significant noun, "is right. I fear his impetuous haste has cut a lot of red tape. But," his fish mouth closed, his cold eye held them. "Red tape doesn't bleed, you know." They gave him their murmuring chuckle, on cue. They shifted their feet in soft confusion on the carpet. "So suppose we go about this in some orderly fashion. Tomorrow is a business day . . ."

"Yeah, that's right . . ." "Good enough for me, Mr. Blair." "Sure, let the office handle it." "I wouldna come out here, only Joe called me." "Proper channels . . ." "Sure . . ."

The little man at the phone had dropped his head on his arm.

"Ah . . . no . . ." he kept moaning. He was cursed with imagination. He contemplated the System, the ramifications, the delicate, vast, and incredibly dainty complexity . . . He stared starkly into the floor with white eyes.

"I'm afraid," said Mr. Blair, with distaste, "this man is unwell . . ."

"Come on, Riley." Somebody scooped up the telephone man. "Give him air." "Come on, you guys. Get him outa here."

Thus, Mr. Blair by a potent and rather frightening magic of his own, got them all out of there. George wiped his face. The jittery butler closed the door. Then, Mr. Blair allowed himself to tremble.

"George," he said, with a fearful quaver. "Was this house here, yesterday?"

"No," said George, and sent Mr. Blair tottering.

"For the love of heaven, boy!"

"I was *going* to explain," said George. "I will. Gee! Now I understand! Poor fellow! No wonder he looked pale! Things must have gotten a little complicated since his day." He pulled himself together and smiled at Kathy. "Wait," he said, "'till I get my carpet bag. Let's go into the library, shall we?"

So George explained.

Now, Mr. Blair lay back on the leather sofa. His hooded eyes were brooding. Kathy, beside him, rested her cheek on her hand. George was sitting on the floor, the other side of the low table on which he'd spread his bagful of uncanny property. The big room was filled with somber light. Outside, it had come on to rain. Leaves rattled in the wet wind. But the high thick book-lined walls around them were ramparts of silence.

Kathy said dreamily, "I suppose when he built a palace, in the old days, it would stand all by itself."

"Sure," said George. "No . . . uh . . . connections." he looked sadly at his collection. "I guess this stuff is kinda out of date. I wish I had the Mirror, though. It was wonderful."

Kathy smiled. "Was it something like television?"

George smiled back at her. "But without any sound. Doesn't it seem as if a lot of things people have wished for, they've got?"

"I guess you tend to get what you wish for," dreamed Kathy, "more or less like magic."

"Too bad . . ."

"Yes, too bad," she mused. "People wished for ways to kill and yet be far away . . . Can you un-wish? What if there gets to be too much of some kinds of magic?"

"Well," said George stoutly, "look . . . magic *can* go out of date and get outgrown. Men go past it. People change the way they think and the day comes . . . we just have no use for some kinds."

Kathy smiled very sweetly upon him.

"Of course," said George, louder, "You'd be able to live pretty comfortably with these things to fall back on."

Mr. Blair raised his head.

"Anyhow, sir," said George to him directly, "now you see why, if there's anything in this house you want, you're welcome to it."

The old man looked around the room. "No," he said. "Not now. I don't want *these* first editions, George. Or that painting. God knows what it is. It isn't human! So what does it mean?" He fidgeted. "The aroma's gone. The patina . . . Do you know what I mean?"

"It's kind of phoney," said George sadly. "Then, I can't bribe you, hm?"

Mr. Blair said nothing for a long moment. His crabbed hands massaged his knees. "Maybe you *can* bribe me," he said at last. "Maybe you can."

George was very quick. "Any of this stuff?" He gestured towards the table "Because I'd rather have Kathy."

Kathy said quickly, "I'd rather, too."

"Money and power," mused the old man, staring at the table, "I have. I've had a long time. Furthermore, I worked for it. I carved it out. No, there's only one of your little gadgets, George, that . . . tempts me, somewhat."

Slowly, George reached out. "You're welcome to this Flask."

Mr. Blair grunted his admiration. "Yes," he said, "I . . . thank you, my boy. I somehow feel you are going to be . . . right for Kathleen. You may take it that I withdraw any objections."

George looked at Kathy joyfully and she smiled like a rosy angel.

Mr. Blair's gnarled hand closed softly on the pink stone Flask. He rested it on his knee. His head dropped forward. Chin on breast, the old man sat dreaming.

George snatched at the Ring. "Would you wear this . . . temporarily?"

Kathy said, "If you want me to."

He put it on the proper finger. He drew her up out of the seat. They skipped off together, out of the amber-colored room entirely. Her shoulder tucked under his, they slipped around the dreaming old man. They closed the door between. In the green and silver music room, they kissed, and then, George, holding her, could not speak, so filled was he with happiness.

In a little while, they sat down on a window bench in a nook behind the silver piano. George just could not say a word. He just kept looking at her . . . dear, darling, delicious Kathy!

Kathy smiled and then her eyes grew moist and then she smiled again. She looked down at the Ring. She twisted it. She put her head on George's shoulder and out of George came a soft sound like a purr, wordless, and not even chopped into thoughts at all.

Kathy sat up a little straighter and blinked her eyes. "I . . . I wish it would stop raining," she said, just aimlessly, groping for the earth.

It stopped raining.

"George," she said, "this Ring winked at me!"

"Hmmmmmmmmmmmmmmm?"

"It seemed so. Oh, I suppose it caught the sun." The sun was shining. Kathy turned her wondering head to look out and George kissed her. She pushed him away a little, laughing. "I feel so funny," she admitted. "Do you? As if it all happened so suddenly. Oh, dear, I wish I hadn't eaten those cucumbers."

The prompt distress on George's face was comical. "Oh, never mind, silly," laughed Kathy. "It isn't import . . ." Lips parted, she looked down with quick suspicion at her left hand. For the taste of cucumbers had vanished. She said, in a funny little voice, "George . . ."

"Hmmmmmmmmmmmmm?" He was still in a state.

"Oh . . ." she burst out. "I wish you'd *say* something!"

"I love you," said George immediately. "I love you so much I can hardly talk. Wheeee! Kathy, darling, I thought I'd lost my voice."

But Kathy was staring at the Ring. "It winked again. George, do you suppose . . . ?" She looked around the room. "George, wouldn't you like to be up in Maine, right now?"

"I don't care where we are," he babbled.

Kathy said, rather slowly, quite deliberately, "I wish we were in Deeport, Maine."

Nothing happened.

The stone in the Ring remained dull and lifeless. It felt heavy on her finger.

"Oh," said George, catching on, "you thought it was a Wishing Ring! Say, maybe it is!"

"Maybe," said Kathy thoughtfully. "One person gets just three wishes. Isn't that so?"

"That's the rules and regulations, the way I heard it," babbled George. "The heck with them." He kissed her.

But Kathy's fingers moved. The forefinger ... rain! The middle finger ... cucumbers! The ring finger . . . yes, indeed! George *had* said something!

"It's a bad habit," said Kathy, when she could, "to go around saying 'I wish' all the time."

There was a middle door of this room and now the knob turned, the door cracked. "Beg pardon, sir. A Mrs. McGurk is here to see you. Are you engaged, sir?"

"Darned tooting, I am!" replied George happily. "Mrs. McGurk here! For heaven's sakes! Come on, Kathy. I want you to meet her. Let's tell her! Gee, I've got to tell somebody!"

Mrs. McGurk was waiting in the drawing room. She was dressed as for church. Her hat was last Easter's madness, and under it her hair was crimped violently. Her face was stiff with peach-colored kalsomine, and she'd left a little lipstick on her long teeth.

It wasn't in George to rebuke the surge of affectionate pleasure that brought her two hands reaching out to him. The hat and the kalsomine did not obscure, from him, the real moisture in her eye. "It's nice to see you," he said cordially, and bent to pick up her handbag off the floor. It was one of those soft suitcases. There was something hard and heavy in it. "Did you get my note?"

"Oh, I did! I did!" She gave him a Look.

But George didn't notice. "Kathy."

Mrs. McGurk became aware of Kathy, graceful in a soft blue wool frock, moving up within George's arm, with her red gold mane so near his shoulder. "Mrs. McGurk, this is Kathy Douglas. Kathy ... Mrs. McGurk ..."

The landlady's head, which had frozen in mid-nod, went on with the gesture it had begun. Then she swerved and tapped George on his forearm. "But oh ... please, George, 'Constance?' My name, you know?"

"Uh ... very pretty name," said George feebly. He took a step back. He had a horrid suspicion.

"Have you come far, Mrs. McGurk?" said Kathy politely.

"Just from the city," said Mrs. McGurk with a lofty sniff. "A friend with a car drove me."

"But how did you . . . ?"

Mrs. McGurk cut George's question off. It could only lead to her surrender of the Mirror. So she ducked it. "Oh, George," she cried. "I thought you should know! A man called. He made the nastiest threats. Something about gold . . ."

"Gold?"

"Coins, you know. He had two of them. He seemed to think you had deceived him."

"Oh, gosh!" said George. In his mind he ticked off the bottomless Purse. Obsolete! "Well, it was kind of you to bother." George whipped back to his main concern. "Mrs. McGurk, what do you think? I'm going to be married. Kathy's promised!"

"I'm so glad," said Mrs. McGurk, with fingers turning white on the handbag. "It isn't going to make any difference," she blurted.

"What?" said Kathy.

"I want you to go on thinking of my house as home," wailed Constance. "And if ever . . ." she now shot a hard suspicious look at Kathy, "you are troubled and need a friend . . ."

"I beg your pardon," said Kathy. "George, dear, is this a relative of yours?"

"No, no. Mrs. McGurk runs a rooming house where I . . . she was very kind," said George desperately. He backed away.

"I understand!" cried Constance, dramatically. "Now, you have all this! The world is at your feet! Only remember, my dear, glitter isn't everything. Kind hearts do count . . ."

"Glitter?" said Kathy, a bit tensely.

"And a pretty face and a hank of red hair," went on the landlady, quite carried away, "may not take the place of . . ."

"What place?" asked Kathy ominously.

"Of one who . . . boo hoo hoo . . . oh . . . hoo . . ."

"George," said Kathy, smouldering, "if you'll excuse me, please . . ."

"Don't, Kathy. Mrs. McGurk, now, you mustn't cry."

Mrs. McGurk's hat was askew. So was her nose, even more than normally. "George, she isn't right for you! Forgive me! But I think of you and you only. See how cold she is! George, think! Before it is too late!"

In Kathy a dam busted. "I'm sorry, but she can't come in here and say things like that!"

"She doesn't know what she's saying," said George in anguish. "Just . . . bear with it . . ."

"Wouldn't it be simplest if she . . . left?" asked Kathy brightly.

"You see!" The landlady clung to George's hand. "She'd turn me out of your life! Your true friend, George . . . the truest friend . . ."

"Now wait a minute." George held out his other hand to Kathy. "She's not to blame, Kathy. She can't help it. I realize what must have happ . . . I can explain."

But Kathy's mane rippled and flared with the swing of her body. "Maybe you'd better take this back." She pulled off the Ring and smacked it into his palm, "until you do!"

"KATHY!"

"Oh, evil temper!" cried Mrs. McGurk.

"Mr. Blair," called Kathy, as she ran. "I want to go home. Mr. Blair, please . . ."

George ripped his hand from Mrs. McGurk's moist grasp and rounded on her. "Now see here! Rose or no Rose, you're going to have to understand, Mrs. McGurk. As far as I'm concerned you were kind . . . sometimes . . . and that's all! You can't insult my girl and I won't . . . WHAT'S THAT!"

At the window there was a profile, pressed against the glass. Its eyes squinted to peer through its own shadow. Like a strange outlandish piece of vegetation, the hair of its beard hung there.

It was Mr. Josef's face of course.

George said, "How . . . ? He . . . ? Who . . . ?" He shoved the Ring on his finger. His hands curled into fists.

Mr. Josef brought me," wailed Mrs. McGurk. "Oh George, don't be mad at me! I can't bear it!" She burst into tears.

"Excuse me," said George. He dashed off towards the music room, the way Kathy had gone.

The old man sat dreaming. Memory, flowing like water, gently exploring the vast fields of past time. Ah, the long, long days of his life! How various they had been. How . . . after all and on the whole . . . he had enjoyed them! How wise he felt! How vividly he could now see the interplay of influences, how he had been deflected, in what ways, and why.

He should be tired. Well, he was tired, the old man thought, often and often. But the fatigue was in his body, his bones, his sinew. Not in the mind. A mind, fortified with so much experience, could play the game of life on a different level. All was illuminated, now. He saw further ahead, further behind. If it were not for the weariness of his flesh . . . what fun! What fun!

Young in spirit, he thought complacently, I have kept, for I have only refined my taste, not lost my appetite.

He roused from his reverie to realize he was alone. They'd gone, the young pair. Gone to embrace, to murmur plans. He knew. He knew. It was a shame and a pity and a waste . . . yes, waste! . . . that all he knew, all he remembered, all he had learned with such difficulty, so many pains . . . all this was tied to a declining body, chained to the span of a creature who must, at the appointed hour, long since struck for him, begin to die.

Mr. Blair took the stopper out of the Flask. He'd seen old flasks of this type. He knew the trick. It was one of the little barnacles of knowledge that had accumulated to him. He sniffed at the neck of the Flask and detected no smell. He looked about him for a vessel. There was his coffee cup. He emptied the dregs into a saucer. He drew out his handkerchief and wiped the cup quite dry.

There were no printed instructions on any label. He shook the Flask. Then he tipped it up and poured a little liquid out into the cup. A fleeting fear of poison or . . . worse . . . flat disappointment (for perhaps it was plain water) crossed his mind. But he faced the chances. Lips touched the rim. He drank.

It was perfectly tasteless.

He put down the empty cup and sat quietly where he was. He closed his eyes. A tree, in early spring, before it pushes forth its buds, must feel a deep interior thrill . . .

Mr. Blair had a moment to think this gentle thought and then he experienced a kind of personal earthquake, a sensation so entangled with that of speed that he was out in the clear at the other time-side of the whole shaking experience before he could tell himself *what* it felt like!

He opened his eyes and the room leapt into clarity. He could see, but how marvelously well! He'd forgotten how it was to see with a depth of focus, without glasses, with young eyes!

He bounded off the sofa. Oh, the spring in his legs! The freedom to move quickly! The strong responding pump of the willing heart!

But his clothes were all askew. His trousers were far, far too loose at the waist. His coat was tight on the edge his shoulders. Its tail was out like a bustle in the back. Mr. Blair unbuttoned his vest. He had to. He flexed his biceps. He held out his hands before him and saw that they were young.

He felt of his face, patting it with loving frantic fingers. He felt of his hair. Ah, the warm plenty of it! The soft thatch, the crisp wave at the temples! (It was blond and parted in the middle.)

George's butler crossed, with grave mien, the kitchen of George's house and said to the cook, who was his wife, "Marie, we've decided right. We give notice."

She nodded. "I don't like it, Edgar. It's odd. Those men running in . . ."

He leaned closer. "It is *very* odd. For instance, the master has a woman by each hand, in the drawing room."

"Tch . . . !"

"There is, also, a man with a beard going around the house, looking in at the windows."

"My!"

"Also . . . don't be alarmed, Marie . . . there is another man, a big fellow, watching this back door."

"Ooh . . ." said Marie. "That is odd, isn't it?"

"And," said the butler, "a strange young gentleman I never saw before is standing on his hands in the library."

"Standing on his hands!"

"As I breathe! Feet in the air!"

"Odd," she said. "No place for us, Edgar."

"Oh, no," he said. "Certainly not!"

Kathy ran through the music room. She fell against the door to the library. "Mr. Blair!"

Mr. Blair, enjoying the sweet coursing of his blood, nevertheless realized that he must stop this mere jumping about. There were bound to be certain problems. He must face them. He must contrive to avoid the hurrah and the vulgarity of public knowledge, and blend this miraculous renaissance into a prosey world without an uproar. He would, somehow, arrange for old Bennett Blair to fade away. Yes, and he would substitute himself as his own . . . what? Grandnephew! Bennett Blair 2nd! He fancied that! He would, for instance, change his signature.

Wait . . . ! Mr. Blair took out his pen, snatched a book, and scribbled his name on the margin. Good heavens! Not so! On the contrary, he must learn to forge his own signature and force this smooth young script into the former crabbed scrawl of his ripened personality.

He laughed out loud. It didn't worry him.

Somehow, Mr. Blair's wise old mind (and it saw and knew and didn't care) was being subtly altered by the vigor of his new young body. That

Cloak, for instance. He'd been indifferent to it. Might be a lot of sport, though, it now occurred to him. He chuckled. He picked up the little box. George had warned them not to touch it, or he would have put the Rose in his lapel out of sheer exuberance.

Good fellow, George! They could be friends, pals, sidekicks, buddies... Amused at the layers of slang that lay like strata in his memory, Mr. Blair, just exercising another of his five rejuvenated senses, lifted the box and smelled the Rose.

He drew in the perfume. Ah ... !

He heard his name. Kathy turned the knob. She opened the door.

Dead silent astonishment held them both.

Kathy caught on quickly. She got her voice back. "M-Mr. Blair?"

"Call me Bennett!" he said in a rich tenor. "Oh please, Kathleen. Oh, how lovely you are! I have never seen you before. Kathleen, do you know me? I am young again, and oh, my dear . . . I am young again for you! Kathleen, beautiful darling, this miracle is ours!"

"OH!" she screamed. "OH NO!" She slammed the door between them. George tore in from the drawing room.

"What's the matter?"

"He's yuh-yuh-young! He's talking about l-love!"

"That damned Rose," said George at once. "Mrs. McGurk, too. It *is* the Rose of Love. It makes you fall . . ."

"Oh!" She was enlightened. "Oh, George, forgive me, I didn't understand. But oh, take me away from here." She was unnerved and trembling with shock.

"Wait, there's a spy . . . that crazy Josef . . ."

She started blindly toward the drawing room. "Not in there," warned George. He whisked her through the middle door to an elbow of the great hall. They were together, and this was good. This was, however, about the only factor that could be called good or even fair among all the existing circumstances, as George soon discovered.

He peered toward the front door. The big Cadillac was still standing in the drive. They might pass swiftly across the arch, ignore Mrs. McGurk ... "Wait a minute," said George. "Nope. He's right out there. Joseph. He's dangerous, believe me. We can't go that way, not that way."

They stood, arm and arm, in a quandry.

Mr. Blair moved swiftly through the empty music room. At the drawing room door he came face to face with Mrs. McGurk.

"Where is she?" "Where is he?" they cried.

"Whoops!" said George, in the hall. He drew Kathy into the morning room on the opposite side of the house.

Mr. Blair strode over the great silky rug, his young feet spurning its fabulous beauty. He burst into the hall, flung open the front door. He cried into Josef's startled beard, "Hey, have you seen a beautiful red-haired girl?"

Mr. Josef, confounded, tried to look as if he were waiting for a streetcar. But Mr. Blair, seeing the Cadillac still there, slammed the door and stood with his back to it. If only he could find her! He'd done wrong. He'd frightened her. Great tides of potential gentleness, deep wells of soothing charms surged restless in his breast. If only he could find her!

George and Kathy slipped from the morning room to the dining room, through the butler's pantry to the kitchen to the back door. The servants might have been so many cupboards. George saw no way to explain this spectacle of the master and his lovely luncheon guest simply flying by, hand in hand.

On the brink of an exit, George reversed them again. "Gogo," he said. "We better not go this way."

"Why don't we use the magic? George, why can't we get the Genie?"

"Say!" said George. He pulled Kathy, another way, into the hall again, the hall that lay like the hole in a doughnut, at the center of everything.

Mrs. McGurk was in the library!

"Wait," said George. "Wait, Kathy." He was most reluctant to face the poor woman. He hesitated. He drew Kathy behind the dining room door to think.

This was an error.

Mr. Blair stood over the second maid. "Went out the back door, did they?"

"No, sir."

"Didn't?" Following a reflex, he chucked her under the chin. "Where then?"

"That way."

"Mr. Blair heaved at his sagging trousers and pursued.

The butler peered palely from the pantry.

Mr. Blair rushed into the hall, dug his heel into the carpet to brake himself, heard breathing in the library, and veered that way.

Someone was breathing. It was Mrs. McGurk. "Seen them?" She shook her head. "They're in the house. They haven't left it." Her woebegone face brightened a little. "How about giving me a hand?" suggested Mr. Blair. "Otherwise we can run circles in this squirrel cage for days."

"I want to talk to George," she quavered.

"Good. Fine." Mr. Blair's legs had temporarily given over to the jurisdiction of his wise old brain. Now he remembered to pick up the Flask and shove it into his pocket. He said, "You come and stand where you can watch the front door and the stairs while I go around again."

Mrs. McGurk nodded. But she was full of suspicion. That was George's Flask! She knew it. Had she not polished it with her own two hands? Who was this odd-looking young man? And what right had he to put George's property into his pocket?

When he had gone ahead, through the music room, then quietly, before she followed, Mrs. McGurk took up the Lamp. She knew its value. George should not lose it! Not while his Constance lived! Yes, it was HIS, and she would defend it! One day he would thank her devotion for this!

When George and Kathy eased into the library, it was too late. The Lamp had gone! George sucked a tooth. His collection was sure getting scattered and it wouldn't do. He had a dreadful sinking feeling, a foreboding. This was just going to lead to all kinds of trouble. He bundled into the carpet bag all of the magic objects that remained.

Kathy whimpered. George said, "Honey, this is just awful! But I can't take you outside with those thugs hanging around." They had reached the hall's elbow again.

"Can't we try upstairs?"

George said, "Upstairs is a dead end, Kathy. You put on the Cloak. Slip out . . ."

"I want to stay with you."

"But—uh—they might shoot!"

"Then *you* must wear the Cloak!"

"No, because if they should grab YOU, I'd . . . I'd . . . I'd . . ."

Kathy pulled herself together. "Why don't I just face Mr. Blair." Her pretty mouth grew firm. "I've been silly . . . yes, I've been silly."

"Honey . . ." George ached to protect her. "There must be a way out of this, if I had the sense . . . I wish," he murmured unhappily, "a little bird would tell me how I could get out of here."

"On the Flying Carpet," said the white cockatoo, tartly.

"Eh? What's that?" said George.

He was wearing the Ring. He had slipped it on his finger, long ago. At his words, of course, the stone in the Ring had become quite clear and shining. George wasn't noticing, however. He was gazing, astonished, at the cockatoo, and the cockatoo stared back, insolently, as if to say, "You dope! You shoulda thought of that!"

"George!" Kathy was jolted out of her nervous reaction. "The Ring! Oh, give me that Ring!"

"Wha . . . ?"

"Quick! I can't expl . . . Oh, quick, before you say another word!"

George gave it to her. "What's the matter?" he said. "By golly, it's the perfect solution! Come on. Upstairs."

Mr. Blair heard Mrs. McGurk give tongue, but too late. George and Kathy scrambled out a window to a flat roof. He spread out the Carpet and they sat down on it.

"Take us to Maine, if you please," said George firmly. "Deeport, Maine." And then they rose. They fell giggling into each other's arms. It was so wonderfully absurd and delightful! Here they were, together. The mad afternoon was over. They floated, free. The sun was sinking behind a band of red . . .

"Well, they're gone," said Mr. Blair.

"Yes," sighed Mrs. McGurk. Her face was calm.

Mr. Blair thought he knew whither the fugitives were flying. He saw no reason to tell this old harridan what he had guessed.

Mrs. McGurk, for her part, knew exactly what she was going to do and how she was going to find them. But she didn't intend to let this wild young man in on her secret.

"I shall go back to town," said he. "I shall just borrow George's car. May I give you a lift?"

"Oh no, thank you," she said. "I have a car."

They parted. It didn't occur to either to wonder why the other was so calm.

The rose and the gold withdrew, leaving a thin gray sky. They huddled

together in the very center of the Carpet, because it was quite small, for two, and steep and empty air was most vividly near, on all sides. Their vehicle was rolling along through chilly space with an undulating flutter that had been a little trying, at first.

Also, there was nothing between them and the stellar distances to keep off draughts. Ah, it was bitter up here! Bitter! Finally, George had hauled the Cloak out of the bag and wrapped it around them both. This helped a great deal, although it was rather frightening and bleak to be invisible. They had to hang on to each other very close to be sure each was not utterly alone, in the middle of the air.

Irritably, George said he wished he knew who the dickens had swiped that Lamp.

Kathy said, "Don't wish, George."

He stretched a cramped leg very cautiously lest a shoe fall into New England. "Say, Kathy, why did you make me take off the Ring? What happened?"

She explained. George found her freezing hand and felt of the Ring with a numb thumb. "Kathy, if it is a Wishing Ring, I can't have used all mine up." He straightened and the Cloak fell back. "Let me get you a sandwich!"

"A sandwich! Of all things, George!"

"But you're hungry! You're starving!"

"I'm not starving," said Kathy. "I just feel as if I were starving. No!" She sat on the hand that wore the Ring. "You know," she went on, thoughtfully, pulling a corner of the Cloak up and vanishing, "you and Mr. Blair make the same mistake. You both want to take care of me. You forget I'm alive . . . and thinking and doing! I have some sense!" She squirmed indignantly. "Whatever made Mr. Blair think I'd let *you* throw my fortune around foolishly? *I'd* be there, wouldn't I? If anybody was going to throw it around foolishly, it would be both of us! You men!" Her body leaned on his. It wasn't as mad as her voice sounded.

"Honey, give me the Ring. This darned thing is too darned draughty and slow . . ."

"First you're going to have to think back. One wish you wasted, I know. That silly bird."

"Bird!" said George feebly.

"You've got a pet phrase. You said . . ." George groaned. "Oh, George, how many times?"

"Once before, in my room. I remember, now. It was a sparrow."

"Two wishes gone!" wailed Kathy. "And all of mine! That certainly settles it! No sandwich, and we'll proceed to Maine the way we're going."

"Honey, please . . . I don't like you to be cold . . ."

"I'm thinking of both of us. We just can't afford . . ."

"I know and you're wonderful and I love you but . . ."

Kathy said she loved him, too, and the point of their dispute got lost, somehow. After a while, Kathy laid her head snug on his shoulder. The Carpet kept rolling along, and miserable as they were, it was peaceful there in the silent sky.

Suddenly, it wasn't silent. George heaved his shoulder. He pointed with an invisible hand.

It was an airliner, a silver thing, speeding the way they were going with a steady roar. It pursued. It caught up. It passed. The Carpet tossed its invisible passengers, as it bucked and staggered in the backwash.

Through the little windows they could see where the dim light bathed the warm upholstered scene. Leaning at his ease in the deep cushioned seat was a young man with blond hair (parted in the middle). He'd been dining. Now he was smoking. A pretty hostess bent to remove his tray. Mr. Blair (for it was he) knocked, as he whisked by in the sky, his lazy ashes off, and smiled up into the pretty face with a quaint turn-of-the-century wolfishness, the image of which persisted on the gray cold air when he had gone.

The Carpet kept lumbering along.

The night wore on. Mrs. McGurk took the Mirror, once more, out of her bag. She was tired and bruised from bouncing through the night in Mr. Josef's old rattletrap of a car, which he pushed so recklessly at a speed beyond comfort. At times, she'd been about to ask him to slow down, but she hated to tamper with his absorption.

"Still east?" he asked.

"Still east, I judge. They seem to be nearing Narragansett."

She and Mr. Josef were, she feared, far far behind. Mrs. McGurk sighed. She was weary and her heart was sore, and she began to suspect that this was ridiculous. She hardly knew, any more, what she hoped. At first, it was only to see George, face to face once more, but now her resolution flagged. She was discouraged. She was . . . and her heart ached . . . growing old. Oh, she'd known *that*, all along. Still, she had hoped that even her middle-aged heart could hold the luxury of devotion. A secret spring of joy, it might have been! Ah, that devil, jealousy, had undone everything!

She had wept already. In her distress, she'd babbled. She'd mentioned magic.

But Mr. Josef didn't believe. He thought they were pursuing a helicopter. He didn't even believe in the Mirror. He'd said, scornfully, that Mrs. McGurk was guilty of reactionary thinking. No doubt, he said, it was simple radar. But when she swore she could lead them to George, he'd been perfectly willing, even eager to go on.

The other one, that Gogo, had left them flat. He'd given a brief total opinion of the whole matter. He'd said, "Nuts!" Mr. Josef had screamed something after him, something like "Traitor!" Traitor to what? she wondered sleepily. She thrust her precious Mirror back into the depths of her bag and this time her fingers stumbled on the Lamp!

For heaven's sake! What a fool she was!

"Mr. Josef," she cried. "Stop, please!"

"At the next gas station, Madame," he said patiently.

Mrs. McGurk bit her tongue. She forbore to correct him. She really could not imagine what the sight of the Genie might do to Mr. Josef. She decided she had better not rub the Lamp until she was alone.

A mangy little roadhouse lay just beyond the next bend. It looked and was a dump. But Mrs. McGurk cried, "Stop here, Mr. Josef. Maybe," she fluttered, "you would care for something to drink? I might take a little myself."

"Ah, perhaps so." They pulled up. Mr. Josef's hand under her arm, and he looking suspiciously on all sides, they went in.

Behind the bar a hairless man with a roll of fat at the back of his neck looked up without expression. The stale smelling twilight seemed otherwise deserted.

Mrs. McGurk asked the bartender and he told her. There was the usual anteroom, the powder table. She took the Lamp out of her bag, pulled herself together, summoned courage. So, in the lady's room of Joe's Bar and Grill, Cocktails, French fries, she met, for the second time, the Slave of the Lamp. This time Constance McGurk did not flinch. She waited calmly while he introduced himself with his formula, until he had asked the conventional question. "What are your commands?"

"Bring George Hale to me," she said.

"I regret, Madame," he replied, "it is not within my power."

"What's that!" Mrs. McGurk was outraged.

"Magic cannot cross magic," the Genie told her.

"Is that so! You mean to tell me, just because he is riding around on that Carpet . . . ?"

The Genie bowed.

"Well!" said Mrs. McGurk in a huff. "A fine thing! Look here, you can do it if he gets off, can't you?"

The Genie bowed.

"Very well," she snapped. "The minute he does get off that thing, *then* bring him to me."

"I hear and obey."

"Wherever I am," she added sharply.

"I hear and obey."

"And never mind that girl. Do you understand? I don't care . . ." The knob on the door behind was rattling. "That's all," she said quickly. "Shoo . . . go on, now."

The Genie vanished. A sullen looking blonde in a fur jacket was entering this sanctuary. Her black eye flickered on the big handbag in Constance's hands. Or did it remark her ruby (relic of Mr. McGurk) solitaire?

The blonde passed on to the inner sanctum. Mrs. McGurk slipped off her ruby and hid it, too, in her bag, which she swung by its long strap over her shoulder. It had occurred to her that she might be among thieves.

Mrs. McGurk was suspicious all over, but she had her own brand of toughness. She demanded a piece of string from the bartender, and she tied the strap of her bag to her slip strap... no silken wisp, this, but a broad band of strong cotton. She even tied the clasp of the bag with several loops of cord. Now! To rob her would involve more serious crime. Let them try it if they dared!

Now she turned commandingly. She said to Josef, "I want to go home."

His beard tipped up. "Dear lady," he soothed, "you must not lose heart."

"I want to go back."

"No, no, we go on!"

"It isn't necessary," she snapped.

"Ah," he purred, "I am afraid, dear lady, you don't quite understand. We ... Go on!" Mr. Josef, locking eyes with the bartender, reached out and grasped her hand.

"Take your hand off me!" said Constance in shrill alarm.

"You see," said Mr. Josef, silkily, "you are to lead me to Hale."

"Lead *you!*"

"Did you think," Mr. Josef laughed nastily, "I've taken so many pains with no motive of my own? Ah, come," he chided. Then he barked. "To the car!"

"Help," said Constance feebly.

"Not in here, Mac," said the bartender. "Outside." He jerked his chin. He turned his back.

"Help! Murder!" cried Constance. She ran.

"Ah, no, my chickadee," said Josef merrily. As she fell out the door he caught her by her arms. She forced them back. With some of the bartender's cord, he was binding her wrists together. Joe's Bar and Grill remained indifferent. Only the neon fluttered over their heads. In this dead of night, the road lay bare.

Josef marched her to the car, forced her to the seat. "My dear woman," he said righteously, "let me assure you, you are only a means to an end. Function as that means and you are perfectly safe." He walked around and got in at her side. "East?" he inquired, calmly.

"East," quavered Mrs. McGurk. "Oh," prayed she, "George! Oh, George!"

When the sun rose, George at last threw off the protecting Cloak and peered over the edge. Below was Maine, and all around was morning, and suddenly George wanted the world to be as clear and crisp as it looked.

"Kathy, let's dump all this stuff! It's no good!" He held up the Rose in its box. "We don't want this around, do we?"

"I don't think you ought to dump it," said Kathy thoughtfully. "You just can't tell. It's not the fault of the *things*, George." She was sitting with her legs crossed, her brown eyes serious. "It's just that the more power you've got in your hand," mused Kathy, "the more careful you have to be how your hand turns."

George took out the Purse. "Gold sure ain't what it used to be."

"But we'll keep it." Kathy put it and the Rose in a deep pocket of her dress.

"Let's see. Mrs. McGurk must have the Mirror. Mr. Blair's got the Flask. One of them's got the Lamp. We're sitting on the dumb Carpet. And you're still wearing the Ring."

"Yes," she said. "I must remember. And here's the Cloak." She folded it over her arm, as one might put on her gloves when the train is entering the station.

"One thing left." George drew out the Sword. The hilt snuggled into his hand as if the blade were begging to dance. "I'd kinda like to ... uh ... hang on to this," said George sheepishly. "But I'm darned tooting going to get rid of this bag!" He buckled the sword belt around his waist. Then he lifted the carpet bag and heaved it over into space. "There!"

He felt better. He lay down on his belly and inspected the terrain. He thought he could spot the Congregational spire. George bet Kathy a dollar his mother would make him shave on an empty stomach. So they lay, giggling, peering down, kicking their heels, and the sun was warm on their backs. They forgot they'd been miserable. They were almost home.

Mr. Blair touched earth long before dawn, hired a car, and drove himself to Deeport. At the Ocean House, he registered, unchallenged, as Bennett Blair 2nd. He reserved a suite for Miss Douglas. He had her luggage put there.

Oh, he was a fox! He chuckled, looking down at George's suit that he had filched from the vast array in the upstairs wardrobe at George's fabulous house. All his own suits were hopeless. He was a fox! He'd thought of this!

Oh, it had been jolly, whipping down the parkways in George's Cadillac, sneaking into his own house, commanding Fraulein in an imitation of his own old voice, over the house phone, to pack for Kathy. Maneuvering the servants out of the way before he made his dash to the streets again. He was postponing, he was evading. First and foremost came Kathleen.

The darling girl had run away and he could not blame her for that. He had overwhelmed her too suddenly, pouring out such talk! Well, he could not blame himself for that, either. That glorious surge of the heart had overwhelmed him. He did not regret it.

All would be well, yet. Mr. Blair felt absolutely invincible.

He breakfasted in his room, alone. This was his first free time with a looking glass. He tried to part his blond hair on the side, but it refused. How old was he, he wondered. A scar, there, at the hairline. He remembered the occasion of it. He must be at least twenty-five. A good age! Just the right age for Kathleen!

Kathleen! Mr. Blair was, actually, in a state of civil war, his physical youth resisting his foxy old brain, so that he swayed between dreams of love and the cooler strategy of conquest.

At last, he realized that even the ancient decrepit Carpet would be ambling into port, soon. So he tore his gaze from the fascinating face in the glass, borrowed binoculars, drove off to an unpopulated stretch of beach. He would take up a post. He would meet the morning Carpet. Mr. Blair chuckled. What a glorious morning! He frisked on the pebbly strand.

Mr. Blair's wise old mind, bouncing, willy nilly, while the rest of him danced, remarked that Wall Street had never been like this!

The Carpet began to lose altitude. It was coming in for a landing on a deserted potato field. George peered anxiously over. He saw a car draw up, the figure of a man got out and ran, arms waving. "Oh, my gosh!" said George in dismay.

"It's Mr. Blair, isn't it?" said Kathy calmly. "Never mind." George squeezed her hand.

The Carpet came softly, softly down. George stepped off, turned to hold his hand to his lady, and vanished.

Mr. Blair came bounding up. "Hello, hello."

"Hello," said Kathy coolly. The fact that George had vanished didn't perturb her at once. After all, they had both been vanishing, off and on, all night long. She was perfectly accustomed to the idea.

"Have a nice trip?" said Mr. Blair pleasantly.

"Not very," she answered severely. "George..." She missed the feel of his hand, the sense of his near shoulder, even more ... "Shall we go home?"

No answer came.

"Where'd he go?" said Mr. Blair, looking about them. But Kathy began to walk straight ahead of her. She was so very tired, so very hungry ... And George ... Why didn't his arm come around her weary shoulders? Tears stung her eyes. She lifted her own arm to mop at them with fabric.

The Cloak hung on her arm!

But then . . . ! "Oh!" cried Kathy. "Oh! Oh!" The Lamp! Now she remembered its loss and terrible power!

"I don't understand what's happened to George," said Mr. Blair, rather angrily, "but if this is the way he takes care of you . . . !"

"I'm afraid . . . there was something," she said forlornly, "he *had* to do."

Mr. Blair's brain beat his body down in a short sharp struggle, for it knew an opportunity when it saw one. He became the soul of tender kindness. *He* would take care of her. He brought her to her room at the Ocean House. Ah, the sweet warm comfort of it, after the vast chill inhumanity of the sky! He commanded them to bring coffee . . . Oh, blessed liquid!

Thus he comforted her with the civilized arts. Now, she must bathe and rest, he said, and then take lunch, perhaps? Mr. Blair's breath grew a trifle gaspy. "Kathleen, won't you call me Bennett, now?"

He was being so kind. Kathy couldn't be ungracious. She smiled and said she'd try.

Mr. Blair's wise old mind fought like a maddened hornet in his skull against his urge to grab her. "Rest well," he counseled, and withdrew.

Sore and bewildered, Kathy nevertheless bathed and dressed herself in fresh clothing. What to do? George was gone! And she could not think how, except by the power of the Lamp. And who, then, had invoked its power but that fatuous old Mrs. McGurk? But what to do? She turned over what magic she had in stock. The Rose and the Purse? She put them in the handbag Fraulein had supplied. George was right. These things were no good. Neither could the Cloak help her. It lay on the bed. The Carpet?

Oh, heavens! It lay abandoned in the field, and what mad adventure waited now for some Yankee farmer, she dreaded to imagine. Oh, George had been so right! This troublesome, troublesome magic . . . She wished . . .

Wished! Wished, indeed! Kathy threw herself down to weep. Here hung the Ring on her finger, and she with no wishes left!

"Oh, George," wept Kathy, "George . . ."

When the sun rose and people began to appear, Mr. Josef abandoned the highways. He made the car slink through back alleys and lanes. It seemed to put one wheel cautiously ahead of the other, like pussy feet. Even the engine whispered along.

He had not gagged Mrs. McGurk. The poor woman was nearly speechless anyhow with misery. She had kept saying, "East . . . North . . ." at random, and he followed her directions with a queer blindness.

He kept talking. He expounded his philosophy, explaining how, by stealth, treachery, and violence, he would help make a fairer world. "No more slaves!" cried Mr. Josef, pounding the steering wheel with his fist. Mrs. McGurk's enslaved ear heard all this, but her unregenerate mind was going furiously around the same old circle. How to get free?

The Lamp was here, still tied to her person. What if Mr. Josef should open her handbag. How could she benefit? if he should accidently rub the Lamp and summon the Genie! Of course, Mr. Josef could not, on principle, acquire a Private Slave. No, no, all must be chained alike to the wheel of the State! Mrs. McGurk wondered to herself if there was an Amalgamated Brotherhood of Oriental Genii with a closed shop. She felt hysterical. She fought down the feeling.

They were slinking along a country lane. "North?" asked Mr. Josef.

"A little east," she answered wearily, as she had been answering for hours, quite at random.

He stopped the car. There was a glade at their right; an old crabapple tree stood among wild grasses. On the left a little wood and the curve of the lane closed them in.

"We have been here before," said Mr. Josef and he turned and behind his eyes there burned a reddish anger.

Mrs. McGurk closed her eyes. He'd come out of his state. He'd noticed they weren't getting anywhere. And what to do or say now, she did not ... did not ... know.

Then, suddenly, George ... George himself ... was there, standing beside the car, leaning on the sill at her side, looking reproachfully into her face. "You shouldn't have done this, Mrs. McGurk," he said, more in sorrow than in anger.

She screamed, "George! Be careful! He ... Gun ... Mad ... Oh ... !"

"Huh?" said George.

Mr. Josef got nimbly out on his side and raced around the hood. A gun was in his hand.

George backed away from the car in confusion and surprise. His feet slipped among the sweet-scented tall grasses of the glade. His hand went, with an ancient instinct, to the hilt of the Sword.

Mr. Josef, gun in hand, charged at him. "Ha!" cried the spy. "Haha! Haha!" His face went into its most menacing leer. His beard wagged. "We shall continue," purred Mr. Josef, "our little chat. I will have the secret of the ray, please. And now! I'll give you two minutes, 120 seconds to explain the process verbally or turn over documents ..."

"Secret! Documents!" cried George. "You dumb bunny! Listen, I cut up that stuff in my room with this old sword."

"Impossible," said Mr. Josef calmly.

George said, "Let me show you! Maybe you'll believe it when you see it. Maybe you'll stop this idiotic Grade-B nonsense!" He pulled the Sword half out of the scabbard.

"Nonsense," said the spy thickly. "That's typical of you stupid Americans!"

Then George really did get mad. "Now, wait a minute," he said. "Shut up a minute, you with the beard! Suppose I had a secret ray? What in hell," cried George, "makes you think I'd give it to such as you? What makes you think I'd let a mutt like you, waving a gun around, steal a better weapon? You're not fit to be trusted with a bow and arrow. I wouldn't give you *any* secret *any* time *any*where for *any* reason . . . You and your corny threats!" cried George. He drew the Sword out all the way. "You obsolete old bully! Get out of the way!"

Mr. Josef raised the gun. The rules of his craft did not permit him to kill dead somebody with a secret. Ideology said, torture. His eyes narrowed calculating pain.

The Sword leapt in George's hand. It glittered across the air like a fork of lightning. It cut the gun . . . and a fingertip . . . from Josef's hand.

Blood flowed.

Mr. Josef looked down. He often had thoughts of blood, but not often was the blood in his thoughts *his* blood. Mr. Josef turned very pale. Holding the wounded hand before him, he tipped, fainting, forward. Fascinated, George watched him fall . . . against the blade! The wicked blade, still poised in George's hand!

Mr. Josef expired at once.

George loosened his hand from the hilt of the terrible toy. It fell on the ground beside the body. His hand was stinging. It was divorced from the rest of him by its independent guilt.

George sunk his face in his hands and groaned aloud.

Mrs. McGurk said, "George, dear George, don't you mind! You couldn't help it! Untie me," she begged. "Oh, George, you don't know! When you hear, you won't feel quite so bad about him. It was self-defense, George. You had to do it."

"Untie you!" said George stupidly. He came to the car. He worked at her wrists. He would not touch that Sword again, even for Mercy's sake. She cut the cord with a dull penknife from his pocket.

Mrs. McGurk, in spite of the pain, moved her hands to her handbag. "Don't worry . . . don't worry . . . you and I will be far far away. See what I have!" she cried, as to a hurt baby. (See! See the pretty Lamp!)

But George shook himself. What's done is done, he thought in some hard sturdy core. Never meant to kill him. Was a kind of accident and in self-defense, besides. I'm not, probably, going to prison. He looked down the long vista of his days, every one of which the memory of this day would mar. No, he would not go to prison, he thought bleakly.

Mrs. McGurk cried out, trying to work her fingers. "Open my bag, George. The Lamp!"

"No," he said. "I can't do that." He put his hand on the bag's tied-up clasp. "This isn't the way, Constance . . . I've got to go straight through everything, now. Or always be sorry. Sorrier, I mean, than I am already.

We'll have to notify the police. You'll . . . help me, won't you?"

"I will! I will!" sobbed Mrs. McGurk. "Oh, George, dear George, I'll tell them how it was. You've saved me!"

A brown animal broke out of the woods. It was a mule. A stout old woman in a dirty gingham garment . . . an old woman with a face like the gray bark of an ancient tree, was holding a rope attached to the animal.

"How do?" she said. "Had a little trouble?"

"Yes, we . . . Yes . . ."

"Seen it," she said. "Sent a kid up to the main road. He'll be back wid somebody," she continued. She leaned on the mule and scratched her tousled gray head with a twig she now took out of her mouth.

"With somebody? You mean, the police?"

"Ay-ah."

"Oh," said George. "Well, thanks very much."

There was a tableau, minutes of no sound and no motion, except the mule's gentle cropping at the grass. Then sound and motion were approaching. George left Mrs. McGurk's side and went to meet the man in uniform.

"What goes on here?" said the Law. "That a dead man over there?"

"Oh, officer!" cried Constance. "He was trying to kidnap me! He had a gun! This young gentleman was forced to . . . do it!"

"He was trying to kidnap you, you say!" said the cop, focusing on her face. Her nose was violently askew, after all she had been through. The cop blinked and looked about him.

"You know me," said the woman with the mule, putting the twig back into her mouth.

"Say! Sure. You're the woman who keeps a bunch of pigs down there in the hollow. You see what happened here?"

"Ay-ah."

"He kill him?" The cop indicated George.

"He killed him, all right. Sliced into him. I seen it."

The cop stepped over the tall grass, looked down, looked up. "Why'd you do it?" said he suddenly, savagely, to George.

"It was . . . more or less . . . an accident . . ." George was feeling sick.

"Nah," said the woman with the mule, spitting out the twig.

"No?" said the cop. "What would you say it was, hey?"

"Murder. That's what it was," said the pig woman, not violently at all. Her dull eyes rested indifferently on George.

About noon, Kathy and Blair Bennett were settled snugly in the bar, sipping sherry. Kathy was the prisoner of inaction. Mr. Blair had agreed that, no doubt, George must have been kidnapped (in a sense that was the word) by Mrs. McGurk. But, he suggested gently, if George did not, now, care for the situation in which he found himself, then, being grown and responsible, he would make his own efforts to change it. Let, hinted Mr. Blair, George do it. While they were waiting for him, in this pleasant meantime, he and she might just explore each other's friendship a little.

Ah, he was a fox! Kathy relaxed. There was nothing else to do. And she was warm and not very hungry any more, and there was the old beauty of the sea, outside, and she snug beside a friend who knew her well.

The manager came into the bar. "Say, Frank, I just heard something over the air. Fellow name of George Hale got picked up over to Snowden." His voice was low, but at that name Kathy was clutching the edge of the table.

"Picked up!" said the bartender. "What for?"

"Homicide. That's murder, to you."

"Murder!"

"Coincidence, eh?" chuckled the manager. "I bet you Miz Hale's phone is going to be ringing."

"Nah," said the bartender. "Nobody's going to think that's *George!* Wouldn't hurt a fly, for gossake. Besides, he's still down to New York."

"Lots of fools in this world," said the manager cheerfully. "Seems this fellow ran a man through with a sword."

"Sword, eh? Kinda unusual. I wonder if somebody hadn't oughta tip George off," mused the bartender. "Tell him to call up his folks and say it ain't him. You think Miz Mar-gret is liable to worry any?"

"Miz Liz and Miz Nell won't let her," soothed the manager. "Just the same, I'd certainly like to talk to George. It could help to talk to George."

"He oughta come back home."

"Frank, nobody knows . . . nobody knows how I wish he'd come back home!" mourned the manager.

"Boys in the band feeling pretty sick, too."

"Going to be a lo-ong winter."

"Sweet guy, that George." The bartender's was a sentimental trade. "I dunno what it was about him... Gee, wouldn't I like to see him walk in...!"

The manager stifled a sob.

Kathy leaned over. "We have to go there," she whispered fiercely. "Now!"

"Suppose," said Mr. Blair cautiously. "I . . . er . . . see what I can find out."

"Just let's go," said Kathy and she rose.

"Kathy, please listen, my dear . . ." He caught up to her. "You can't go there!"

"But of course I can!"

"No, no, dear." His hands were kind but they held her. "It's a nasty mess. Didn't you hear him say homicide? George is evidently in jail. You can't go there."

"Why not?" she blazed.

"Because you mustn't be involved. Think of the newspapers! The whole moronic public licking its lips . . . Kathy, consider. George wouldn't *want* you to go through all that. You are too precious. *I* don't want . . ."

"What you want," said Kathy coldly, "and even what George would want, is not the point exactly. *I want!* Did you ever think of that? You don't even consider I'm alive! Also," her hair swung in a gleaming arc, "you don't mean 'precious.' You mean delicate and breakable! Well, I'm not breakable! I'm me! And if *I* want to be there when George is in trouble, I am going to be there!"

"Oh, no," said Mr. Blair, losing his head.

"Oh, yes," said Kathy, turning her back.

"Oh, no," he cried, seizing her arm.

"Oh, yes," she cried, twisting away.

"Kathy," he blurted. "He isn't worth it!"

"Oh, isn't he?" said Kathy, very, very dangerously.

Mr. Blair groaned, regretting error. He let her run up the one flight of stairs. He followed. She ran to her room. He took a stand in the corridor.

He tried to think what to do or say now. If she insisted, why, he'd better take her to Snowden, defend her from what annoyance he could, regain what ground he had just lost, so foolishly. He wouldn't lose his head again!

Kathy opened her door, wearing her jacket, purse under her arm. She was so beautiful! Mr. Blair's head went looping away from him like a collar button under the dresser.

"Kathy!" he cried in his throbbing tenor. He took a step as if he would surge on one knee with hands up to plead . . .

She slipped back behind the half closed door. She picked the Cloak off the bed.

Had Mr. Blair not been so furiously occupied, retrieving his head for the second time and jamming it fiercely back in place, he might have noticed certain dainty depressions, dotting alone along the padded floor.

It was a crude little jail, but George was tight in a cell just the same, the only prisoner at the moment.

Beyond a thick door, he knew there was a kind of anteroom, and that there, side by side on hard straight chairs, Mrs. McGurk and the pig woman were waiting. He knew this because every now and then someone connected with the law would walk through this corridor. Whenever the end door at the left swung in, he could see that bare and dusty place, and the two of them.

George stared at the wall. The cell block smelled dismally of antiseptics. He felt anesthetized. He would rouse himself and his thoughts would go spinning around the circle of his anxieties. Kathy . . .

whether Mr. Blair was being a problem . . . whether to insist that his people be notified . . . His mother and the Aunts, he knew, would march in close formation, right beside him, heads up, mouths firm, right through this trouble. Yet, if he could spare them any confusion before it was clear just what kind of trouble this was going to be, George felt he must.

Then there were the pig woman and Mrs. McGurk, both problems, and his legal status at their oddly assorted mercies. And there were the complications he'd left behind, about the big house . . . And other complications ahead. There was Mr. Blair. So his thoughts went around and came out at the same place and meanwhile, there arose about him the carbolic flavored, dreary, and somehow official smell of delay.

An attendant of some kind pushed the end door inward. Mrs. McGurk sailed around his bulk. She cried, "George!"

George rose politely. "What's happening?"

"They're waiting. As soon as somebody or other comes back, then they'll start asking questions. Oh, George!" Her strange nose was pink from weeping and wrangling. "Remember," she whispered, "remember we can still get away."

George roused in alarm. "No, no. Don't do that, Constance, please!"

"We can leave all this behind," she breathed. There was a light in her eye he groaned to see. "Everything behind us! Some desert isle . . . far, far away . . ."

George felt the impulse of his hair to stand on end. He could look right into her dream. He could see the hibiscus in her hair.

"That would be the worst thing you could possibly do," said George in a stern desperate whisper. "No, please. You'd better give me the Lamp."

"They'd only take it away from you. George, you must trust me!"

George tried very hard not to look as frightened as he felt. "I do," he said. "I know *you* know I can't spend the rest of my life a fugitive. I must clear my name. *You* understand!"

"I suppose so," she sniffled. It was on the tip of George's tongue to point out that he'd been whisked into that strange duel. It had been *her* doing. But he dared not. "Don't you know," he pleaded, "every time that trick is worked it only causes trouble?"

"Trouble for you, but oh, George, it wasn't trouble for me. It was my salvation!"

Mrs. McGurk had it all twisted around. She'd forgotten that Josef had been after George. She saw herself in the juiciest role, naturally. She was the Heroine. George was, of course, Her Hero. It was maddening.

George changed the subject. "Could you do anything with that pig woman?"

"Pig woman!" spat Constance. "I've talked and talked! She won't listen. We know she's lying. They'll have to believe us. They'll have to!"

But George thought to himself, No, they won't either have to. It was a queer thing, but Mrs. McGurk's obvious partisanship was going to make the truth sound like a lie, while the pig woman's lie, because she told it without heat, was going to shine forth as a simple impersonal objective statement of fact.

He shook his head. "There'll be some way to prove the truth," he soothed, trying to sound serene and confident. "Don't worry. Don't do anything. Nothing to do, but wait till they ask for our story."

Mrs. McGurk nodded. She straightened her tired back. "We'll tell our story," said she. But George saw right through to the female squirm of her judgment. "But if they don't believe it," Mrs. McGurk was saying darkly to herself, "I shall act! I, Constance, shall save him, in spite of himself!"

George stifled a groan. And as Mrs. McGurk, not entirely without realizing the drama of it all, let herself be led away, he beat his head on the bars. Tell their story, eh? Including one thing and another? George closed his eyes and winced all over.

Kathy's voice said, "Hello."

The end door was swinging shut. He seemed alone. "Kathy, where are you?"

"George, have you had any food?"

"No," he said. "Yes. I mean, no. Kathy!"

"I brought you a couple of sandwiches," said she in business-like tones. He felt the package in his hand. As she let go of it, it became visible.

"Ham! Cheese! Darling!"

"And a thing of coffee." The hot carton came out of the air.

"Kathy, how . . . ?"

"I'll tell you while you eat." He could feel her presence, just outside his bars. "Golly, George, do you know something? Being invisible isn't what it's cracked up to be. I'm so battered. I took a bus and five people nearly sat on me. I was leaping from seat to seat the whole time. And it's 70 miles. You see, I didn't have any money, except this old gold, and it would have just caused a commotion. And Mr. Blair had the keys to his car in his pocket. George, I stole the food. Is it good?" The only advantage when you're invisible is that you really can steal things quite easily."

George, even among the sandwiches, was a grin all over. He felt so much better he could hardly believe it. "Kathy, this coffee is delicious!"

"Did I sugar it right?"

"Oh, perfectly! Just perfectly!" How dear and close they were, even in so small a thing! Oh how much cosier was even trouble when it was built for two! "Kathy," he said, "we can get through this, somehow, if she only won't . . . take us apart."

Kathy said, "I want you to tell me. I'm trying to wait till you're not so hungry."

Angel! thought George, and washed down a big bite. Then he told her.

"Oh, dear!" said Kathy at last.

"Honey, was Mr. Blair ... uh ... ?"

"Well, not very," she said. But George knew the problem of Mr. Blair was not diminished. "Well." He could feel her brace up as she spoke. "What *can* we do? Let's see. George, I think I'll go and steal the Lamp."

"Say!"

"That would help, wouldn't it?"

"Boy, would it!"

"All right. That's one thing we can do. Of course, there's this." He felt the warm metal circle slip into his palm. The Ring! "We're pretty sure you've got one wish left," she reminded him. "The only trouble is ... George, what should you wish?"

"Oh, Kathy, I w ..."

Her warm hand stifled his mouth. "Sssssh .... Sssssh! For goodness sakes! This time, we've got to figure it out carefully."

"I guess that's right."

"Don't even speak," warned Kathy, "because ... for instance, you could wish we had the Lamp, but it would be silly not to try to steal it first. Because maybe you'll need the wish to make the pig woman stop lying... but then... There are so many angles ..." she wailed. "I think we better try everything else first and save the Ring for an emergency."

George wondered, for a moment, what she called an emergency. Then he pressed his lips tight. He agreed. For if, he thought, Mrs. McGurk were to whisk him off to a desert isle, *that* sure would be the emergency of all time!

Kathy's hand touched his goodbye. "Call the man, so he'll open the door." George diverted the attendant for a moment or two. Oh, wonderful Kathy!

Say!

"What if he and she ... George and Kathy ... were to be magically transported to a flowery isle? There was an idea. George stared at the wall. He knew right away it wasn't any good. A man can't leave what life is, in the name of life. No, if they were not to be with their kind, to mix in, to take part, to struggle humanly in the great complicated mesh that made the world of men, then what was life for? No ... no good.

The Ring hung heavy on his hand. One magic wish! Just one! Darned if George could think what it ought to be.

In the anteroom, an unseen Kathy hovered over the ladies in their chairs. Mrs. McGurk was cross-examining. "Now," she said, "when you first caught sight of the car, what was happening?"

"You was screaming," said the pig woman readily.

"Why was I screaming?"

"Because the fella wid the sword just come outa the woods at ya."

"No, no, no," protested Mrs. McGurk.

"Fella wid the beard goes running around to get rid of him."

"Exactly! So it was self-defense."

"Sure it was. Fella wid the beard was defending the both of ya."

"No," screeched Mrs. McGurk. "Listen . . ." she began again.

Kathy saw no lamp-shaped bulges in the landlady's print dress. The Lamp must be in that fat handbag. And it, she discovered, was tied tight to Mrs. McGurk. No way to steal the handbag. Kathy touched the clasp with a careful forefinger. Alas, the clasp itself was tied around and around with cord.

Kathy drew back to think it over. Very well. Attack the problem another way. Ah, suppose Mrs. McGurk were not so sentimentally attached to George? Then, would she even think of whisking George and herself away where they couldn't be found? No, of course she wouldn't! Kathy took the Rose, invisibly, out of her own purse. It was worth trying, she thought in excitement. If only she could induce Mrs. McGurk to sniff the Rose a second time and then let her eye light on another, *not* George . . .

On whom? Kathy looked about her. Why, on the fat attendant, of course. He would do quite well. Kathy crept closer on quiet feet.

A great loop of Mrs. McGurk's hairdo had come loose and it bobbed and dipped with the vehemence of her continuing arguments. She paid no attention to the Rose, as Kathy tossed it into her lap.

"My wrists were tied behind my back!" she fumed. "Tied, mind you! I can prove it! Was it George who tied them?"

"I dunno," said the pig woman. "Was it?" Her flesh sagged all around the inadequate surface of the narrow chair. Her coarse hands were folded across her stomach. Her bulk was inert. Mrs. McGurk, in comparison, bounded like a pingpong ball. The Rose bounced in her rayon lap. Just then the attendant got up and went to the door, off on one of his mysterious strolls down George's corridor. Kathy reached for the Rose.

So, yawning, did the pig woman. Her big hand closed. Her thick fingers were in possession. Now the dainty blossom (Kathy watched it, helpless with dismay) moved in that coarse grasp towards the stub of her nose.

"Purty flower," said the pig woman. "Where'd this come from?" She sniffed. The hulking bosom heaved a sigh.

The attendant was returning!

He swung the door inward, as it must go, against himself. The pig woman's little eyes rested, naturally, on the opening gap. Her gaze passed through it, to where, snug in his cell, smack in the line of her sight, sat George.

The blob of flesh in the pig woman's chair began to surge. Somehow, it organized itself roughly into the figure of a woman. Kathy snatched back the Rose, but . . .

"Say!" said the pig woman. "How long do they think they can keep that kid in this lousy clink, hey?"

"What!" Constance's jaw dropped.

The pig woman heaved to her feet. "You, Fatso, take me in there. I wanna see if he needs anything. Somebody oughta take care of him."

Constance gasped.

"Lissen, sister," said the pig woman, turning. The air churned like water under the Queen Elizabeth. "How come you're so interested? Old enough to be his grandmaw, ain't you?"

"Whose grandma?"

"HIS grandmaw. George's. George . . ." repeated the pig woman with a holy softness. Her weatherbeaten face was warm . . . nay, sunny . . . with affection. "Nothing bad is going to happen to a nice kid like HIM. I'll see to that!"

"YOU will!"

"Shuddup!" said the pig woman. "You been making a fool outa yourself long enough."

"Well, I . . . ! You old fat pig!"

"Rather be fleshy than a scrawny old crow," said the pig woman, ominously. "You let HIM alone."

"Who?"

"George."

"Oh?"

"Ay-ah."

"Hah!"

The pig woman's big mitt made a feint at the McGurk puss. The McGurk clawed for the scant and scrambled coiffure of the enemy. But the pig woman got a firm grip in return and Mrs. McGurk's switch left her.

By now, the attendant, with loud male shouts, had interposed himself. Reinforcements poured in from another room. With huffing and puffing, with yelps from their victim, with contributing screeches from Mrs. McGurk, at last they dragged the pig woman away. One of them humanely opened the door to reassure a frantic George that there had been only a little bloodshed.

Kathy slipped back to him. "Oh George . . ." she sobbed. "Oh . . . oh . . . look!"

The door had become wedged open. They could see Mrs. McGurk, settling her ruffled feathers. Pale with outrage, she perched on the edge of her chair. The cops were all busy, elsewhere, subduing their billowing witness. Mrs. McGurk was alone. Through the door, George and Kathy, watching with a horrid fascination, saw the landlady's hands and teeth begin to work on her handbag. She undid the cord. She dove into the bag. She took out the Lamp.

"Kathy ... Kathy ..." Their hands clung.
"Wish!"
"But what'll I wish?"
"Call to her ... Stop her ... !"
"Constance!"

Bosom heaving, eyes flashing, Mrs. McGurk was in no state to respond. She didn't hear. She was lifting the Lamp to ...

There came a sharp rap on the outer door.

It was a reprieve. "I beg your pardon," said a familiar tenor. "Oh, I say, it's you, isn't it?"

"How do?" said Mrs. McGurk, unenthusiastically.

"My name is Blair." He cleared his throat. "Is Miss Douglas here, anywhere, do you know?"

"Douglas? Oh, you mean that red-headed girl? No, no, she is not." Mrs. McGurk was brusque.

"But Hale is here?"

"In there," said Constance and her eyes blazed.

"Yes, I ... er ... see ..." Mr. Blair swept the cell block with enough of a glance to see how empty it seemed of Kathy. He brushed by George with a formal lttle nod. (George, who stood with his hands held through the bars in so odd, so tense a position.) "Ah ... I see you have the Lamp there," said Mr. Blair pleasantly.

Her hand tightened.

"Powerful little gadget, isn't it?" He gave her a magnetic smile and sat down beside her.

"Y'know, I have an idea."

He had, too. Kathy's hands writhed, if possible, closer to the hands of George. Their four hands were all bruised on the Ring ...

"*I* could use that Lamp," drawled Mr. Blair, "whereas *you* might have some use for ... this!" He took the Flask from his pocket. "This," he said and no salesman ever spoke with softer lure, "is water from the Fountain of Youth ..." The last syllable fell on the sanitary air like the serpent's whisper in Eden. "You see, Mrs ... er ... ?"

"McGurk," she murmured, hypnotically.

"I am *Bennett* Blair, you know."

Her gaze slid on the pink stone bottle. "Thought he was an older man . . ."

"He was," came the seductive voice. "I *was* old. Now, it appears to me that you . . . are fond of George? Isn't that so?"

"I am," she snuffled. "Oh, Mr. Blair, he is in such trouble and that horrible woman, she . . . bahoo!"

"My dear lady, there is nothing to worry about. Not now that I am here."

"You mean you can help?" she quavered. "He killed a man!"

"I'm sure he never meant to," soothed Mr. Blair. "Why, of course, I'll help. I would like so much to have that Lamp," he continued with a glide of tone that pointed up the connection. "And you'd rather like to be . . . young again?"

"Young?" *Pig woman,* thought Mrs. McGurk, *ha ha!*

"George, George, he mustn't have it!"

A series of futile wishes paraded in George's head. Futile . . . futile . . . inadequate all.

"I can't find Kathleen, you see," Mr. Blair was murmuring. "I want so much to find her and . . . er . . . keep her."

"I see," said Mrs. McGurk, eyes riveted on the Flask. *Redhead, ha ha!*

"Wish, George! Wish!"

"But *what?* Oh Kathy, what will I wish?"

"I'm not so sure," said Mrs. McGurk, suddenly recalling her best self. "Now, I can use this Lamp to take George right out of this. But . . . er . . . the thing I had in mind . . . We'd need the Lamp, there. I won't," she said with stubborn devotion, "have George doing without well-balanced meals and the comforts of civilization."

"Oh, my dear girl!" cried Mr. Blair, reading her dream. "Don't do that! Pray don't! How much better to clear him of these charges, simply clear him. And then, both of you so young . . ."

She raised her tempted swimming eyes to his face. "How do I know you can get him free?"

"It will be simple. I happen to know certain officials of this state rather well. I believe I could exert pressures on people in even higher places, if necessary . . ."

"You're sure, now!" said Mrs. McGurk, lifting the Lamp in both hands.

"I am Bennett Blair," he laughed, reaching for it.

"But . . . Bennett Blair's an *old* millionaire. How will . . . ?"

"Exactly," said he, very quickly indeed. "Think of it! Only the day before yesterday, I was an old millionaire!" He dazzled her with a smile. "You, too," said Mr. Blair with the flawless technique of the radio commercial, "can be young again . . ."

Her mind was paralyzed. Her hands began to loosen.

But so did George's. He pulled them free. Now he knew what the wish must be!

Out there in the anteroom, the Lamp and the Flask hung in the air, passing. George spoke aloud in a shaking but solemn voice.

"I WISH," said George, "THIS WAS THE DAY BEFORE YESTERDAY."

The Ring winked. " But in the morning!" cried George, belatedly. (Oh, was it adequate, after all?) Their hands were locked again. The Ring blazed in the tangle of their fingers. "And oh . . . don't . . . don't . . ." pleaded George, "don't let me forget! Not again! Don't let me forg . . ."

Time swirled in a kind of stew. All dissolved.

Thus, it became the day before yesterday.

"If you wish," said the proprietor, "sixteen dollarss and thiss . . ."

"What's in it?" said George.

"Ssee?"

"Nuh-uh. What would I want with . . . ? Hey, what's that?" George spied the hilt of the Sword. What a magnificent old thing! He was attracted. Maybe . . . his mind was reaching for a good reason . . . maybe he ought to consider this deal. There might be something valuable in this carpet bag.

As he touched the hilt, something thrilled through his hand. This blade in the crimson scabbard was old, very old. It was evil.

"No, no," murmured George mechanically.

"Maybe iss antique?" said his tempter. George didn't answer. Evil? The shadows all around him were drawn over evil unknown. He looked at his hand, where it merely touched the sword. There was no reason for this shiver, this ghost of horror.

George took his hand away and rubbed it on his trousers. He shook his head slightly to dispel this misty fright that was growing up around him. Silly! Nothing to be afraid of! Just a lot of old junk. He fished into the bag to see what else it held.

He drew out a little box with a sliding lid. George looked down at the rose. What was it, anyhow?

"You take?" whispered the old old man.

George stared at him dumbly. Time rustled by, like feathers dragging. There was something wrong. Something was pricking on his nerves.

But, in George's upbringing, there was no tradition of nerves. One went ahead and did the right thing, regardless of how one felt. That was his training, and it stiffened him, now. Maybe this was a chance . . .

He stood, hesitating. It was strange how time hung, as if the unwinding ribbon of it snagged on a point. As if George was balanced between two futures. And was it real? Were there two real futures? Does it matter, when we try? Are we free to choose? Looking back, we think we see . . . we *seem* to learn.

George thought, Yes, it matters. What we do, how we choose, where we push, how we aim . . . Being men, we must, to call ourselves alive, believe it matters. Dreaming, he swayed on the point of decision, teetering there, held in this whirling gust of strange unbidden thoughts.

Then the proprietor chose to push at the balance. "Thiss," he said, shifting closer, "thiss rose . . ." His ancient finger gave it a sly poke. He turned his wrinkled face up and it broke into a smile George didn't like, "iss Rose of Luff!" said the man with hideous glee.

(It was glee for George. George didn't need anybody's glee. George didn't like it.)

"You let girlss smell thisss . . . they luff!"

George closed the box. He felt a little ill of his distaste. "No, thanks," said George quietly. "I don't think I need anything of this sort."

He turned and burst back through the heaps of stuff towards the light. He ran out into the street and gulped the fresh air. He was shaking a little, as if he'd just almost had an accident. "Don't *need*," he heard himself saying. Well, now, how true that was!

He came to a drugstore; he found the phone booth; he put in his nickel. His throat all but closed up when he heard her voice.

She wasn't angry. He could tell.

"Kathy," said George, slowly and clearly, "when you said you wouldn't wait, *what did you mean?*"

"I thought you'd never ask!" Her voice was strong and fresh and glad. "I meant I don't *want* to wait. *I want . . .*"

"Kathy," cried George, "Darling! Marry me! Right away!"

"I certainly will! I certainly will! That's it! That's what I meant! Oh, George I'm so glad you c-called . . ."

"If Mr. Blair keeps back all your money," groaned George.

"You don't want it, do you?"

"Who! Me?" cried George, horrified.

"Well, I thought not. So, pooh!" She switched in the most enchanting way. "We'd better run away," she said practically, "to Maine, I think. The cheapest way. We'll take a bus, George."

"Oh," said George, "dearest Kathy, meet me . . . oh darling . . . meet me on the corner!"

Mrs. McGurk stood behind her front room curtains with the sign in her hand, savouring this moment of delicious power. George was off, bag and baggage, and a cute red-headed trick besides. Sister? Mrs. McGurk thought cynically, not. Bride? Well, if so, *she* wanted no newly-weds in her house. Always so much in love . . . never had any leverage on them.

Now, she thought, take him. This one, coming up the steps to the stoop. Very prompt with the rent, he was. And serious minded. "How do, Mr. Josef," she greeted him pleasantly.

He bowed. "Good afternoon, Madame." He fingered his beard. His eyes slanted to the card. "Someone has left us?" He implied that he deduced it.

"Hale. Fourth floor."

"Ah," said Mr. Josef. "And the next occupant?" He watched her face slyly for any hint of a plot.

"I'll tell you one thing about the next occupant," said Constance cheerfully. "He will have a full month's rent in advance."

She raised her hand. She put the sign, the symbol of her power, in the window. That simple, potent, magic word, "Vacancy."

Fraulein stood in Mr. Blair's lair, twisting unhappy hands. "So I pack for her, Mr. Blair. What else can I do? Oh, sir, do you think . . . once they marry . . . that she will want me?"

He grunted.

"Can she afford me?" asked Fraulein boldly.

Mr. Blair looked up over his glasses. He took them off. He rubbed the vague persisting ache in his knobby knees. "Of course she can afford you," he said irritably. "I can't keep the child's fortune from her. I used all the pressure I could bring to bear," he continued waspishly, "but the young won't listen, they'll make mistakes." He brooded. "Sometimes," he said to Fraulein's listening face, and knew not why he said it, "I shudder to think of the mistakes one makes, being young." He shook his own (bald) head.

"I am glad if she is happy," said Fraulein stoutly. "This George is a good man?"

A thin, reluctant smile approached the old fish mouth. "As a matter of fact," he admitted, "this George . . . and I have checked . . . *is* a good man."

"And they love!"

"That, of course, makes everything rosy!" said Mr. Blair sourly.

But not as sourly as he might have.

Darkness gathered over New England. The chill sky pressed down.

Inside, the bus reeked of gasoline, tired people, old candy bars. Gum wrappers and scratchy little gobs of cellophane grated under shifting feet. There was a baby, of course, and a man with a rasping snore. Now and then, the bus screamed to a stop. Clumsy folk blundered in and out, stirring the stale air with piercing draughts. Again, they would slam on through the night.

But Kathy was snug in a seat by the window. Her hair was a pool of gold on George's shoulder. ". . . know what you'd call success," she murmured sleepily, "when everybody in the whole town, probaby the whole state of Maine, adores you. And me, too, besides . . ."

George filled his soul with the sweet warm scent of her hair. He wasn't really worried about success right now. For him, the bus was flying, gossamer light, through the soft cool night. It was a dear chariot, carrying ALL. And all within . . . the baby fretting pinkly up ahead, the old man, sleeping in noisy peace across the aisle, the middle-aged wife with the beautiful worry lines on her mother-face, the work-soiled, black-nailed, strong man's hand on the back of the next seat, all, all he knew and loved. All their pale faces in the weak light yet were aglow and gilded with something more.

For he loved her, loved them, loved all.

"Why it's like Magic!" thought George. "It *is* Magic!" And he saw the world, and all its knots and problems, transformed, illuminated, and the pattern changed, by the beautiful blaze of the magic enchanting his eyes.

The bus winged on.

The Authors

Richard Matheson

Richard Matheson (1926-   ) was born in Allendale, New Jersey, and earned a bachelor's in journalism from the University of Missouri at Columbia. Many of his science fiction, fantasy, and horror novels have been filmed, including *I Am Legend* (1954). His screenplays include *The Night Stalker* TV movie (1972) and many episodes of the *Twilight Zone* television series.

"The Children of Noah" first appeared in *Alfred Hitchcock Mystery Magazine*, Mar., 1957.

Seabury Quinn

Born in Washington, D.C., and educated in law and medicine, Seabury Quinn (1889-1969) was the most popular writer for one of the Twentieth Century's most influential magazines of fantasy and horror, *Weird Tales*. Much of his work (ninety-two stories and a novel) features a team of occult detectives, Jules de Grandin and Dr. Trowbridge.

"The Phantom Farmhouse" first appeared in *Weird Tales*, Oct., 1923.

Edgar Pangborn

Edgar Pangborn (1909-1976) was born in New York City and educated at Harvard University and the New England Conservatory of Music. After a varied career, which included farming in Maine from 1939 to 1942, he began writing in the early 1950s. His best-known science fiction novel, *A Mirror for Observers* (1954), is a tale of Martians who secretly guide humans. It won the International Fantasy Award. Much of his shorter work is collected in *Good Neighbors and Other Strangers* (1972).

"Longtooth" first appeared in *The Magazine of Fantasy and Science Fiction*, Jan., 1970.

Stephen King

The world's most famous and best-selling writer of the horror genre, Stephen King (1947-   ) was born in Portland, Maine, and earned a baccalaureate in English from the University of Maine at Orono. *Carrie*, his first novel, was published in 1973.

"One For the Road" first appeared in *Maine Magazine*, Mar.-Apr., 1977.

Ruth Sawyer

Ruth Sawyer (1880-1970) was born in Boston and earned her bachelor's from Columbia University. A specialist in folk tales and children's literature, she produced more than thirty-five books and numerous short stories, winning, among other literary awards, the Newbery Award, the Caldecott Medal (twice), and the Laura Ingalls Wilder Medal. During later life she lived in Hancock, Maine. Margaret Sawyer, her daughter, is married to Robert McCloskey, Maine's most famous children's artist and writer.

"The Four Dreams of Gram Perkins" first appeared in *American Mercury* in Oct., 1926.

Harriet Prescott Spofford

Harriet Prescott (1835-1921) was born in Calais, Maine, and educated at Putnam Free School in Massachusetts. Encouraged by the educator Thomas Wentworth Higginson, she began writing to help support her family and for four decades placed a steady stream of stories, poems, and critical pieces in the leading magazines of the day.

"Circumstance" first appeared in *The Atlantic Monthly*, May, 1860. It is reportedly based on an incident in the life of Mrs. Spofford's maternal grandmother, Mrs. Sarah Hitchings. The version of the story appearing in this anthology is an abridgement by the editors.

Edward Page Mitchell

Edward Page Mitchell (1852-1927) was born in Bath, Maine, and earned his bachelor's degree from Bowdoin College. Most of his career was spent on the editorial staff of the *New York Sun*. He is the author of *Memoirs of an Editor: Fifty Years of American Journalism* (1924), an autobiography, and several science fiction stories about computers, invisibility, and time travel. They were virtually forgotten until collected in *The Crystal Man* (1973).

"The Last Cruise of the *Judas Iscariot*" first appeared in the *New York Sun*, Apr. 16, 1882.

Carlos Baker

Carlos Baker (1909-   ) was born in Biddeford, Maine, and earned a Ph.D. in English from Princeton University. A professor emeritus at Princeton, he is the world's leading Hemingway scholar. His books include *Hemingway: The Writer as Artist* (1952), *Ernest Hemingway: A Life Story* (1969), and *Ernest Hemingway: Selected Letters* (1981).

"The Prevaricator" first appeared in the collection *The Talismans and Other Stories* (1976).

Jane Yolen

A specialist in mythic fantasy, Jane Yolen (1939-   ) was born in New York City and earned a master's degree in education from the University of Massachusetts. She has produced more than eighty books and is the president of the Science Fiction Writers of America. Her many literary honors include the Society of Children's Book Writers' Golden Kite Award and the Mythopoeic Society Award.

"One Old Man, with Seals" first appeared in *Neptune Rising: Sons and Tales of the Undersea Folk*, 1982.

Donald Wismer

Donald Wismer (1946-   ) was born in Chicago, Illinois, and earned master's degrees in comparative religion from Indiana University and library science from Southern Connecticut State College. He is deputy state librarian at the Maine State Library in Augusta. His science fiction novel *Starluck* was published in 1982.

"Safe Harbor" first appeared in *Tin Stars*, an anthology edited by Isaac Asimov, Charles G. Waugh, and Martin Harry Greenberg, 1986.

Thomas Easton

Born in Bangor, Maine, Thomas Easton (1944-   ) earned a Ph.D. in biology from the University of Chicago. He is an assistant professor of biology at Thomas College, Waterville, Maine. The author of many science fiction stories, he has also written several textbooks including *Bioscope* (1979, 1984) and *Careers in Science* (1984).

"Mood Wendigo" first appeared in *Analog Science Fiction*, May, 1980.

Fredric Brown

Fredric Brown (1906-1972) was born in Cincinnati, Ohio, and was educated at the University of Cincinnati and Hanover College. Best known as a mystery writer, he won the Edgar Allen Poe Award and had several works turned into movies including *Crackup* (1942). In his most popular science fiction novel, *What Mad Universe* (1951), a science fiction editor becomes trapped in the dreamworld of a demented fan.

"Death Is a White Rabbit" first appeared in *Strange Detective Mysteries*, Jan., 1942.

Fritz Leiber

One of the most honored writers of science fiction and fantasy, Fritz Leiber (1910-   ) was born in Chicago, Illinois, and earned a bachelor's degree from the University of Chicago. He followed his similarly named father into movies during the 1930s, but soon turned to writing. He has won science fiction's Hugo and Nebula Awards numerous times. His novel about witchcraft on campus, *Conjure Wife*, has been filmed three times.

"Yesterday House" first appeared in *Galaxy Science Fiction*, Aug., 1952.

Charlotte Armstrong

Charlotte Armstrong (1905-1969) was born in Vulcan, Michigan, and earned her baccalaureate from Barnard College. She was a prominent mystery and suspense writer, winning the *Ellery Queen Mystery Magazine* short story contest in 1951 as well as the mystery writers' Edgar Allen Poe Award for both short story and novel.

"Three-Day Magic," in the form in which it is presented in this anthology, first appeared in *The Magazine of Fantasy and Science Fiction*, Sept., 1952.